# THE DISORDERLY SOCIETY

# THE DISORDERLY SOCIETY

## Rethinking Global Governance in an Age of Anarchy

BOBO LO

**agenda**
publishing

*To my darling Siriol – inspiration, advisor, shrink*

First published in 2026 by Agenda Publishing

Agenda Publishing Limited
PO Box 185
Newcastle upon Tyne
NE20 2DH
www.agendapub.com

ISBN 978-1-78821-465-0 (hardcover)
ISBN 978-1-78821-844-3 (paperback)

**British Library Cataloguing-in-Publication Data**
A catalogue record for this book is available from the British Library

Typeset by Newgen Publishing UK
Printed and bound in the UK by TJ Books

EU GPSR authorised representative:
Logos Europe, 9 rue Nicolas Poussin, 17000 La Rochelle, France
contact@logoseurope.eu

# CONTENTS

# PROLOGUE: A PARABLE OF GLOBAL DISORDER

On 5 November 2024, Donald Trump secured a decisive victory in the US presidential election. Confounding predictions of a knife-edge contest, his win was comprehensive. He defeated his opponent, the incumbent Vice-President Kamala Harris, by 86 electoral college votes (312–226). He won the popular vote. And his Republican Party regained the Senate while holding on to its majority in the House of Representatives.

The most remarkable aspect of Trump's triumph was that it defied all the conventional rules of political success. He stood as a convicted felon, with multiple other charges hanging over him. He had barely survived impeachment proceedings after he tried to overturn the result of the 2020 presidential election, including inciting a far-right mob assault on the US Capitol. Earlier as president, he had botched the federal government's response to the Covid-19 pandemic, a failure that contributed to the deaths of 1.2 million Americans – by far the highest death toll of any country. Between 2017 and 2021, his administration became a byword for endemic corruption, serial incompetence, rampant disinformation and bureaucratic chaos. Yet in the face of all these handicaps, the American public chose in their tens of millions to put their trust in him once again.

Trump's resurgence has been portrayed as part of a larger phenomenon of electorates around the world throwing out incumbent governments.[1] But this rationalization undersells the change that is taking place. It is not merely that people are dissatisfied with their rulers; it is that the very idea of order is much diminished. Order, and especially democratic order, no longer equates with good governance. Disorder has become normalized. People voted for Trump, or against Harris, because he was an iconoclastic figure who promised to upend the established way of doing things. And similar trends are playing out in other Western democracies.

This shift from order to disorder has far-reaching implications for global governance. For the best part of three decades, the main story of the post-Cold War era has been of a universal "rules-based international order", led by the United States and shaped by Western liberal values, norms and institutions. But well before Trump came onto the political scene, this construct was already in trouble. Today, it holds little appeal for much of the world, where many see it as a piece of sophistry designed to promote Western interests at the expense of others. Like the Trump-supporting public in America, but on a vaster scale, non-Western countries are profoundly dissatisfied with what passes for order. They crave major reforms to the international system, and reject the presumption that the West knows best.

Crucially, the United States itself has given up on the rules-based international order, at least in its post-Cold War form. The first year of the second Trump presidency has highlighted his belief in the primacy of power over international law and norms, let alone universal values. He has asserted US territorial claims to the Panama Canal and Greenland, called for Canada to become America's 51st state, declared that the United States will take over the Gaza Strip and convert it into prime beach-front real estate, and sanctioned the International Criminal Court. No less significantly, leading Western democracies have been reluctant to call him out for his open disregard for international order.

The reputation of the West has rarely been lower. Yet that is not the worst of it. Politicians like to employ phrases such as "international community" to signify a world that is globalized, interdependent and imbued with a strong sense of shared interests. However, the polarized reactions to recent events, notably the Russian invasion of Ukraine and the conflict in Gaza, point instead to a *disorderly society* in which the feeling of community, much less a common purpose, is almost entirely absent. UN Secretary-General Antonio Guterres has warned of an impending "Great Fracture", characterized by systemic political, economic and ideological splits.[2] But that reality is already upon us. "Rules" and "order" have become disposable concepts, reflecting the dominance of narrow national interests and the often arbitrary exercise of power. For all the hype and drama surrounding Trump, he is only the latest embodiment of this worldwide trend, as much a weather-vane as an influencer.

The landscape appears unremittingly grim, with precious little sign of the cooperation needed to tackle multiple threats and challenges – from runaway climate change to geopolitical confrontation, delinquent international behaviour and large-scale disinformation. Today's zeitgeist is characterized by extreme views, malice and a despair amounting at times to panic. Western policy-makers are in full-on reactive mode, hoping against hope that the storm will pass without inflicting terminal damage to the international system.

But it is too late for short-term views and band-aid "solutions". We find ourselves in our present parlous condition largely because we have chosen to ignore, deflect or underestimate the challenges before us. As shocking as they are, events in Ukraine and Gaza, and the return of a vengeful Donald Trump, underline the obvious – the time for procrastination and wishful thinking is over. We need to fundamentally rethink our approach to global governance.

The good news is that we have a real opportunity to effect a transformation for the better. In this book I set out the vision of a new internationalism as the foundation of revitalizing global order. We should have no illusions about the hard road ahead. But nor do we have to accept the inevitability of bad outcomes out of a misguided belief in historical determinism. We owe it to ourselves and future generations to at least strive for a more stable, prosperous and equitable world. To do anything less would be shamefully negligent.

# ACKNOWLEDGEMENTS

Writing is supposed to get easier with practice and age. That, however, has not been my experience. Completing this book has been (un)comfortably the toughest intellectual challenge of my life. The vastness of the subject is one reason; the sheer pace of change is another. It has been a never-ending struggle just to keep abreast of developments across multiple domains, let alone understand how they fit in with broader trends of global order and disorder. Working on this book has been humbling.

My wife Siriol has been an enormous influence on me for more than two decades. She is the life-force that has made this book possible. As a constantly reassuring presence, she has held me up in times of despair while encouraging me to stretch and even go beyond my limits. Siriol has read multiple versions of the manuscript, giving invaluable comments on approach, substance and style. Her criticisms have not always been easy to accept, but they have invariably improved the text. Without her, there would have been no book, and as a human being I would have been much the poorer.

Several people have contributed greatly to the making of this book. I owe a particular debt to Erik Jones, Anthony Bubalo, Angela Stent, Cynthia Stahl, Jeannette Hung, and an anonymous reviewer for their observations at various stages of the process. They have helped focus much of my thinking, and pushed it in more practical and interesting directions. They have also helped me avoid serious errors and misjudgements. I am extremely grateful to all of them. The role of the editor is central to the fate of any book. Alison Howson of Agenda Publishing has been a most encouraging and patient commissioning editor, while Clare Owen of Newgen has been a model of efficiency and flexibility in finalizing the proofs.

There are others whose influence on this book is more indirect, but no less crucial. The late, great Glenn Waller and the legendary Kyle Wilson have been key to my intellectual development over many decades. Without their support and friendship, I would never have had the chutzpah even to attempt this enterprise. And then there are those heroic figures whose efforts may not always meet success, but whose example is utterly inspirational and will long outlive us. Lena Nemirovskaya, Yura Senokosov, Inna Berezkina – I salute and love you.

La Rochefoucauld famously said that "a true friend is the greatest of all blessings." I have been undeservedly lucky in this respect. At such a time of acute pessimism and fatalism, friends and family are more important and cherished than ever. Although I cannot count them all here, I wanted to mention in particular Lyn and Bruce Minerds, Linda Kouvaras and Richard Ward, Lizzy Fisher and Jim Ross, Stephen Shay and Nicola Cade, Helen and Hugh Jones, Steve and Aileen Carroll-Turner, Leo Littman and Sharon Hamlin, cousin Cynthia and Ralph, cousin Jean and Ashok, Hung Koon ("Uncle Doc") and Auntie Kathy, cousin Jenny and Wah, Ole and Berit Lindeman, and Agnès Waller. I should also recognize our dogs past and present – Lyosha, Riley, and Martha – whose joy and sense of humour have so enriched our lives. Thank you all for your gift of love and friendship.

# INTRODUCTION

In his seminal 1977 work *The Anarchical Society*, the great Australian scholar Hedley Bull wrote of an international order on which there was broad consensus. As he put it: "Most states at most times pay some respect to the basic rules of coexistence in international society, such as mutual respect for sovereignty, the rule that agreements should be kept, and rules limiting the resort to violence".[1] The notion of an international *society* was crucial, with its understanding that states, "conscious of certain common interests and common values ... conceive of themselves to be bound by a common set of rules in their relations with one another".[2] Tellingly, for Bull these rules transcended strategic competition and ideological differences. The United States and the Soviet Union were then engaged in a multi-dimensional confrontation, but one that was played out according to rules and conventions both sides understood. During the Cold War, they managed to co-exist. They rarely interfered in each other's domestic politics. They developed an arms control regime that enshrined strategic stability. And they avoided direct conflict with each other. In short, there was an order, one based on certain minimum "rules of the game".

Today, the situation could hardly be more different. We live in a disorderly world, where there is no consensus over the rules of engagement and coexistence. Western leaders pontificate about "the rules-based international order", but recent conflicts have highlighted its vanishing legitimacy and credibility – a process underlined by the second coming of Donald Trump. Beijing and Moscow promote a "multipolar order", but this is more a rhetorical aspiration than a practical reality. Commentators speak of a new age of great powers (or "empires"), but recent years have revealed a diminishing capacity to advance their agendas, let alone manage global problems. The United Nations system that arose in the aftermath of the Second World War is undermined at every turn, amidst a general malaise of multilateralism. And the quality of national leadership – in democracies as well as authoritarian regimes – has sunk to lows not seen since the 1930s, as decision-makers resort to crude expediency and shabby populism.

Meanwhile, the world faces an unprecedented set of dangers – a "perfect storm".[3] What distinguishes the current period from past, sometimes more violent eras is the global reach and diversity of these threats, their compounding effect on each other, the exigencies they place on problem solving, and, simultaneously, their immediate urgency *and* long-term nature. They encompass the directly existential, such as anthropogenic climate change, pandemic disease and global poverty. They are often elusive, as in the case of disinformation. Even historically familiar phenomena, such as geopolitical confrontation and military conflict, are unusually complex, reflecting the involvement of myriad actors across multiple regions, and set against the backdrop of fluid power relations.

There is a natural temptation to rationalize away such problems as unexceptional features of international politics. Realist thinkers argue that states have always behaved selfishly in the pursuit of national interests and are constantly striving for advantage and primacy. Conversely, professional optimists such as Steven Pinker assert that the world has never had it so good. We are, he argues, healthier, safer, more prosperous and happier than at any time in history.[4]

So, are we over-reacting to individual events and crises? If selfish national interests and strategic rivalry are constants, why not simply look to manage them responsibly, for example through "guard-rails" preventing military conflict, while boosting defence capabilities to ensure effective deterrence against actual and potential enemies? And if the world, for all its troubles, is still doing relatively well, there is perhaps no need for radical measures that might risk making things worse. After all, since the end of the Second World War, we have experienced arguably the most peaceful and prosperous period in history – the so-called Long Peace. Provided we act sensibly, why should this state of affairs not continue indefinitely?

In this book, I argue that such a position is untenable. "Tried and tested" recipes, from the US-led "rules-based international order" to great power "Concerts", are hopelessly ill-suited to the increasingly disorderly world of the twenty-first century. It is fanciful, and self-destructive, to imagine that we can muddle through on the basis of discredited habits and mechanisms. In past eras, such sleepwalking has led to disaster.[5] And the future is unlikely to be any more forgiving of the complacency of governments and societies.

There is no time to lose. Revitalizing global order is the central task of our time. Not because order is inherently virtuous, but because without some measure of it we will scarcely be able to address the challenges before us. On present trends, the temperature of the earth is set to climb above 3 degrees centigrade from pre-industrial levels by the end of the century[6] – a reality that is already inflicting tremendous physical (and economic) harm on the planet. We have just experienced the worst pandemic in a century, resulting in the loss of more than 7 million lives in two years. And the scientific evidence suggests that such outbreaks will become more common *and* more lethal.[7] Global poverty, which had been falling in the decades after the Second World War, has become static in recent years,[8] aggravating the largest unregulated movement of people in more than three quarters of a century. Technology is changing the world faster than anyone could have imagined. We are only at the beginning of a revolution in Artificial Intelligence (AI) whose long-term implications are largely unknown. Information has exploded, and so has disinformation. And geopolitical confrontation – between the United States and China, and between Russia and the West – has reached a pitch not seen since the height of the Cold War. It is a measure of how far such tensions have escalated that talk of an impending major power war, long a taboo, has become routine.

These challenges, formidable in themselves, are also threat multipliers, impacting on every aspect of the human condition. Thus, climate change has increased the incidence of zoonotic diseases and the likelihood of further pandemics. It has also exacerbated poverty and inequality in many developing countries. Technology has sharpened US-China rivalry and opened up abundant opportunities for mass disinformation, corroding public life in democracies and authoritarian regimes alike. And the degradation of governance – national and international – has weakened the will and capacity of leaders for problem solving.

## A new internationalism

We need a new international order, but what should it look like? What would be its defining principles? And how might state actors – the essential building blocks of any functioning system – be persuaded to buy into it? The US-led post-Cold War order is disintegrating because many nations see it as neither morally legitimate nor politically authoritative. Any future order would need to appeal not just to the major powers, but also to emergent middle powers as well as to developing nations in the Global South. It would also have to reflect the realities of a world where non-state actors, such as Big Tech, are increasingly influential.

A viable international order depends first and foremost on the perception of *self-interest*. Ideals and values matter, but it is self-interest that ultimately stimulates cooperation and constrains disruptive behaviour. The United States drove the creation of the post-Second World War order and, later, the liberal international order because it recognized that American national interests would be best served by global arrangements shaped out of Washington. Altruism was tangential to the case. No less important, a critical mass of other countries, including in the non-Western world, agreed that the benefits of the US-led global order outweighed its disadvantages. This ensured their cooperation or at least acquiescence.

That time is over. We are witnessing a fundamental shift in attitudes. A growing number of nations, including democracies such as India and South Africa, regard the "rules-based international order" as inordinately favouring the West at the expense of the rest. They view this order as unjust, prejudicial to their interests, and inconsistent with the steady diffusion of international power over the past two decades. And they have developed the will and self-confidence to challenge or circumvent its dictates.

A new international order needs to take account of these "facts on the ground". It has to be an order that most countries, most of the time, view as beneficial. But that will not happen without addressing the twin issues of *representativeness and inclusiveness*. The future of international cooperation is contingent on a much broader range of nations having the opportunity to participate actively in global decision-making.

It is often claimed that inclusiveness is incompatible with effectiveness.[9] The more parties involved in negotiations on a given issue, the harder it is to achieve consensus, and the more remote the chances are that any decisions will be implemented. The torturous history of the COP (Conference of the Parties) on climate change would seem to support this argument. Yet the alternative to inclusiveness is much worse: an expanding number of malcontents bucking against an international order they see as neither fair nor useful. This collective resentment has tangible consequences. The belief of many Global South countries[10] that their interests are routinely disregarded within the "rules-based international order" is a major reason why they were reluctant to condemn Putin's invasion of Ukraine or Hamas for its October 2023 assault on southern Israel. The international order described by the West is not theirs, so they have little incentive to defend its norms and institutions. Lack of representativeness equates to an absence of legitimacy.

*Flexibility* is key to a working international order. In a diffuse world, it is unfeasible to impose rules and norms from above. The United States is the most formidable power in history, and yet its capacity to influence the actions of even the weakest and most dysfunctional states has declined markedly – as highlighted by its humiliating exit from Afghanistan in August 2021. The fixation on universal values carries within it the seeds of failure. It sets impossible standards that even the most advanced Western democracies regularly fail to meet, thereby inviting charges of hypocrisy and undermining the whole enterprise of order-building. Such universalism has become all the more implausible since Trump's return to the White House and his dismantling of American democratic institutions and norms.

A flexible international order would proceed from the reality that the only practicable approach is one able to accommodate diverse and sometimes conflicting value systems. It would rethink the concept of "leadership", moving away from the usual focus on the United States or a self-appointed group of great powers, and emphasize instead a wider collective responsibility for problem solving. It would incorporate a variety of multilateral structures and mechanisms, from tightly knit organizations such as the European Union to looser groupings like the Quadrilateral Security Dialogue (the "Quad") and the BRICS framework. It would prioritize establishing and sustaining international rules of conduct instead of promoting "universal" values, such as democracy. Most of all, it would grow organically out of the global environment rather than attempt to impose artificial "truths".

Such an order would be imperfect and anarchic to some degree. For order is not a self-standing or objective phenomenon, but an elusive and fragile political construct buffeted by competing interests. There would be policy failures, bitter divisions and even wars. Adherence to international rules would continue to be selective and arbitrary. Nevertheless, this order would represent a signal improvement on today's disorder of collapsing norms, escalating tensions, and bankrupt policy-making. Crucially, it would offer a foundation from which to tackle the challenges of the twenty-first century.

## From decline to revival

This book divides into two parts. Part I centres on context, beginning with the *rise and fall of the post-Cold War liberal order*. In highlighting the undoubted failings of liberal internationalism, we tend to underestimate its achievements. For the most remarkable aspect of the liberal order is that it succeeded as well as it did. By the late twentieth century, it had become synonymous with international order. This was hardly a foregone conclusion, notwithstanding the remarkable rise and exceptional power of the United States. In the course of two centuries, liberal ideas and norms of governance gradually superseded the classical Westphalian hierarchy of states, the post-Napoleonic Concert of Europe, the Bismarckian balance of power of the late nineteenth century, and, finally, the Soviet-led Communist order. To succeed, the liberal order had to outperform more established rival systems. This it did to an astonishing degree. No other order has had a comparable global impact.

Another notable aspect of the liberal order was its resilience in the face of tremendous pressures and formidable opposition. In the lead-up to his historic 1972 visit to Beijing, US President Richard Nixon was in a state of high anxiety about the decline of the West and of the United States in particular, and the threat to its primacy.[11] Yet the liberal order saw off all challengers. It is a testament to the enduring power of liberal norms and institutions that even the most authoritarian of regimes have sought to benefit from them. The rise of China owes much to the US-led global order and economic globalization. Accession to the World Trade Organization (WTO) in 2001 allowed it unprecedented access to the global commons, supercharging its economic growth and, in an ironic twist, helping to legitimize Communist Party rule with the Chinese public.

The tragedy of the liberal order is that it has been a victim of its own success. It has over-extended itself by assuming, and then clinging on to, a universalist mission.[12] It has also indulged in a sustained embrace of "suicidal statecraft" over the past 20 years. Leading Western democracies have betrayed liberal values, and the growing disjunction between rhetoric and practice has undermined the competitive advantages of the liberal order. The 2003 invasion of Iraq, the global financial crisis, the feeble response to Vladimir Putin's 2014 annexation of Crimea, the chaos of Trump's first presidency, the West's disastrous response to the Covid-19 pandemic, and Joe Biden's foreign policy missteps – all these were stages in the dismantling of the post-Cold War order and the discrediting of liberalism.

Liberalism's trials have opened up opportunities for powers such as China and Russia. But a new post-liberal order has yet to emerge. Instead, the contemporary international system is defined by *a world disorder*, the most important feature of which is the breakdown of rules. Today, there is little consensus on what the rules are, who should make them, and how they should be applied and to whom. Core principles, such as the sanctity of national sovereignty and territorial integrity, have been eroded. A growing number of nations see international "rules" as being grounded in power relations. The powerful make (and ignore) the rules, while the rest must adapt to an environment where rule-breaking has become normalized.

The absence of moral authority is compounded by the difficulties in implementing norms, however partially. The paralysis of the United Nations Security Council is emblematic of an acutely dysfunctional international system. Some observers hope for a potential strategic accommodation between the great powers, along the lines of the nineteenth-century Concert of Europe. Yet the animosities between Washington and Beijing, and between Russia and the West, are conducive to disorder, not order. With little agreement on the rules of the international system, and even less hope of enforcing them, today's global condition bears more than a passing resemblance to Thomas Hobbes's "state of nature" back in the seventeenth century: "where there is no common power, there is no law; where no law, no injustice. Force, and fraud, are in war the two cardinal virtues".[13]

Most of the book, Part II, is about how we get out of the mess we're in. Given the extent and depth of the world's problems, it would be easy to surrender to despair and to dismiss the prospects of global order out of hand. But it is precisely because the challenges facing us are so great and so urgent that we cannot afford to lapse into fatalism. The issue is not that we lack the capacity to take meaningful action. It is that we are not doing so, largely because we are in denial about the gravity of the crisis and cling to the hope that somehow things will work out.

The natural starting point for rethinking global governance is to expand on the *principles of a new internationalism* – self-interest, representativeness and inclusiveness, and flexibility – that I flagged earlier. But immediately we come up against a critical conundrum: how does one turn national self-interest, something that is often a constraint on enlightened policy-making, into a driver of positive change and reliable foundation of international order?

It would be foolish to pretend there are straightforward answers. However, we can move in the right direction by recognizing, and acting upon, the interconnectedness of interests among nations and peoples. This interdependence is not solely or even primarily economic, as per the mainstream Western understanding of globalization, but also political, ideational, technological, informational and physical. Covid-19 exposed the futility of attempts by countries to cordon themselves from global forces; the pandemic cut across all borders, making no distinction between "us" and "them", rich and poor, "free" and "unfree".

Equally, conflict, poverty and hunger are no longer solely the concern of what used to be known as the "Third World", but have significant repercussions for the stability of even the most prosperous Western democracies, with uncontrolled migration fuelling the rise of far-right populism. More dramatically still, AI and social media are driving an extraordinary expansion of the global information space. The world has never been "smaller" or more interconnected. And this interconnectedness is transforming the local and the national into the transcontinental and the global.

Adapting to this complex and often anarchic world demands not only broader views, but also a practical empathy that has been conspicuously absent. State actors, including the most powerful, need to gain a better understanding of alternative perspectives and competing agendas, however unpalatable. Unfortunately, much of contemporary international politics has been reduced to a series of convenient but misleading binarisms – democracy versus autocracy, "rules-based order" versus "might is right", "right" and "wrong" side of history. Such simplicities distort our perceptions of the world, and are inimical to the prospects of a functioning global order. They have not only exacerbated US-China confrontation, but also the gulf between the Global North and the Global South. Lack of empathy is not just a moral and intellectual failure, it is antithetical to the effective pursuit of national interests.

The key, then, to effective order-building lies not in attempting to transcend self-interest – an impossibility – but in channelling it in ways that serve the greatest number.[14] That necessitates an international system which is sufficiently representative and flexible as to give diverse state and non-state actors a real stake in its success. It also means identifying how different players can best contribute to this goal.

As the strongest and most influential actor, *the United States* faces the largest task of all: to adapt its primacy and leadership to a post-unipolar world. While the era of American hegemony is over, no other power or set of countries is ready to assume its responsibilities. For at least the next two decades and probably longer, the United States will remain the world's most influential player. This condition is both a boon and a burden for Washington. On the one hand, it puts it in prime position to shape a future international order, and to take advantage of this to promote American interests. On the other hand, a position of such superiority makes it a magnet for the accumulated resentments and jealousies of others.

Exercising geopolitical and normative self-restraint is counter-intuitive when the gap between the United States and others remains so large. Washington has to navigate between two extremes: an expansive liberal internationalism that risks strategic and normative over-reach; and an "America-first" nationalism that jeopardizes not only international order, but the security and prosperity of the United States itself. Finding the right balance of engagement will be difficult, especially given the inclinations – and lack of restraint – of the Trump administration. But over time this balance can and indeed must be achieved.

One of the tenets of US foreign policy is that *China* aims to establish a Sinocentric global order that would supplant the US-led system. This belief owes much to anxieties about China's enhanced capabilities, assertive foreign policy behaviour and strident rhetoric. It is also a reflection of larger American and Western insecurities arising from the unravelling of the post-Cold War order.

But part of the problem stems from contradictions in Beijing's foreign policy. Although President Xi Jinping envisages China as a global leader, it is far from clear what he understands by this. Is Beijing ready to assume the responsibilities that such a role implies, especially given its domestic preoccupations? China's economic heft has grown impressively in recent decades, but its role in global governance remains modest and sometimes peripheral. A fully engaged China is critical to addressing challenges such as climate change, AI governance and debt relief, but this necessitates dilution of its intensely self-centred worldview.

There is a further catch: the more China involves itself in matters of global order and governance, the more nervous the United States, Europe and China's neighbours will become. The challenge for Beijing is to move from the rim to the centre of global governance without aggravating the current world disorder, all the while advancing Chinese national interests. The task before the West is no less demanding: to rise above its geopolitical and economic anxieties and co-opt the world's second power in collective problem solving. The quality of *US-China engagement* will be pivotal here. Their relationship will continue to be fiercely competitive, but some sort of functional normality is attainable. Washington and Beijing owe it to the world, and most of all to themselves, to manage their rivalry sensibly.

No less vital to a future international order is the role of *powers in flux* – important players that are either declining, rising or undergoing some kind of transition. Throughout history, major powers have found it difficult to adjust to the loss of status and influence. Russia vividly illustrates the point, but there are other modern examples, notably former colonial powers such as Britain and France. Denial is generally the default response to decline, sometimes reinforced by military adventurism as in the case of Russia in Ukraine or Britain and France in Suez 1956. But sometimes major powers are able to re-invent themselves, as in the cases of Japan and Germany after the Second World War. The key to a successful transformation lies in moving on from delusions of "greatness" and self-entitlement to maximizing actual strengths.

Adjustment is also a challenge for *rising powers*. Under Prime Minister Narendra Modi, India has promoted itself as the leader of the Global South and an independent centre of global power. However, it has found it difficult to persuade others of its vision. Few in the Global South wish to be led; India's neighbours view it as an overbearing would-be hegemon; and Washington has lost patience with Modi's "multi-aligned" foreign policy. Like Beijing, New Delhi also faces the problem of matching capabilities and intentions. It speaks of India being a new type of global actor, but it is unclear whether it is ready to reinvent itself and think beyond conventional metrics of power.

The failures and shortcomings of the United States and Europe, and the excesses of China and Russia, have created openings for *middle powers* such as Türkiye, Brazil, South Africa and Saudi Arabia. But to do what exactly? In the past, middle powers were mainly content to maximize their sovereignty and freedom of manoeuvre by balancing between larger powers; former CIA Director William Burns has described them as the "hedging middle".[15] But now we are seeing signs of greater ambition, both in terms of power projection and problem solving. Under President Recep Erdoğan, Türkiye has played a pivotal role in addressing collateral issues from the war in Ukraine, such as the passage of grain exports from Ukraine and Russia through the Black Sea. Meanwhile, Brazil is positioning itself at the head of efforts to alleviate climate change and poverty in developing countries.

As international power becomes more diffuse, middle powers are likely to find growing opportunities to influence global governance. However, there is nothing certain about their success. Ambition itself is insufficient without a proven ability to contribute to problem solving. The distribution of influence across multiple players makes for an intensely competitive "market-place", with the winners likely to come from those state actors that are able to see beyond narrow self-interest and add materially to the global commons.

It is difficult to recall a time when *multilateralism and its institutions* have been in such poor standing. Fairly or not, they have become synonymous with many of the worst vices of governance – unrepresentativeness and inequity, bureaucratic inefficiency, cronyism and impotence. At the same time, multi-lateral cooperation has never been more indispensable. The universality and urgency of contemporary challenges demand nothing less.

In a globalized yet fragmenting world, international institutions come in all shapes and sizes. This diversity is a mixed blessing. On the one hand, it weak-ens the notion of a broader community by encouraging tribalism. On the other hand, a patchwork of many different and sometimes conflicting bodies offers nations a menu of options – and incentives – to engage multilaterally. Given the impediments to reform of the Security Council and the Bretton Woods institu-tions (IMF, World Bank), the way forward may lie in an eclectic approach to cooperation, whereby various institutions and mechanisms serve complemen-tary purposes. Those structures and arrangements that meet the needs of their constituents will prosper, while those that do not will become marginalized. With greater choice and competition, the quality of international institutions may improve, as countries rediscover the habit of working together towards common goals.

*Non-state actors* have long played an important, if underestimated, part in global order and governance. But in coming decades, their role is set to grow exponentially. This influence will be decisive across much of the global policy agenda, from the development of renewable sources of energy to AI governance and countering disinformation.

The expanding role of non-state actors raises two particular issues in build-ing a new international order. The first is finding a balance between encour-aging initiative and creativity, and ensuring accountability and responsibility. Managing this tension is central to the future development of AI. The second issue is more structural: how best to involve non-state actors in decision-making. Even in Western democracies, governments jealously guard a near-monopoly over this. But if non-state actors are to invest in future solutions, such as the development of renewables, they will need to become full partici-pants in the policy process.

More generally, addressing the twenty-first-century global agenda will require an all-of-society approach. One of the constraints on effective policy-making is that governments struggle to gain public support – and legitimacy – for difficult decisions. This leads them to opt for lowest common denominator populism or, just as unfortunately, to keep people in the dark. But there is another way, which is to incentivize public interest and engagement. This goes against almost every instinct of government. Yet such involvement improves the chances of implementing difficult decisions. Instead of being a passive and often resentful recipient of top-down fiats, the public becomes an active stakeholder.

This book concludes with an epilogue. In imagining *tomorrow's world*, it has become customary to speak of being at an "inflection point". Joe Biden employed the expression to distinguish between "those who argue that, given all the challenges we face … that autocracy is the best way forward … and those who understand that democracy is essential".[16] However, the true inflection point is far more significant and encompassing than the ideological struggle suggested by Biden. The very future of international society is at stake. The Long Peace of the post-Second World War era may be coming to an end, giving way to a new age of conflict, including between major powers. But we have also reached a pivotal moment – a potential tipping point – in the struggle against climate change, the management of global pandemics, and in the technological and information revolutions.

These immense challenges cannot be ignored or wished away. Nor can they be successfully addressed by resorting to the standard playbook – intoning the verities of the liberal international order, ratcheting up geopolitical and ideological confrontation, or putting one's faith in great power "bargains". Changing realities necessitate more enterprising and, above all, more *relevant* approaches. The notion of international cooperation may seem utopian in the current climate. However, we are not doomed to live out some dystopian Hobbesian future, whereby force and fraud become normalized. Tomorrow's world is one of abundant promise. But only if we are ready to abandon obsolete thinking and recast global governance for the demands of the twenty-first century.

# THE UNRAVELLING OF INTERNATIONAL ORDER

1

# THE RISE AND FALL OF THE LIBERAL ORDER

In thinking about the future of international order, it makes sense to begin by re-examining the liberal or "rules-based" model. After all, it has been the dominant paradigm of the post-Cold War era. But a more important reason still is that the liberal order exemplifies many of the qualities and shortcomings of global governance. Its mixed fortunes offer an instructive tale about the nature of order and disorder in the modern world.

The liberal rules-based order has been widely pilloried, including within the West, for its inadequacies and iniquities. And with good reason. Yet it is also one of the most successful systems in history. Although the liberal order has privileged Western democracies, it has benefited many non-Western and developing countries as well. The biggest winner of all has been China, which has emerged as the next global power on the back of the stability and prosperity this order has offered. But nearly every country has profited from it in some degree. It is important, therefore, to see the liberal vision of a rules-based international order in proper perspective, to acknowledge its achievements as well as highlight its failings.

**The universalist moment**

The "rules-based international order" is a somewhat slippery concept. For one thing, the term itself is relatively new, entering regular usage only in the 1990s. During the Cold War, the United States led a liberal order founded on certain norms and institutions, but this was a limited and indeed self-limiting project. It was highly successful in many respects, but it was not globally dominant. Its rules not only had no remit in the Soviet bloc and associated client states, but also did not apply to many other parts of the world, including China and India. There was little effort to universalize liberal values. Instead, as the International Relations scholar John Ikenberry notes, the United States pursued two separate order-building projects: one, the "Western project to reorganize and strengthen the foundations for liberal democracy within the advanced industrial world"; the other, the "Cold War project, oriented toward building political partnerships and alliances in the struggle with the Soviet Union".[1]

That all changed with the end of the Cold War, and the arrival of America's "unipolar moment".[2] The end of bipolarity opened the way for a new, unitary global order to emerge. As Ikenberry puts it, the "inside" (Western) order became the "outside" (global) order.[3] It remained, however, Western in essence, reflecting the dominance of Western interests and values. As the sole superpower, the United States set, enforced and sometimes disregarded the rules of the international system. Other countries occasionally sought to dilute its dominance, but for the most part accepted this as an inescapable reality. US power was at its zenith; at no stage was the gap between America and other major powers greater than in the 1990s. Its political authority and self-confidence appeared unchallengeable.

*The keys to success*

The authority of this new order was boosted by the fact that it had emerged triumphant by employing predominantly non-military means. Contrary to some revisionist views of history, it was not American military might (and the Strategic Defense Initiative – SDI or "Star Wars") that brought down the Soviet Union. Rather, it was the vast disparity in what the two rival systems were able to offer their respective constituencies. Whereas the US-led order during the Cold War presided over an unprecedented increase in economic prosperity and social welfare for the populations of the West, the Soviet order stagnated, particularly from the late 1970s. The triumph of the liberal international order was, above all, one of Western – and liberal – soft power.

Subsequently, the US-led post-Cold War order was able to further internationalize its benefits, delivering well beyond its core constituencies. The 1990s were great years for democratization, but also for economic growth and development, peace and security, and public health across the planet. There were atrocities, such as the 1994 Rwandan genocide and the Balkan conflicts, but the overall direction of travel was positive. The liberal international order was seen to be more powerful, more effective, and more humane than any other. This gave it a dual legitimacy: that of power *and* performance. Countries might object to individual Western policies or actions, sometimes vehemently, but they still wanted in.

This contradiction was exemplified by China, which angrily condemned the US bombing of its embassy in Belgrade during the 1999 Kosovo war, and later entered into a stand-off with Washington over the EP-3 spy-plane incident near Hainan island in 2001.[4] And yet it became increasingly integrated into a global order whose rules were shaped by American power and influence. Beijing recognized that US leadership was essential to the international stability on which China's growth depended and, by extension, to the continuing popular legitimacy of Communist Party rule. The dividends of membership of Western-dominated institutions like the WTO – enhanced access to global markets, natural resources, and foreign investment and technology – far outweighed concerns about US hegemony or the subversive influence of Western liberalism.

Two further features underpinned the early success of the US-led liberal order. One was that no other country was capable of offering a viable alternative. True, in 1997 Presidents Jiang Zemin and Boris Yeltsin issued a Sino-Russian declaration calling for a "multipolar world" and the "democratization of international relations".[5] But this charade fooled no-one. Yeltsin was forced to admit the reality of NATO eastward enlargement, and as "compensation" was allowed to bring Russia into the G-8 as the sole non-Western member. Meanwhile, China pressed hard to join the WTO, finally acceding in 2001.

Another aspect of the post-Cold War order that contributed to its success was that it was genuinely liberal. Although US President Bill Clinton (1992–2000) was committed to democracy promotion, his touch was a relatively light one by the standards of his predecessors and successors. There was no Grenada-type invasion such as occurred under Ronald Reagan,[6] let alone the huge military commitments in Afghanistan and Iraq that later defined the presidency of George W. Bush. The major military operations of the Clinton era – Bosnia 1995 and Kosovo 1999 – were intended as humanitarian interventions ("responsibility to protect"). Both were time-limited and successful in achieving their main objectives, which ensured that the idea of the liberal international order, virtuous and powerful, remained broadly plausible.

Despite talk of promoting democracy and stability, the Clinton presidency mostly stayed clear of attempts at regime change. (It targeted Serbian President Slobodan Milošević, not because he was authoritarian, but because he presided over genocidal policies in Bosnia and Kosovo.) Washington believed, wrongly as it turned out, that economic and social modernization in China would lead to political liberalization. Naïve though these assumptions were, the attitude of the White House was one of deep faith in the power of liberal norms and institutions, and that others would in time come to appreciate their value.

Finally, the liberal international order captured the spirit of the age. Following decades of geopolitical confrontation and systematic domestic repression in many countries, people were ready for a more positive vision. More than three decades on, it is easy to forget the idealism and optimism of that time – whether in ex-Soviet republics, emancipated former Warsaw Pact members, a post-apartheid South Africa, and even an economically modernizing China. Dictatorships and authoritarian regimes still abounded, but there was a definite mood that not only facilitated a liberal international order, but made it necessary.

### The seeds of failure

How, then, did we go from America's "unipolar moment" and the triumph of the liberal order to today's wholesale trashing of international norms and escalating disorder?

The very strengths that made the liberal order so successful in the early post-Cold War period contributed to its subsequent difficulties. In the first place, the idealism, emotional excitement, and great hopes associated with the end of the Cold War have long since dissipated. We live in an altogether more cynical age, in which the vision of a just and generous international order seems quixotic. Even within liberal democracies, the language is about national interests, geopolitical competition, and strategic containment, with the threat of major confrontation closer than it has been in decades. It is as if the world experienced a brief Kantian moment in the 1990s, only for events to drag it back to the Hobbesian reality that was always present, if ignored.

But to say the world has lost its idealism begs the question why. What went wrong? Who messed up? Could things have gone differently and, if so, how?

One explanation arises from the changing relativities of power. The United States no longer dominates the world as it once did, and consequently has been unable to impose its vision of order. This is less a matter of US and Western decline than of the "rise of the rest" – major powers such as China, Russia and India, and key players in the Global South like Türkiye, Saudi Arabia and South Africa.[7] To some extent, this represents a return to a pre-Western normal. Before the European powers achieved global dominance in the nineteenth century, there were multiple centres of influence. And even during the heyday of Western imperialism, there was no one hegemonic power. Viewed through this prism, America's "unipolar moment" was an aberration, and inevitably short-lived. Yeltsin's liberal foreign minister, Andrei Kozyrev, was already warning back in 1994 that "the international order of the 21st century will not be a Pax Americana ... The United States does not have the capability to rule alone".[8]

When in September 1990 President George H. W. Bush announced a "new world order",[9] the only significant limit on America's global influence appeared to be itself – whether it would seek to implement an expansive internationalist vision or adopt a more inward-looking national agenda. Now, however, we are reverting to the historical mean: multiple players vigorously asserting their interests, and resisting direction or instruction from a would-be hegemon.

The result is a more diversified, fragmented and disorderly environment, in which any attempt to impose a unitary international order is unnatural and unsustainable.

This trend is separate from America's performance as global leader. The point is that China and Russia would have asserted themselves over time irrespective of US actions. They are countries, indeed civilizations, with strong traditions of messianism and exceptionalism. As soon as they developed the heft and self-confidence to pursue more ambitious goals, they were going to challenge the post-Cold War status quo. Thus, Xi Jinping's aim of "the great rejuvenation of the Chinese nation"[10] reflects a mission to restore China as a great power and global civilization, and right the wrongs inflicted during the "century of humiliation" (between the Treaty of Nanjing in 1842 and the founding of the People's Republic of China in 1949). In the case of Russia, the humiliation was much more recent and briefer – the fall of the Soviet Union and the decade of the 1990s – but no less powerfully felt. And the desire to return things to their "natural" condition is just as strong. The 2022 invasion of Ukraine was motivated primarily by the urge to rectify historical "errors", in particular the existence of an independent Ukraine separate from the Russian empire.[11]

Well into the 2000s Western governments continued to misinterpret Chinese and Russian acquiescence to the post-Cold War order as reflecting a sincere conversion to its principles. However, Beijing's approach to international relations has always been grounded in a hard-bitten pragmatism, albeit wrapped up in platitudes about "win-win" cooperation. It never had much time for Western pieties about rules, yet recognized the practical value of the liberal order to Chinese interests. Moscow, by contrast, barely bothered to pretend. Putin's speech at the 2007 Munich Security Conference, in which he accused America of disdaining international law, laid down a clear marker that Russia would pursue its own interests as it saw fit, and without care of giving offence to the (self-appointed) rule-givers.[12] The speech shocked its audience, but it shouldn't have. The signs had been there for some time.

## How the wheels came off: six stages of suicidal statecraft

Western leaders like to believe that it is the moral and political example of the West that is most inspiring to others: the emphasis on individual human rights and freedoms; the openness and dynamism of civil society; and the equity and justice that come from the rule of law. Yet, while these virtues are certainly influential, the chief selling-point of liberal democracies is that they have far outperformed other types of government according to *material* metrics. Being rich, powerful and stable has been the best advertisement of all.

Correspondingly, nothing has discredited the liberal vision of a rules-based international order more than the policy failures of the United States and Europe over the past two decades. Even with better decision-making, such an order could not have survived in its original post-Cold War form. But the missteps or rather "suicidal statecraft"[13] of Western governments have accelerated its decline. Six developments, in particular, have played a decisive role in the undoing of the liberal order: the 2003 invasion of Iraq; the global financial crisis; the weak response to Putin's 2014 annexation of Crimea; the acute dysfunctionality of the first Trump administration; Western mismanagement of the Covid-19 pandemic; and Joe Biden's mishandling of the wars in Ukraine and Gaza.

### Rules are for other people: the 2003 invasion of Iraq

The invasion of Iraq was a fiasco on several levels. Most obviously, it disregarded international rules and processes. Although the George W. Bush administration attempted to replicate the UN consensus that had underpinned the international response to Saddam Hussein's 1990 invasion of Kuwait, it quickly realized this would not be possible. Not only was Russia more self-confident and less cooperative than an imploding USSR, but Putin was also less committed than Mikhail Gorbachev to working with the West – especially after his attempts to promote Russia as America's global partner of choice in the wake of 9/11 had been rebuffed. The strong anti-war stance adopted by Berlin and Paris meant also there was no consensus within the West. The US-led "coalition of the willing" became reduced to an Anglosphere-plus.[14] This damaged the legitimacy of the enterprise from the outset. The notion of a rules-based international order was further undermined when the ostensible reasons for intervention – Baghdad's alleged possession of weapons of mass destruction (WMD) and its involvement in international terrorism – were later shown to be bogus, and it emerged that Western intelligence had been manipulated or "sexed up" to justify military action.

That said, the unsound basis of the Iraq intervention was not in itself fatal to the credibility of the liberal international order. Had the success of the opening military phase been followed up, it might have been possible to gloss over the moral arguments. But the intervention proved to be an abject and prolonged operational failure. The counter-insurgency was a disaster; the initial welcome given to coalition troops soon turned into bloody hostility. Efforts to promote democracy in Iraq led to crony and sectarian politics of the worst kind. The elimination of the Saddam Hussein regime, and the dismantling of the structures of the Ba'athist state, created a strategic vacuum that Iran was quick to fill. And the dysfunctionality and corruption of successive Iraqi governments opened the way for Daesh/ISIS (Islamic State of Iraq and Syria) to wreak further devastation.

The Iraq invasion also had wider knock-on effects. Most critically, it distracted attention from the US-led Operation Enduring Freedom in Afghanistan. Early on, the latter had appeared to be a rare example of a successful foreign military intervention. That promise soon evaporated, and after two decades of mostly fruitless endeavour, Western forces carried out a hurried final withdrawal from Kabul in August 2021 that left the Taliban once again in control of the country. The conflict caused the deaths of around a quarter of a million combatants and civilians on all sides, while the political gains in developing democracy, women's rights and the rule of law were quickly reversed.

What most harmed the liberal international order was that the West was seen to be impotent as well as immoral. The world witnessed the United States, arguably the greatest power in history, being frustrated at every turn by assorted insurgent groups (in Iraq) and one of the most backward regimes on the planet (the Taliban). If America and its European allies could not impose themselves in conditions where there was such a disparity of power, how could they hope to sustain a rules-based order across the globe?

By exposing the limitations of American power, the cumulative experience of Iraq and Afghanistan shook the self-belief of proponents of a liberal order, and gave encouragement to all those resenting US primacy and leadership. These considerations were later to play out in relation to the 2022 Russian invasion of Ukraine. Putin understood that Western appeals on behalf of the rules-based international order would be dismissed as rank hypocrisy by much of the non-Western world. For him, the US-led invasion of Iraq has been the gift that keeps on giving.

### The end of "West is best": the 2008 global financial crisis

The damage to the liberal order caused by the global financial crisis was at least as significant as the Iraq war, if very different in character. The main failures were systemic rather than moral or operational. The financial crisis was "born in the USA", beginning with the collapse of the American sub-prime mortgage market. But this was just the tip of the iceberg. The crash revealed excessive risk-taking in the banking sector and the extreme volatility of financial markets across the West. More than that, it highlighted the downsides of a global economy overly reliant on the United States and the so-called "Washington Consensus", with its neo-liberal emphasis on free markets, deregulation and privatization. The worst recession since the Great Depression of the 1930s was not just ruinous to many in America, but had worldwide consequences. A total system meltdown was only avoided by the injection of huge national stimulus and recovery packages, and unprecedented policy coordination between the world's leading economies through the mechanism of the G-20.

In the years that followed, it seemed the worst was over. Washington was able in some measure to draw a line under the financial adventurism of the past. But the damage was wider and longer-lasting than appreciated. While the United States recovered relatively quickly, many European economies continued to suffer the after-effects of the crisis over the next decade. Most fundamentally, it undermined global trust in one of the aspects of the liberal order that had previously been the most reliable, namely, the Western financial and economic system.

The crisis also suggested that there were alternatives to the Washington Consensus. For example, the Chinese economy continued to grow, albeit at a reduced tempo. The Communist Party leadership put in place a 4 trillion RMB stimulus package (equivalent to $587 billion or 13 per cent of China's GDP in 2008), and China emerged from the crisis in better shape than almost any other country. This had several ramifications. It legitimized China's approach to governance, not only with its own population, but also in much of the developing world. Beijing was able to argue that its brand of state capitalism offered a stable basis for economic growth and social welfare. The financial crisis dramatized the contrast between Chinese resilience on the one hand, and Western systemic failures and policy shortcomings on the other. The psychological impact was considerable. The confidence of Western governments and especially publics took a battering, while that of the Chinese Communist Party soared.

2008 was a light bulb moment. Before the crash, there was a general assumption that the West was "best". It represented the gold standard in military power, economic prosperity and political stability. The United States and its European allies might be selective and self-serving in their interpretation of international order. But US global leadership was still the dominant reality. The world continued to run on Western time and according to Western rules.

The financial crisis revealed major flaws in liberal institutions and practices, and weakened Western societies. It had a lasting negative impact on vulnerable social groups, exacerbated economic inequality, and undermined public faith in political elites.[15] Although the United States remained the sole superpower and by far the most influential actor, its vulnerabilities – and those of the liberal order – were laid bare. The West lost its post-Cold War monopoly on economic wisdom, and was no longer unchallengeable. International society became more disorderly, as a growing number of actors became increasingly assertive in pursuing their individual agendas.

*The stamp of impotence: Western responses to Putin's annexation of Crimea*

Russia's annexation of Crimea in February–March 2014, and subsequent occupation of parts of the Donbass region, were a precursor to its full invasion of Ukraine eight years later. It was the first direct assault by a non-Western power on the liberal international order. Russia broke multiple rules. It invaded a neighbouring sovereign state on the flimsiest of pretexts. It ignored its commitment, in the 1994 Budapest Memorandum co-signed with the United States and the United Kingdom, to safeguard the territorial integrity of Ukraine.[16] It broke its own 1997 bilateral treaty with Kyiv, by which the latter extended the lease for the Russian Black Sea fleet in return for Moscow formally recognizing Ukraine's post-1991 borders.[17] And in July 2014, Russian proxies in the Donbass shot down an international civilian airliner (Malaysia Airlines MH17).

Given events since February 2022, the annexation of Crimea does not now seem especially shocking. But at the time Western policy-makers were dumbfounded by the brazenness of Putin's actions. The annexation was a textbook example of a major power deciding that its national interests overrode any international rules or strictures. It indicated the Kremlin's confidence that its rule-breaking would incur no serious costs. In a world where the "weak get beaten",[18] what mattered most was power – whether you had it and were willing to use it, and whether others were able to stop, counter or punish you. The annexation of Crimea and its aftermath crystallized this Hobbesian worldview, in which "notions of right and wrong, justice and injustice, have … no place".[19]

In 2014, Putin bet that the West's appetite to defend Ukraine – and international order – would not match his determination to annex Crimea and undermine the new Ukrainian administration of President Petro Poroshenko. He judged correctly. The United States and the European Union issued statements condemning Russia, and imposed various sanctions.[20] US President Barack Obama dismissed Russia as a "regional power" whose actions demonstrated weakness rather than strength.[21] But Western efforts to raise the costs for Putin had negligible impact. Berlin and Paris sought to protect bilateral ties with Moscow, and Germany became even more energy-dependent on Russia.[22] Franco-German efforts to mediate a political solution through the Minsk process[23] had the unintended consequence of consolidating Russian territorial gains by, in effect, treating the two combatants as morally equivalent. Meanwhile, the Obama administration continued to block the delivery of light defensive weapons to Kyiv.

Both Russia's aggression and the West's supine response were consistent with patterns of behaviour both sides had exhibited in preceding years. As early as 2004, Putin attempted to reverse Ukraine's Orange Revolution by pressuring the outgoing Ukrainian President, Leonid Kuchma, to crush the challenge of Viktor Yushchenko. In 2008, he used the opportunity of a brief war with Tbilisi to formalize the secession of two breakaway Georgian provinces, Abkhazia and South Ossetia. French President Nicolas Sarkozy subsequently brokered a settlement that made this a fait accompli. In August 2012 Obama declared that the use of chemical weapons by the Syrian regime of Bashar al-Assad would cross a "red line" – and then failed to act when this line was crossed a year later.[24]

With the annexation of Crimea, Putin demonstrated that the liberal vision of a rules-based international order had no practical force unless supported by a genuine commitment to defend it. He gambled that the United States and the leading European powers were no different from Russia in prioritizing self-interest, except that they dressed this up as ethical behaviour. Unfortunately, the Western response to the Crimean crisis confirmed Putin's point in very public fashion.

## Donald Trump "makes America great again" (part I)

Few individuals did more to undermine the liberal international order – and US global leadership – than Donald Trump during his first presidency (2017–21). This order was already in deep trouble before he swung a wrecking ball at its norms, values and institutions. It was his particular art, though, to seize on the new spirit of the age, one of growing cynicism and expediency. His actions stripped away many of the pretensions surrounding the US-led order and exposed the emasculation of liberal values within the West itself.

Trump made it clear from the outset that he had no time at all for liberal or indeed any version of internationalism. His "America-first" narrative saw the world as a feral environment in which almost everyone was either a competitor, rival, enemy or, in the case of most of America's allies and partners, a backsliding freeloader. Accordingly, he set about dismantling the post-Cold War order. The United States abrogated or withdrew from more international agreements than under any of his predecessors. High-profile casualties included the Joint Comprehensive Plan of Action (JCPOA) over Iran's nuclear programme; the Trans-Pacific Partnership (TPP); the Paris climate agreement; and the Intermediate Nuclear Forces (INF) and Open Skies treaties with Russia. Trump also pulled the United States out of various UN bodies, including UNESCO (United Nations Educational Scientific and Cultural Organization), UNRWA (UN Relief Works Agency), UNHRC (UN Human Rights Council) and the WHO (World Health Organization). He began the withdrawal of US troops from Iraq, Afghanistan, Syria and Europe. He sidestepped the WTO to impose unilateral trade tariffs against China. And he threatened to pull the United States out of NATO and alliances with Japan and South Korea, and publicly identified the European Union as a "foe".[25]

Trump's disregard for international agreements and institutions underlined the primacy of power over rules in his worldview. If Biden was later to speak of the power of example,[26] then for Trump power itself was the ultimate example. In this respect, he had much in common with Putin and other authoritarian leaders. The United States would pursue its foreign policy interests as far as it could, unconstrained by concerns about international order. Trump borrowed from the nationalist/isolationist tradition in US foreign policy, but took things much further. There was no pretence about common Western (much less liberal) values; instead, the unapologetic pursuit of US interests spoke to a different political culture, based on narrow self-interest and the maximization of power relations. It became apparent, too, that Trump did not much believe in American rules and institutions either – as demonstrated by his efforts to overturn the result of the 2020 presidential election.

Trump's contempt for a rules-based order was a boon to authoritarian regimes around the world. One of the most striking features of his first presidency was a preference for engaging personally with authoritarian leaders – Xi Jinping, Putin, Saudi Crown Prince Mohammed bin Salman, North Korean leader Kim Jong-un – and his conspicuous disrespect towards Western counterparts such as German Chancellor Angela Merkel, British Prime Minister Theresa May, and Canadian Prime Minister Justin Trudeau.

The damage Trump inflicted on the liberal order extended well beyond America's role within it. With the United States – the cornerstone of this order – no longer subscribing to it, other Western democracies were incapable of filling the void. With few exceptions, European leaders either pandered to Trump or were impotent in the face of American force majeure – as illustrated by the collapse of the JCPOA. As a result, such moral advantage as the democratic West still enjoyed over authoritarian regimes had largely evaporated by the end of his presidency.

Trump's excesses injected an added element of uncertainty and unpredictability – disorder – into the international system. For decades, the world had been used to Western leaders, and especially US presidents, behaving more or less normally. They might be hawkish or make bad decisions, but they were seen as essentially rational actors. This enabled others to frame policy around reasonable expectations and probabilities. Trump changed all that – but not to America's advantage. With no likelihood of consistent decision-making in Washington, powers such as China, Russia and Iran had little incentive to be responsive to US (and Western) substantive policy concerns, since any agreement reached might later be cancelled.

In the end, the most damaging aspect of Trump's foreign policy during his first term was that it did not work. For all his macho posturing, the Trump years saw a significant weakening of US power and influence in the world.

Allies were publicly humiliated and alliances were called into question. Enemies and opponents became more assertive – from China and Russia to the Taliban, Iran and North Korea. The United States was more overbearing than at any time in living memory, but also surprisingly impotent. Its reputation for functional competence, already damaged by the global financial crisis, was shredded by serial maladministration in the White House.[27] American claims to virtue became risible. The consequences for the liberal, rules-based international order were crippling. By the end of the Trump presidency it had become evident that this order was neither orderly nor liberal nor based on any meaningful rules.

### Devil take the hindmost: responding to the Covid-19 pandemic

Trump's worst failure was his disastrous mismanagement of the Covid-19 pandemic. Domestically, it cost him re-election in 2020. Internationally, it inflicted enormous reputational damage on the United States and the wider West.

The pandemic not only exposed the shortcomings of the "rules-based international order", it also highlighted the human costs of its breakdown. To a greater extent even than the 2008 financial crisis, it demonstrated that bad governance had material consequences. By May 2024, more than 7 million people worldwide had died as a direct result of Covid-19.[28] The disruption to economic activity led to the worst global recession since the Great Depression. And geopolitical tensions between the United States and China, already high, were fanned by mutual recriminations over responsibility for the virus and its extraordinary death toll.

The pandemic should have been an opportunity to showcase the advantages of liberal democracies – political transparency, democratic solidarity, and technological superiority – in contrast to the secretiveness and relative backwardness of authoritarian regimes. After all, the virus originated in Wuhan, China, apparently as a result of unhygienic conditions in a local "wet" (live animal) market. The city and provincial authorities, and subsequently the central government in Beijing, first attempted to cover up the outbreak and then underplayed its severity, before belatedly admitting the gravity of the situation.

Despite the delay caused by the lack of transparency of the Chinese authorities, Western governments nevertheless had time to put measures in place to contain the pandemic. But they were slow to act, instead responding with a mixture of denial, complacency, confusion and a startling lack of solidarity. In the early months of Covid-19, there was minimal coordination between the Trump administration and European governments, while the EU degenerated into a rabble of 27 different states, each pursuing individual approaches to the coronavirus. When they did eventually come together to work on an economic recovery package for the EU area, they bickered long and hard over the details. It was only intense public scrutiny that eventually embarrassed them into agreeing a deal after the second longest EU summit in history.

Worse still were the West's dismal efforts at global vaccine diplomacy. In principle, Western policy-makers appreciated the importance not only of developing vaccines, but also of ensuring their worldwide distribution. If Covid-19 was not contained globally, then even countries with advanced health systems would be acutely vulnerable to new strains of the coronavirus. As the former British Prime Minister Gordon Brown put it, "no one is safe until everyone is safe".[29] But although the scientists developed vaccines with remarkable speed, vaccine nationalism defined the response of governments. Mechanisms for international vaccine distribution were established, such as the COVAX (Covid-19 Vaccines Global Access) programme, but Western nations then hoovered up most of the global supply. The result was that vaccination rates in developing countries, particularly in Africa, were extremely low at the height of the pandemic in 2020–21.[30] Meanwhile, Germany and several other European governments joined multi-national pharmaceutical companies in blocking moves to loosen patent restrictions on vaccine technology, something that would have helped address the shortfall in vaccines to the developing world.

Despite their wealth, as well as their advanced health systems and world-class research capacity, Western democracies were nonetheless some of the worst performing countries during the pandemic. During 2020–21, the United States and the United Kingdom had the highest per capita mortality rates among large nations, greater even than Brazil and Mexico, whose populations suffered directly from the denialism of their leaders. In America, public health became hostage to conflicts over identity and culture – a development stoked by the Trump White House. In Britain, the casual approach of Prime Minister Boris Johnson encouraged neglect, gross inefficiency and corruption.

The Covid-19 pandemic was not just a public health failure; it became emblematic of the degradation of governance within the West. It revealed how easily rules-based systems – and liberal values – could break down under pressure. The damage to the standing of the liberal order was immense. Quite apart from an inability to protect their own populations, the lack of empathy shown by rich Western democracies towards poorer nations accentuated the divide between the Global North and Global South. It made a mockery of the notion that the West could preside over a functioning global order or offer a model of best practice for others to emulate.

## *The Biden disconnect*

It may seem strange to identify Joe Biden's foreign policy as one of the stages of "suicidal statecraft" that accelerated the decline of the post-Cold War order. His presidency boasted some impressive successes. Biden reversed the decline in transatlantic relations. He was instrumental in marshalling a united and vigorous Western response to Putin's invasion of Ukraine. He brought a consistency of purpose to US policy on China. He was responsible for several landmark initiatives, notably the Inflation Reduction Act and the CHIPS and Science Act.[31] And, at least in the beginning, he improved America's global reputation, restoring greater professionalism to its conduct of foreign relations and resolving the crisis in public health management that had so undermined the federal government's response to Covid-19.

Yet, despite these achievements, the Biden presidency became notorious principally for its failures: the shambolic US withdrawal from Afghanistan; the unravelling of its Ukraine policy; its limp response to the humanitarian disaster in Gaza; and Biden's own personal decline.

Taking each of these in turn, the pull-out from Afghanistan was damaging to the United States, and the liberal international order, because of the way it was carried out rather than because the decision itself was necessarily mistaken. In overestimating the strength and resilience of the Afghan National Army, Washington failed to anticipate the speed and extent of the Taliban's victory. It also omitted to brief allies in the International Security Assistance Force (ISAF) on the US plans for withdrawal. The optics were terrible. The final, desperate exit recalled the US pull-out from Saigon nearly half a century earlier, and presented a stark contrast to the orderly Soviet withdrawal from Afghanistan. Worst of all, it conveyed the message that America was an unreliable ally and partner.

During the 2024 presidential campaign, the Republican Party lost few opportunities to claim that the US withdrawal from Afghanistan had emboldened Putin to invade Ukraine. Ironically, though, Ukraine's remarkable resistance gave Biden an early opportunity to salvage America's reputation. And, for a time, he managed to do this. The US-led Western response was stronger and more cohesive than many, including Putin, expected, and transatlantic cooperation reached levels not seen since before the 2003 invasion of Iraq.

However, as the war turned attritional, there was a widening discrepancy between American (and Western) rhetoric and real outcomes. Biden promised to support Ukraine "for as long as it takes", and supplied it with copious amounts of military and economic assistance.[32] But he also placed significant restrictions on how this aid could be used. He blocked progress towards Ukrainian membership of NATO,[33] and offered Kyiv no meaningful security guarantees. It became clear that, while Washington did not want Ukraine to lose the war, neither did it wish to see Russia defeated. Periodic hints by Putin that he might resort to nuclear weapons paralyzed US decision-making. Without a coherent strategy in place, the Biden White House drifted as Ukraine's armed forces lost ground on the battlefield.

This was harmful both for US credibility and the notion of a rules-based international order. As 2024 drew to a close, Putin became increasingly buoyant about his chances of victory, and sought to drive home his advantage – aiming not only to build on Russia's territorial gains, but also to fatally weaken Ukrainian sovereignty, reshape the map of Europe, and fracture the Western consensus. Biden looked bereft of ideas in the face of this reversal of momentum.

If Biden's response to the Russian invasion of Ukraine was initially successful, then his approach to the Gaza conflict was a failure from the outset. At virtually no stage was he able to temper Israeli actions or mitigate the humanitarian tragedy unfolding in the territory. Israeli Prime Minister Benjamin Netanyahu was able to act with impunity, secure in the knowledge that Washington possessed no effective leverage over him. Even allowing for the difficulty of Biden's position, his tolerance of Israeli excesses in Gaza made a nonsense of America's commitment to a rules-based international order.

All this was aggravated by the spectacle of Biden's personal decline. Well before the disastrous presidential debate performance that forced an end to his re-election bid,[34] he was visibly faltering. The comparison with other major leaders, such as Putin and Xi Jinping, was brutal. Biden became a metaphor for a weakened West, while his authoritarian opponents appeared vigorous, self-confident and decisive. His refusal to give way to a younger, more capable Democratic Party candidate until it was too late also paved the way for the return of Donald Trump to the White House. This, ultimately, was Biden's greatest defeat. For it created the conditions for the final collapse of the liberal international order, while imperilling the future of American democracy and the rule of law.

## Drawing the lessons

From the end of the Second World War to the early years of the twenty-first century, the United States (and the wider West) was the epitome of success. In the aftermath of 9/11, its international standing was at a historic high. Al-Qaeda's terrorist attacks were shocking, but had the effect of rallying support behind America. Putin was the first international leader to offer his sympathies to George W. Bush, and later endorsed the military intervention in Afghanistan. US-China cooperation expanded rapidly under the Bush administration, leading some observers to describe the state of relations as the best in history.[35] The prospects for the post-Cold War order had never seemed better.

It offered a vision that attracted friends and admirers and deterred (most) opponents.

Perhaps the most surprising aspect of the subsequent unravelling of this order is how quickly it happened. A little over two decades after 9/11, the international system is unrecognizable in many respects from what it was. Instead of order, disorder is everywhere. US strategic and normative dominance has given way to a fiercely competitive geopolitical environment. The economic globalization of the Washington Consensus is being supplanted by mercantilism, protectionism and state interventionism, including in the United States itself. The West is no longer identified with good governance, while the liberal order has lost its moral authority.

Looking back at the decline of the post-Cold War order, the greatest threats to it have not been external – the rise of China, Russia's resurgence, Islamist extremism – but internal. Western policy-makers routinely accuse China and Russia of "malign" behaviour, but it is their complacency, misjudgements and blunders that have provided the openings for Beijing, Moscow and others to exploit. The post-Cold War order would certainly have come under attack sooner rather than later, but Western shortcomings ensured that its plight would become existential.

Much of this was rooted in an almost boundless arrogance. Having triumphed in the Cold War, many in the United States and Europe believed that "history" had ended with the final victory of liberal democracy and free market capitalism. Like Francis Fukuyama, the originator of the "end of history" thesis, they thought that other countries would either embrace liberal norms and values, or else would be left behind. Either way, the outcome was incontrovertible: the West, and the rules-based international order, had won. The idea of history as something fluid, dynamic and contested was lost.

Arrogance led to a loss of introspection and critical thinking. Western policy circles assumed they had a virtual monopoly on political and economic wisdom. There was little appreciation of the diversity of the world beyond the Manichaean simplicities of good governance versus bad, democracy versus authoritarianism, progress versus backwardness.

Western governments also forgot a key reason why the liberal order was appealing in the first place – namely, a genuine commitment to its ideals. It was this commitment that was responsible for perhaps the greatest success of the post-Cold War era: the smooth integration of many former Communist states and ex-Soviet republics into the EU and NATO. But it was not long before these progressive ideals became hollowed out. Western leaders resorted to platitudes, and instrumentalized "rules" and values to justify adventures such as the invasion of Iraq. America's approach, in particular, became characterized by a "do as I say, not as I do" mentality. Charges of Western double standards and hypocrisy were airily dismissed as "whataboutism".

Western leaders were guilty of a lack of empathy. In the full flush of victory in the Cold War, they showed no capacity or inclination to see events from the perspective of others. This was more a failure of attitude than of individual policies. For example, the eastward enlargement of NATO did much to promote political stability and economic prosperity on the European continent, while avoiding the strategic and security vacuum that would have ensued had Central and Eastern Europe been excluded. But the West mistakenly assumed that Russia would meekly acquiesce in the new European order and eventually become a "normal" country – democratic, liberal capitalist, and post-imperial. Western governments lost their sense of jeopardy, and only began to recover it in recent years when Russian (and Chinese) actions forced them to belatedly recognize the dangers. Lack of empathy amounting to heartlessness was especially evident during the Covid-19 pandemic. Nothing did more to destroy the notion of an international order *for all* than the spectacle of Western democracies hoarding vaccines.

The crisis of the liberal order has been a cumulative process. It is the result not of a single mass-extinction event, but of multiple trends, policy failures and accidents; of myopia, self-delusion and egoism. To reverse or check the decline of liberal norms and values will therefore be a protracted endeavour. While Trump poses a significant threat to liberalism, his (eventual) departure will not solve its deeper problems. For he is more a product and symptom of its failings than the cause of them. The biggest lesson of the past 20 years is that liberal democracies and institutions need once again to demonstrate their worth, to articulate and implement a compelling vision. The West won the Cold War because it outperformed the Soviet Union in every dimension of power and influence. A similar burden of proof exists today, in the face of even more formidable opposition and exacting circumstances.

## 2

# A WORLD DISORDER

Following the fall of the Berlin Wall in 1989, the distinguished scholar Ken Jowitt wrote about the emergence of a "new world disorder" that was much more fluid, dynamic and unpredictable than the bipolar order which had preceded it. This world was "increasingly unfamiliar, perplexing, and threatening; in which existing boundaries are attacked and changed; in which the challenge will be to establish new national/international boundaries".[1] To Jowitt, the new world disorder was not ipso facto good or bad, just different. He welcomed some of its features, such as Eastern Europe's discovery of "political ethics" and "human dignity".[2] Jowitt's concept of a "new world disorder" was intended also to rebut the certainties of Francis Fukuyama's then popular "end of history" thesis, which viewed the end of the Cold War in triumphalist terms – as signalling the decisive victory of liberal democracy and capitalism over all other political and ideological systems.[3]

More than three decades have passed since Jowitt set out his ideas, during which the international environment has undergone a far-reaching transformation. Nevertheless, much of what he said then still holds true. Established norms have been eroded, but new "truths" are yet to take root. Conventional hierarchies have been undermined by the diffusion of power among a growing number of state and non-state actors. Global challenges appear ever more "perplexing and threatening".

A certain amount of disorder is intrinsic to the human condition. Throughout history, even the most regulated of orders have been disorderly to some degree. The difference today, however, is the *extraordinary* degree of uncertainty and ambiguity in the international system. The contemporary global environment is considerably more anarchic than Hedley Bull's "anarchical society". It is also much darker than Jowitt's post-Cold War disorder, the optimism of that era having given way to disillusionment and deep pessimism.

The biggest issue is not the lack of rules or rules-based traditions. There is an abundance of both. In addition to the US-led order and the UN system, there are multiple other frameworks in existence. These include a world economy, regional and global trading arrangements, arms control regimes, and innumerable bilateral and multilateral agreements. There are also assorted constructs of global governance, such as the "multipolar order" (or "polycentric system"), Xi Jinping's "shared future for humanity", and modern variations on the theme of a "Concert" of great powers.

The real problem of international order is instead threefold. First, although alternatives to the post-Cold War liberal model have been proposed, their thrust is aspirational rather than practical. They deal in generalities and are short on specifics. Second, we are no closer to achieving consensus over the rules and norms needed to underpin a viable international order. What are the rules and on what principles are they based? Third, there is a systematic failure of implementation, leading to a world where the breaking and evading of rules has become normalized, not just among the so-called "great powers", but with nations of all sizes and types.

## The poverty of alternative orders

Critics of the West are inclined to see the unravelling of international order as essentially a crisis of US primacy and leadership, part of the broader trend of Western decline. However, the problem of disorder is far more comprehensive. Yes, the post-Cold War, US-led "rules-based" order is on life-support. But the bigger issue is that there is no overarching international system, much less a "common power", to discipline the behaviour of state actors.[4] Various alternatives to the liberal international order have been proposed. But none are grounded in reality, and consequently have little hope of gaining serious traction.

### *The UN-based order*

The United Nations appears to possess many of the attributes of a functioning global order. Apart from the Vatican and North Korea, all the sovereign states of the world are represented within it. Its principles, enshrined in the UN Charter and related documents, are universally accepted – in theory. Its institutions embrace every area of human activity. And governments of all kinds formally recognize the United Nations as the principal source of moral and political authority in the world.

So why not put our faith in a UN-based global order? Because *this order never actually existed*. The real post-Second World War order was bipolar. The United Nations and its institutions – in particular, the Security Council – played important and sometimes vital roles, most notably in de-escalating the 1962 Cuban Missile Crisis.[5] But the primary business of global politics took place in Washington and Moscow, not New York. The United States and the Soviet Union were the major decision-makers, not a storied UN "community".

Although the United Nations is often described as the chief decision-making body in international politics, few people believe this to be true. Washington has demonstrated under successive administrations that it sees the United Nations as, at best, a rubber stamp for decisions it has already reached. The notion that a UN system of any kind might replace the US-led post-Cold War order is as unthinkable among Democrat liberal internationalists as it is among "America-first" Republicans. Beijing and Moscow are hardly more supportive. They exploit the myth of UN primacy as a counterpoint to American "hegemony" and "unilateralism". For them, the United Nations is a battleground, not the basis for a new (or renewed) global order or a place where serious decisions are made.

To advocate a UN-based order also elicits the question of "which one". The UN system created in the 1940s that was dominated by Western liberal ideals and institutions? Or the one shaped and compromised by the Cold War rivalry of the United States and the Soviet Union? Or a new order reflecting the very different world we live in today? If the latter, then this would involve a radical transformation of, among other things, the Security Council and the status and privileges of its five permanent members (P-5). Foundation documents like the UN Charter would have to be revised. The functioning of Bretton Woods institutions, such as the International Monetary Fund (IMF) and World Bank, would need to be overhauled. Amidst such a revolution, only one thing would be certain: there would be bitter conflicts over the substance and authority of this order, and the absence of anything approximating a consensus. Decades of futile effort to reform the UN Security Council indicate that attempting to build a more modern and representative "UN-based order" would be immensely difficult.

### The multipolar order

Lately, the "multipolar order" has acquired a growing following as the principal alternative to the "rules-based international order". Yet the concept itself is so loose as to be virtually meaningless. It is a slogan rather than an idea with real content.

The most common understanding of multipolarity implies the existence of several centres of global power. A multipolar order would be co-managed on the basis of a strategic ("great power") accommodation or compact between them. Notable examples of this include the post-Napoleonic Concert of Europe and the Bismarckian balance of power of the late nineteenth century. Key here is a rough equilibrium between the various principals. Some may be stronger than others, but the disparity is never so large as to allow one or two powers to dominate proceedings.

Such multipolarity bears no relation to contemporary realities. Despite its "suicidal statecraft", the United States remains much the strongest power in the world. As such, it wields a degree of influence significantly greater than that of any other power or group of powers. It is one of two nuclear superpowers along with Russia. It has the most powerful and expensive military in the world, with more than 750 overseas bases (compared to China's one). It possesses the largest and most diverse economy, comprising around 25 per cent of global GDP (the same share as in 1980), while the US dollar accounts for nearly 90 per cent of global foreign currency transactions.[6] Despite recent Chinese advances, the United States remains the number one technological power. American social media providers – Meta (Facebook), X (Twitter), Alphabet (Google/YouTube) – dominate the global information space, while American popular culture touches every corner of the earth, aided by the fact that English remains the global lingua franca.

The world, then, is not multipolar in any practical sense.[7] Moreover, there is no consensus as to who (or what) qualifies as a "pole". In Beijing and Moscow, use of the term multipolarity or "polycentrism" denotes their common opposition to American dominance. But that is as far as it goes. The Chinese do not regard Russia as possessing anything like the same importance and influence as themselves; their benchmark is the United States. In similar spirit, Moscow scarcely views the Europeans, India, Japan or Brazil as equals in the global firmament. The Kremlin's vision is tripolar – the United States, China and Russia. Meanwhile, New Delhi envisages a multipolar order in which India stands as an independent centre of global power, meriting as much consideration as anyone else.

It is more problematic still to speak of a multipolar *order*, since this denotes something purposeful and cooperative, as in the nineteenth-century Concert of Europe. But there is no chance of this emerging in the foreseeable future. Washington views the very idea of multipolarity as an affront to American primacy, and opposes its basic premise of collaborative governance by the great powers. This is truer than ever under Trump. It is one thing to do individual deals with Moscow over Ukraine or, potentially, with Beijing over Taiwan. It is quite another to admit others as equals and allow them, in "Concert", to limit its freedom of action.

The emphasis on multipolarity exemplifies the wishful thinking that clouds the judgement of some policy-makers and observers. It is rooted in a desire to see the United States cut down to size and a concomitant hankering for enhanced status. However, multipolarity is a fiction. US primacy is not what it was, and its capacity for global leadership is much reduced. But other major powers have shown nothing to suggest they are able to fill the vacuum of authority and make a multipolar order work.

### Xi Jinping's "shared future for humanity"

Ever since he became paramount leader in 2012, Xi Jinping has sought to position China as a global player. The comparative modesty of his predecessors has been jettisoned. Under Xi, China is no longer concerned about hiding its capacities, biding its time or never claiming leadership (as Deng Xiaoping famously advised).[8] This shift has encouraged a consensus in Washington that China aims to displace the United States as the global leader, and institute its own version of international order.[9] Such speculation has been fuelled by a series of declarative documents coming out of Beijing: the Global Development Initiative in 2021, the Global Security Initiative in 2022, the Global Civilization Initiative in 2023, and the Global Governance Initiative in 2025. These all come under the banner of Xi's "shared future for humanity", aka "global community of shared future" or "community for common destiny".[10]

However, the notion of a China-centred global order is largely abstract. Beijing lacks the wherewithal to translate a vision of global governance into reality. China remains deeply integrated into existing international structures and networks, and dependent on a global financial system dominated by the United States. Unlike Washington, which retains close alliances and partnerships across the world, Beijing's only serious strategic relationship is with Moscow, while many countries regard China as their principal security challenge. These include not only the United States and leading European nations, but also several of China's neighbours – India, Japan, South Korea, Vietnam, Australia, to name just a few. Even those countries that welcome the erosion of US and Western dominance, such as Russia, are not keen to see a new Pax Sinica in its place.[11]

But perhaps the main reason why a Sinocentric order is improbable is that the Chinese themselves are not committed to global leadership, at least in the sense usually understood in the West. There is a big difference between wanting to be a global player and aspiring to be *the* global leader. The former is about promoting China as an independent centre of power. The latter means taking on the responsibilities and burdens of global governance.

Xi's "shared future for humanity" is more an exposition of principles than an attempt to establish a new world order. The four Global Initiative documents – Development, Security, Civilization, Governance – deal mainly in generalities: "win-win", respecting the sovereignty and territorial integrity of all countries, abiding by the principles of the UN Charter, the peaceful resolution of disputes, and so on. The lack of detail is deliberate. Beijing portrays its approach to global governance as inclusive and flexible, contrasting it to the prescriptive-ness and high-handedness of the United States. Its overriding message is that international norms and rules cannot be imposed by any one power (the United States) or small group of powers (the West).[12]

Viewed in this light, Xi's vision is about maximizing China's freedom of action, status and influence in the world, and, correspondingly, diluting the authority of the United States. But Beijing does not seek to build a (mythical) "Chinese model" or overturn the international system, from which it continues to benefit enormously. When it comes down to it, China is a revisionist power, not a revolutionary actor.[13]

### The Empire strikes back: Donald Trump's dystopian world

In his second presidency, Donald Trump has pursued something of a "shock and awe" approach to international relations. Yet many of his actions have been fairly predictable, not least because he foreshadowed them during his 2024 election campaign and even in his first presidency. He has lost no time in threatening – and imposing – hefty tariffs against a swathe of countries, including US allies. He has drastically curtailed US support for Ukraine. He has given Benjamin Netanyahu *carte blanche* to level Gaza and ethnically cleanse it of Palestinians. And he has called into question America's commitment to NATO and to European security.

Somewhat more surprising has been the emergence of a new American imperialism. Belying predictions of foreign policy retrenchment, Trump has travelled in the opposite direction. He has asserted territorial claims over the Panama Canal and Greenland, backed if necessary by the threat or use of force. He has ratcheted up the pressure on Canada to become part of the United States. Trump and other senior administration figures, such as Secretary of State Marco Rubio, appear determined to impose a twenty-first-century version of the Monroe doctrine, whereby America exercises hegemonic control over the western hemisphere. In this connection, Trump has referred admiringly to William McKinley, US president 1897–1901, who led the last great American territorial expansion,[14] and was an enthusiastic proponent of tariffs.

It is uncertain how committed Trump is to pursuing America's irredentist claims. We are frequently enjoined to take him "seriously, but not literally", and there are huge obstacles to taking over Canada (the world's second-largest country, population 40 million, NATO member state) or seizing territory from another NATO member state (Denmark in the case of Greenland). It may be that Trump is a devotee of the "madman theory" of international politics, whereby

the real purpose of extreme statements is to intimidate others into making concessions, often in unrelated policy areas.

This much remains murky. What is clear, however, is that Trump's view of global
order is sui generis. His rejection of universal rules and norms, and loathing of
multilateralism, set him at odds with the notion of a UN-based order. The liberal internationalist vision of a rules-based order is similarly noxious to the White
House. Xi's "shared future for humanity" seeks to undermine US primacy and is
consequently unacceptable. Trump's partiality to great power diplomacy suggests,
at first sight, that he might be amenable to some form of multipolar order, centred
on a Concert of great powers. His eagerness to settle the war in Ukraine on terms
favourable to Russia has encouraged speculation about a new "age of empires".[15]
But, as noted earlier, such an arrangement would contradict the central premise
that the United States must be, and always remain, the indisputable world number
one. This notion is especially important to Trump, since it is intimately connected
with his sense of self-worth, in particular an irrepressible desire to win (see below).

There is a danger of over-thinking Trump's vision of global order. For this is
more a set of personal instincts and reflexes than a cohesive or coherent body of
ideas. There are documents, such as the Heritage Foundation's Project 2025, that
provide a quasi-intellectual foundation for various conservative policies. But
there is little evidence so far they have had much impact on Trump himself. For
example, Project 2025 says nothing about acquiring foreign lands.[16] In Trump's
world, ideas are transient – readily instrumentalized and disposable – whereas
instincts are permanent.

It has become commonplace to describe Trump's mindset as transactional.
But this term is misleading. Trump is transactional in that he prioritizes his
interests over larger human values, and believes that everyone and everything has their price; there is always a deal to be made. But Trump's brand of
transactionalism is not about give-and-take. Compromises may sometimes be
necessary if the other side's position is strong, but *the prime imperative is to
win*. That may be achieved through persuasion, or a shared perception of common interests (for example, working with Putin to "solve" Ukraine), but it can
also be secured through threats, sanctions and even the use of force. Morality
and justice, rules or law, are moot. The outcome is everything, whatever the
means.[17]

The self-centred absolutism of the Trump vision makes it wholly ill-suited as
the basis of a viable global order. Simply put, it offers very little to other parties.
Carried to its logical conclusion, America (or rather Trump) wins, but almost
everyone else loses. Even if other parties gain something in the short term, as
in the case of Russia over Ukraine, they remain vulnerable to the vagaries of US
decision-making. As Trump demonstrated during his first presidency, a "deal"
can always be modified ("re-negotiated"), suspended or cancelled. Since the only

true "law" comes from the exercise of power, no country bar the United States can rest easy. It is worth noting that Trump's extreme version of America-first is even more unipolar in spirit than the "unipolar moment" of the immediate post-Cold War period.

And that means a Trumpian world is a non-starter. Compared to the 1990s, the United States is far less able to bend others to its will, even assuming that it perseveres in the face of mounting opposition. Nearly every country in the world, from leading powers such as China to the most modest developing nation, will resist becoming mere objects of American foreign policy. Washington may win out in individual tests of will, for example, extracting a promise by NATO member states to spend 5 per cent of GDP on defence and defence-related priorities,[18] or browbeating the European Union over tariffs.[19] However, it will find it increasingly difficult to achieve long-term strategic goals, whether it is reasserting its dominion over the American hemisphere, pacifying the Middle East, defeating China, circumventing Europe, ignoring the Global South, or dictating the future direction of the global economy. Instead of a Pax Americana – or American imperium – Donald Trump's dystopian vision promises only further disorder and conflict.

## De-universalization and the challenges of consensus

It may seem contentious to claim that there is little agreement over the rules of international order when, for decades, the UN Charter has codified norms of interstate behaviour. This appears to show that, whatever their differences, states can agree on certain fundamentals: the inviolability of sovereignty and territorial integrity; non-interference in the domestic affairs of other states; the non-use of force to resolve differences; the sovereign equality of all states; the right of all peoples to self-determination; and the protection of human rights. These norms are deemed universal because they apply to everyone, irrespective of political orientation, level of economic development, or cultural specificity.

Why, then, are we witnessing a breakdown of international rules? So much so that the former British foreign secretary David Miliband has described the current era as an "age of impunity".[20] Part of the answer lies in failures of implementation and enforcement, discussed later in the chapter. But there is a more structural explanation: the progressive de-universalization of norms.

The notion of universalism is problematic in itself. We have become so accustomed to talking about universal norms and values that we do not bother to subject this orthodoxy to proper scrutiny. Arguably, universalism has always been something of a myth, perpetuated by a collective suspension of disbelief. It has been convenient, perhaps necessary, for states to cultivate it as a foundation truth, part of what makes us human. Accordingly, leaders and regimes of all types have formally subscribed to the UN Charter and the Universal Declaration of Human Rights. And nearly all the countries of the world are members of the United Nations (193 out of 195 states), IMF (191), World Bank (189) and the WTO (166).

But for universal norms to mean something they have to possess moral and political authority. This is conspicuously lacking today. Universal norms are often so abstract as to encourage an almost unlimited latitude of interpretation. For example, Article 2.4 of the UN Charter states that "all members shall refrain in their international relations from the threat or use of force against the territorial integrity or political independence of any state".[21] Yet this rule is routinely broken. The 2022 Russian invasion of Ukraine and the 2014 annexation of Crimea were blatant transgressions. But so was the 2003 US-led invasion of Iraq, while the legal basis of the NATO interventions over Kosovo in 1999 and Libya in 2011 was dubious at best. And there are myriad other examples of "the threat or use of force" being used against the "territorial integrity or political independence" of UN member states.

Similarly, Article 1.3 of the Charter speaks of "promoting and encouraging respect for human rights and for fundamental freedoms for all without distinction as to race, sex, language, or religion". What norm could be more universal? However, it is hard to think of more than a handful of countries that genuinely subscribe to it. What is one to make of Xi's persecution of the Uighurs in Xinjiang; Indian Prime Minister Narendra Modi's discrimination against Muslims; Putin's clampdown on political expression; the forced separation of children from their refugee parents on the US-Mexican border during the first Trump presidency; or the institutionalized discrimination against women in Iran and Afghanistan?

Many of these contradictions come down to the clash between universalism and relativism. Notwithstanding their formal obeisance to the values of the UN Charter, member states claim priority for their own particular interpretations of human rights, democracy and international order. They invoke cultural and civilizational norms, in effect appropriating or "nationalizing" international rules. Such relativism is death to the idea of a global order based on universal norms. If we return to Hedley Bull's definition of international society as being founded on the appreciation of "certain common interests and common values",[22] then such a society no longer exists. When Beijing talks up the diversity of political paths and civilizational traditions, when Washington proclaims specifically American values, or when Moscow emphasizes Russia's "traditional spiritual and moral values", they are demarcating the extent to which they feel bound by allegedly common norms. And that is very loosely indeed. The only rules they are prepared to countenance are those that do not constrain their ability to pursue national interests to the fullest extent possible.

This raises another issue: "universal" is in the eye of the beholder. The United Nations was established when three-quarters of the countries in today's world had not yet come into being. In 1945, there were only 51 member states, mostly from the Americas and Europe. The UN Charter grew out of negotiations involving the United States, the Soviet Union, the United Kingdom and Nationalist China before the end of the Second World War. The 1948 Universal Declaration of Human Rights was drafted by a nine-person committee led by Eleanor Roosevelt. All but one member of this committee – the Soviet representative – was either from a Western country or had been educated in the United States.[23] The Declaration and the UN Charter are extraordinary documents, whose authors were enlightened and open-minded people. But the ideas they enshrine necessarily grew out of the wellspring of Western liberal thought.

Today, the make-up of the world is transformed. Africa (54) and Asia (51) now have more countries than Europe (44) and the Americas (35). The number of democracies has been declining steadily over the past 19 years.[24] Although the influence of Western liberal ideas remains powerful, it is no longer dominant. Ideationally, the world is an infinitely more complex and contested space than it was in the 1940s, even taking into account the presence then of the Soviet Union. Under these circumstances, the international order has lost its universality; its "rules" and institutions are increasingly seen as a holdover from the past – not just anachronistic, but biased towards Western interests. Even within the West itself, a pronounced values-gap has opened up between Trumpian America and much of Europe.[25] The notion of a unitary "West", with shared values and a common allegiance to international norms, has rarely looked more suspect.

The thorniest disagreements are over sovereignty. Countries such as China and Russia understand this very narrowly, determining that other state actors have no right to comment on, much less intervene in, their domestic affairs. So, whatever Beijing does with the Uighurs or with popular dissent in Hong Kong, or how the Kremlin deals with its domestic critics, is entirely their own affair. In stark contrast, for much of the post-Cold War era, Western governments operated in the belief that there were higher values that transcended sovereignty. This conviction lay at the heart of the doctrine of "responsibility to protect" (R2P), which supplied the ethical and intellectual basis of multiple Western-led "humanitarian interventions" – in Bosnia 1995, Kosovo 1999, Iraq 2003 and Libya 2011.

Then there is the question of sovereignty *for whom*. The UN Charter with its emphasis on "sovereign equality" makes no distinction between states, great and small. But in the real world it is a different story. There, as Thucydides said, "the strong do what they can and the weak suffer what they must".[26] 2,500 years later, in a dispute over the South China Sea, then Chinese foreign minister Yang Jiechi reminded his Singaporean counterpart that "China is a big country, and other countries are small countries, and that is just a fact".[27] Nor are such attitudes solely the preserve of authoritarian regimes. When he was US president, Joe Biden contrasted the rules-based approach of democracies to international order with the "might makes right" mindset of countries like China and Russia. But the United States, supported by other Western powers, has undertaken numerous foreign military interventions in the post-Cold War era because it had the capacity to do so (or at least thought it did). Most recently, Trump has underlined that sovereignty is a malleable construct. In laying claim to the Panama Canal and Greenland, he has made clear his view that true sovereignty rests only with those who are able to exercise and maintain it.

*The Ukraine effect*

The de-universalization of norms has come out very clearly in the course of the war in Ukraine. On the face of things, Putin's invasion should have bolstered the case for universal norms and rules to govern the behaviour of states. In addition to its flagrant disregard for Ukrainian sovereignty and resort to extreme violence, Russian aggression was globally destabilizing. Developing countries suffered particularly badly from the disruption of food supply chains, spiking energy prices, and the general downturn in the world economy.

Yet Western efforts to enlist the support of the Global South against Putin have been largely in vain. While most of these countries backed the UN General Assembly resolutions condemning the invasion, none followed through with sanctions against Moscow. Formally, they recognized the principle of respecting the territorial integrity of Ukraine, but that was as much as they were prepared to do. (Indeed, a number of them have continued to trade with Russia, undermining the effectiveness of Western sanctions.)

Some governments acted out of fear or narrow self-interest. But most refrained from choosing sides because they were unconvinced by the West's legal and ethical arguments. They perceived no qualitative difference between the Russian invasion and the US intervention in Iraq nearly two decades earlier, however much Western policy-makers protested to the contrary.[28] And they were unreceptive to claims of Russian imperialism, given the colonial past of the European powers and what they saw as the bogus morality that packaged Western self-interest.[29]

For many in the Global South, the Western focus on Ukraine was also part of a larger trend whereby non-Western interests are invariably marginalized. As the war extended into its third year (2024), many developing countries became increasingly resentful about the band-width it was absorbing, diverting attention and resources away from critical priorities such as debt relief and climate financing. They could hardly fail to notice, too, the contrast between the generous welcome afforded by European nations to Ukrainian refugees, and the hostility to asylum-seekers from other conflict countries, such as Iraq, Syria and Afghanistan. In the circumstances, it is hardly surprising that Global South countries should come to view the Ukraine war, not as a struggle for the soul of international order, but as an unwelcome distraction.[30]

There is a further, somewhat paradoxical dimension to the "Ukraine effect". Although the war has caused serious economic harm to developing nations, it has enhanced their political agency. For the first time since the heyday of the Non-Aligned Movement (NAM) in the 1950s and early 1960s, the Global South has emerged as a genuine constituency in world affairs, courted by America and Europe, China and Russia. This newfound attention reinforces the message that a contested, unruly world offers Global South countries more opportunities – and leverage – than one dominated by Western-led "universal" norms.

## The rule of lawlessness

Rule-breaking has become ubiquitous. The issue goes far beyond a little national exceptionalism here and there. Over the past quarter of a century, we have witnessed a remarkable growth in lawlessness, both in terms of the gravity of the breaches and the range of offenders. There is also a broader sense that rules per se do not matter. International law has become a critically endangered species.[31]

Traditional great powers have been among the worst offenders, often appearing to operate according to the principle, "I can, therefore I will". As we saw in the previous chapter, during Trump's first presidential term, the United States led the way in driving a new "rule-less" international system. Trump rammed home the message that rules were dispensable, and that only the weak were bound by them. Great powers and especially the United States, the strongest of them all, could do as they pleased – deciding what rules, if any, to follow. Trump's actions since returning to the White House in January 2025 have only doubled down on this conviction.

That said, despite the radical nature of his rules-busting, Trump's behaviour is not such an outlier in the American experience. The George W. Bush administration (2001–09), notoriously, disregarded the United Nations over Iraq and overrode the opposition of European allies such as France and Germany. In doing so, it made it quite clear that observance of international norms was subordinate to the American national interest. The United States, not the United Nations, would decide what rules to follow.

Beijing's slogans of "win-win" and "a shared future for humanity" reflect a decades-long campaign of reputation-laundering, pitching China as a good global citizen compared to a "unilateralist" America. But it, too, operates on the exceptionalist basis that rules are for other people. This is especially evident on the vexed question of South China Sea territoriality. Unlike the United States, China is a signatory to the UN Convention on the Law of the Sea (UNCLOS). Yet it is just as averse to multilateral oversight. In 2016, it refused to recognize the jurisdiction of the Permanent Court of Arbitration (PCA) in The Hague, which had gathered to consider an application by the Philippines regarding the legal status of maritime features in the South China Sea. Inevitably, it rejected the PCA's judgement that Chinese territorial claims were illegitimate, instead insisting on its "historic rights" to sovereignty on the basis of the so-called "nine-dash line".[32]

China has adopted a similarly voluntarist attitude towards bilateral treaties and agreements. Xi's clampdown on Hong Kong contravened the commitment in the 1997 China-UK Joint Declaration to leave the territory's political and economic system unchanged for 50 years. Beijing's discarding of this arrangement highlighted its belief that considerations of national sovereignty outweighed any international "rules" or bilateral commitments. It also acted in this fashion because it *could*. China was no longer the weak and humiliated nation on which colonial powers such as Great Britain had foisted the "unequal treaties" of the nineteenth century. It was in control of its own destiny.

Although Trumpian America and Xi's China have trampled over international rules, Russia under Putin has been the most consistent transgressor. Since 2008, it has launched four external military interventions – in Georgia 2008, Ukraine 2014, Syria 2015, and the 2022 full-scale invasion of Ukraine – while Russian "mercenaries" have been involved in several other conflict zones, notably Libya and the Sahel. Russia is the only country since the end of the Cold War to have seized and annexed territory from another sovereign state (Ukraine in 2014–15 and 2022). During the Syrian civil war, it colluded in the Assad regime's use of chemical weapons. It has engaged in major cyber-hacking operations against foreign governments. It interfered blatantly in the 2016 US presidential and 2017 French presidential elections. Russian security agencies have also pursued a programme of assassinations against assorted overseas targets, from Russian opposition figures to former intelligence officers. Even prior to the latest invasion, the extent of Moscow's rule-breaking was astonishing.

Why, then, do countries engage in such behaviour, to the extent that they scarcely bother to cover their tracks? There are essentially three main explanations: the belief that others routinely flout international norms, so why shouldn't they; realpolitik; and the lack of consequences for themselves. These reasons not only merge into one another, they are mutually reinforcing.

## Double standards

Claiming double standards is the first line of defence for authoritarian regimes against accusations of rule-breaking. The Kremlin, in particular, loses no opportunity to recycle its condemnation of the US-led invasion of Iraq, the NATO interventions over Kosovo and Libya, and the West's operation in Afghanistan. It compares US rhetoric about the rules-based international order with Washington's disregard and sometimes open contempt for the United Nations. Similarly, Beijing rebuts American calls for China to respect freedom of navigation under UNCLOS by pointing out Washington's refusal to ratify the Convention. In 2023, Moscow and Beijing dismissed Biden's support for the International Criminal Court (ICC)'s indictment of Russian leaders for war crimes in Ukraine, pointing out that the United States itself rejects the authority of the court.

Common to these cases is the belief that the United States and other Western governments have little compunction in telling others how they should behave, but are not prepared to abide by the same rules. Crucially, this complaint is shared by many non-aligned countries. For them, nothing exemplifies the hypocrisy of the United States, and of the West in general, more than the response to the conflict and humanitarian crisis in Gaza.[33] This predates Trump's return to the White House. Biden, despite his emphasis on the "rules-based international order", indicated that the United States would never bring Israeli Prime Minister Benjamin Netanyahu to book, however egregious his actions. More than that, it condemned the ICC for issuing arrest warrants against Netanyahu and (now former) Defence Minister Yoav Gallant, and even threatened the court with possible sanctions.[34] Trump has since escalated matters, but in this he was following in Biden's footsteps.[35]

## Realpolitik

The indulgence Washington has shown to Israel is part of a broader pattern whereby the application of rules is determined by reasons of state rather than moral or legal considerations. Enemies are targeted, while allies and partners are protected. Under Biden, Washington overlooked India's growing restrictions on press freedoms, persecution of domestic critics, and anti-Muslim discrimination in the cause of enlisting it as a strategic counterweight against China. The United States and Britain actively supported Saudi Arabia's brutal war in Yemen in order to counter Iranian influence. And the Biden White House scaled down its nominal sanctions against Riyadh for the extra-judicial murder of the journalist Jamal Khashoggi because it sought Saudi cooperation in controlling energy prices.[36]

The United States is hardly alone in sacrificing principle for strategic and political ends. Beijing's response to the Ukraine war is telling. Chinese foreign policy trumpets its commitment to national sovereignty and territorial integrity. However, at no stage has Beijing criticized Putin's invasion for violating these norms. Instead, it asserts that Moscow was "provoked", and blames the West for stoking the conflict. The point, of course, is that China's position on sovereignty is not "principled", as Beijing claims, but self-interested. In the context of the war in Ukraine, that means preserving the Sino-Russian partnership, strengthening its leverage over Moscow, and discrediting the United States.

Putin's Russia is a unique case. Although it styles itself as a defender of international law and is a stickler for UN procedure, it revels in being the disruptor. Viewed from the Kremlin, unpredictability and the ready resort to violence expand rather than limit Russia's opportunities. They demonstrate resolve and daring, and discombobulate the West, in particular the Europeans with their excessive faith in soft power, international law, and "rules". More than any other contemporary leader, Putin personifies Machiavelli's belief that "if you have to choose, it's much safer to be feared than loved".[37]

## Lack of consequences

Few states suffer significant consequences for breaching international norms. This is especially true of the major powers which have generally acted with impunity: the United States (and the "coalition of the willing") in Iraq; Russia in Georgia, Syria and Crimea 2014; and China in relation to Taiwan and the South China Sea. When the offender has been sanctioned, as in the case of Russia, the punishment has either been symbolic or simply ineffective.

The Western response to Putin's 2022 invasion of Ukraine might, at first sight, appear to be an exception. The level and range of counter-measures, from suspending Russia's participation in the SWIFT financial messaging system to large-scale military and economic support for Kyiv, has been unprecedented. Yet the longer the war has gone on, the more Western decision-making has become characterized by dithering, exaggerated fears of Russian escalation, and "Ukraine fatigue". For all the self-congratulation about Western unity and resolve in the defence of norms, the course of the conflict has seen their further weakening.

It is not only major powers who believe there is little penalty for rule-breaking, but also countries like North Korea and Iran. Sanctions have done nothing to rein in Kim Jong-un's nuclear weapons programme or to moderate Pyongyang's threatening rhetoric against Seoul and Tokyo. Despite recent setbacks, Iran acts as a relentlessly destabilizing force in the Middle East, while supporting Putin's war in Ukraine with missiles, drones and munitions. Importantly, the June 2025

Israeli assault on the Iranian regime was driven not by a desire to enforce international "rules", but by strategic opportunism. The Netanyahu government judged that Israel would never have a better opening to change the geopolitical map of the Middle East in its favour

The fragility of norms is visible even in the most legalist and institutionalized of contexts, namely the European Union. Far from subscribing to fundamental values such as the rule of law, transparency and accountability, the "illiberal democracy" that is Hungary continues along its merry way – interfering with the judiciary, suppressing civil liberties, harassing the independent media, and undermining EU foreign policy – mostly without consequence. Indeed, the subsidies that Budapest continues to receive from Brussels strengthen Prime Minister Viktor Orban's hold on power. He is effectively being rewarded, not punished, for breaking the rules.

This brings us back to Thucydides – "the strong do what they can, the weak suffer what they must". Those who possess power have greater latitude in observing, disregarding or manipulating the rules than those who do not. There is, however, one critical difference from past eras. International power has become much more diffuse, and the "weak" feel more empowered than ever before. States *of all sizes* believe they will face few if any consequences for rule-breaking behaviour, and that even if there is a punitive response of some kind it will be bearable, and certainly not strong enough to make them change their ways.

The widening sense of impunity stems in part from the bad example shown by the leading powers, but it is also a result of the weakening of enforcement mechanisms, such as the United Nations Security Council. During the Cold War, the Council was able to function in this capacity from time to time. The United States and the Soviet Union transcended their strategic and ideological rivalry to cooperate on containing conflict in the Middle East. And until relatively recently Russia supported efforts to restrain the nuclear weapons ambitions of North Korea and Iran.

But all that is past. The Security Council has neither the capability nor the legitimacy to act as a mechanism for implementing international norms. On the contrary, it has become part of the problem, broadcasting its conflicts – and impotence – to a worldwide and increasingly dismissive audience. Meanwhile, the moral standing of the so-called "great powers" is at its lowest point in decades. The idea they can lay down the rule in enforcing international norms has become thoroughly implausible.

## The end of rules?

Order is part of the secular cult of international relations. Governments of all political hues fetishize it as a self-evident good. European leaders emphasize their commitment to *the* rules-based international order, comparing this with the "rule-breaking" behaviour of non-Western powers such as China and Russia. By contrast, Beijing and Moscow declare their fealty to the "UN-centred international system" and "world order based on international law".[38]

These disputes have become somewhat sterile. They do, however, raise the question of whether it is still useful to talk about a global order. There are dangers in setting the benchmark too high or too low. As noted earlier, all orders are disorderly to some extent, with conflicts, normative fissures and widespread rule-breaking. On the other hand, the breaches of international norms may become so numerous as to make a mockery of the principle. There has to be a reasonable standard of practice, perhaps along the lines of states observing most of the rules most of the time – as Bull suggested in *The Anarchical Society*.[39]

If one looks back at past examples of international order, we find that this condition was generally met. For example, the Concert of Europe established an authoritarian order over the continent for much of the nineteenth century. This did not prevent wars, revolutions or even significant territorial changes from happening. But in the main there was an identifiable European society, conforming to broad conventions of behaviour.

The principle of an international society abiding by certain rules was also integral to the post-Second World War global order. This order was fragile, and was almost overturned on several occasions – during the Korean War (1950–53), the 1962 Cuban Missile Crisis, and in the 1980s when the United States and the Soviet Union came close to (an accidental) nuclear confrontation over NATO's Able Archer exercise.[40] There were multiple conflicts, as the Cold War frequently turned hot by proxy – in Asia, the Middle East, Africa and Latin America. Nevertheless, even at its height, Washington and Moscow saw themselves as playing by certain rules. This not only guided their bilateral relationship, but also set rough parameters for global management.

Today, such understandings are absent. Even if we set a low bar and speak of a loosely applied code of conduct, it is clear this has been unravelling for some years now. Many of the aspects of inter-state behaviour we have long taken for granted are in question. The old rules are no longer seen as fit for purpose by a growing number of states, but a new consensus has yet to form. The result is a vacuum of normative authority, in which different countries do not merely play by different rules, but operate increasingly on the tacit assumption that there is no international law and no overarching international order.

The most worrying aspect of the breakdown of rules is that many countries don't seem to care. States – democratic and authoritarian alike – pay lip-service to the importance of international order, but casually abuse or ignore the rules whenever it suits them. Breaches are readily rationalized by catchall phrases like "national security" and "legitimate interests", as with Russia's invasion of Ukraine and Trump's claims to the Panama Canal and Greenland. We are living out a twenty-first-century version of Hobbes's "state of nature", in which there are few ethical constraints, let alone the sense of being part of a larger international community and having a responsibility towards it. Governments are conditioned primarily by the possibilities and limits of power.

There are parallels here with the 1930s, when there was a similar breakdown of agreed norms. The international emergence of the Soviet Union; the rise of Nazi Germany, Fascist Italy and the Japanese Empire; the Great Depression; the slow collapse of the Versailles Peace Treaty and impotence of the League of Nations; and isolationism in America – all these contributed to an essentially rule-less, anarchic world. Well before the outbreak of the Second World War, it was apparent there was no international order, but rather a disorder in which the exercise of power far outweighed any formal or informal code of conduct.

It is tempting to seek comfort in the thought that a world where rules and norms are sometimes observed is better than having no rules at all. But there are two obvious problems with this Panglossian attitude. One is that chronic cherry-picking of rules negates the whole idea of a rules-based order; how much rule-breaking and rule-bending is sustainable before order collapses into disorder? Second, an *à la carte* approach to the observance of rules invites whataboutism, enabling governments to justify their behaviour on the grounds that it is, at the very least, no worse than that of their critics. The result is a race to the bottom.

Looking ahead, the biggest challenge of order is to conceptualize it in more generous and inclusive terms. For only then will it become more than an abstraction and acquire practical substance and influence. That necessitates looking at international norms and rules through a different, more positive lens – less as an irksome restriction on our freedom of action than as the ultimate safeguard of our security and prosperity. It will mean rethinking not just the content of the rules themselves, but also how they are made and implemented. With this in mind, we now turn to Part II of the book – revitalizing global governance.

**PART II**
# REVITALIZING GLOBAL GOVERNANCE

# 3

# PRINCIPLES OF A NEW INTERNATIONALISM

In his "Man in the arena" speech in 1910, former US President Theodore Roosevelt proclaimed that "it is not the critic who counts; not the man who points out how the strong man stumbles, or where the doer of deeds could have done them better. The credit belongs to the man who is actually in the arena … who strives valiantly; who errs; who comes up short again and again, because there is no effort without error and shortcoming".[1]

It was to be expected that, as a man of action, Roosevelt would have little patience with those "cold and timid souls" carping from the side-lines. But his basic point was nevertheless fair: it is easy enough to point out the mistakes of decision-makers, but it is far harder to take effective action in response to diverse threats and challenges. Political leaders must juggle competing priorities and absorb intense pressure from multiple directions. It is unsurprising, then, that they should so often fall short. And, as difficult as government was in Roosevelt's time, it is a vastly more complex and demanding enterprise today.

Difficult, though, does not mean impossible. We can and must recast international order, not out of an abstract attachment to order, but because it is key to addressing an array of global challenges. Accelerating climate change, pandemic disease and major power confrontation are existential threats, their consequences no longer hypothetical but already evident in the here and now. Poverty in developing countries is not just a Global South problem, but is impacting the Global North like never before. And technological transformation and the information revolution are changing our lives at an extraordinary pace and in countless ways.

In this time of turbulence, international order has never been more critical. And yet it has rarely seemed so lacking. The inadequacies of the contemporary system have been brutally exposed. Indeed, in a fractious world this is one of the few points on which there is broad agreement. Almost no-one, it appears, is content with the current state of order, largely because it has slipped into chronic disorder.

But if the "why" of reforming global governance is clear enough, the matter of "what" and "how" is much less so. So in the rest of the book I want to set out how we might translate a generalized acceptance of the need for change – the feeling that "something must be done" – into substantive action. Many of my suggestions concern particular players and constituencies, from the United States and China to middle powers, multilateral institutions and non-state actors, and are the subject of subsequent chapters. But first it is important to outline some guiding principles of what I call a new internationalism – a practical approach to order and governance in an anarchic world.

## Moving on from the old

The first principle is the simplest in theory, but the hardest to implement. We need to jettison the failed prescriptions of the past. Despite the setbacks of the post-Cold War era, liberal internationalists have kept faith in their vision of a "rules-based" order and America's global leadership mission. By contrast, "realists" believe that history has vindicated their view of a world in which geopolitics is king and great power rivalry is inevitable. In their narrative, security and stability are to be achieved, not through a misplaced liberal utopianism but through a clear-headed mix of strategic containment and accommodation.

In fact, both sides are equally wrong. A viable international order cannot be built by rehashing recipes and shibboleths well past their use-by date. What worked or, more often than not, didn't work in the past does not offer a reliable playbook for the twenty-first century. It is time to move on, first by rethinking established, but increasingly untenable, propositions about international politics.

### The chimera of US global leadership

Chief among these propositions is the messianic conviction that the United States "must lead"[2] – a variation on the age-old theme of "born to rule". Such exceptionalism reeks of arrogance, yet that is not its main defect. Washington's capacity to make good on such ambitions is highly questionable. It is one thing for the United States to be the pre-eminent power; it is quite another to bring others along in a common purpose. The international response to the war in Ukraine and the conflict in Gaza have highlighted the limits of America's authority.

Washington's "suicidal statecraft" since 2003 has undercut American claims to leadership. But in any case, few countries, including some of its closest allies, wish for a return to the kind of dominance we saw in the 1990s. Europeans hope the United States will remain the ultimate guarantor of their security. But many resent the pressure Washington is putting on them to take a hard line on China. They also reject its interference in European domestic politics,[3] and disruption of their attempts to counter disinformation on social media. Asian allies and partners welcome active American involvement in the Indo-Pacific, not least as a hedge against Beijing. But they do not want to be forced into an either/or choice between their main protector (the United States) and their largest trading partner (China). They are prepared to accept US leadership, but on their terms – terms very different to those envisaged by the Trump White House.

China, Russia and other foes of the United States are, of course, keen to see real limits on US influence, while the generally neutral position of Global South countries towards the war in Ukraine is driven partly by the perception that they benefit from a world where America is no longer so dominant.

Most important of all, the United States itself has jettisoned the idea of global leadership within a unitary international order. Even before Trump's outright repudiation of liberal internationalism, Joe Biden had already prioritized the consolidation of a strategic consensus behind America in its struggle with China. His packaging of this as democracy versus autocracy had little merit, and convinced few. Nevertheless, it reflected tacit recognition that the United States could not hope to lead the world, but only its allies and partners – and then only some of the time.

### The unreality of realism: the "great power" myth

Realists, as the name would suggest, like to think of themselves as grounded in hard truths, free of the illusions that coloured the internationalism of the early post-Cold War era. The re-emergence of great power rivalry between the United States and China has reaffirmed timeless verities, such as the Thucydides' trap – the likelihood of conflict when a rising power challenges the leadership of the incumbent power.[4] In the realist narrative, the great powers make the rules of international politics, and everyone else must adapt as best they can. The only important variables are, first, which great power comes out on top and, second, whether great power rivalry ends in conflict or some sort of compromise.

The past two decades have belied such simplicities. While the liberal internationalists of the 1990s were guilty of self-deception and hubris in thinking that humanity had evolved into a "higher" post-geopolitics stage, the so-called realists have been no less misguided in their anachronistic belief that the world revolves around the "great" powers. In fact, the latter have rarely looked more fallible, unable to achieve many of their objectives, let alone set the rules in an increasingly anarchic world. The limitations of their influence have been repeatedly exposed – in Afghanistan, Ukraine, across the Middle East, in the Indo-Pacific, and throughout much of Africa and Latin America.

History is not static. The world of the twenty-first century is radically different – more complicated and disorderly – to nineteenth-century Europe or the Cold War bipolar order. This is not a time of giants, dispensing largesse and punishment as they see fit. Major powers are routinely humbled; they have little desire or ability to work together; their world-views are incompatible; and their capacity to address global problems is outweighed by an irresistible urge to make political capital from them. To frame international politics around their collaboration, as realists seek to do, is to put our faith in something that has virtually ceased to exist.

The persistence of the great power delusion is reflected in the renewed emphasis on "Concerts", the premise of which is that a (self-)chosen few can, given time and patience, arrive at a strategic accommodation based on a reasonable balance of interests. However, there is nothing to suggest that the twenty-first-century global agenda – from non-traditional security threats such as climate change to long-standing preoccupations like conflict management – can be addressed through plutocratic mechanisms constructed for very different times and circumstances. Any attempt to ignore this reality will meet fierce and sustained resistance, especially from those excluded from the magic circle.[5] The rest of the world will not accept dictation from their supposed betters, especially when the latter have so amply demonstrated their failings.

It is worth reminding ourselves that the most ineffectual international mechanism operating today, the UN Security Council, originated as a de facto great power Concert. As UN Secretary-General Antonio Guterres has observed, it reflects a form of governance "stuck in time".[6] A reheated elite institutional framework would not bring about better outcomes. For it would suffer from the same problems that have hamstrung the Security Council, namely, the obsessive concern of its members with status, acrimonious divisions, lack of broader legitimacy, and diminishing relevance to challenges that require *global* responses.

Major powers will continue to play significant roles in global governance. Their actions may destabilize the international system, and their obstructive and destructive power should never be underestimated. But when it comes to creating or reviving world order this depends not only on them, but on a host of other players: middle powers, smaller states, multilateral institutions and non-state actors.[7] The time of top-down, great power-centred governance is over, and has been for at least 20 years. It is time to look elsewhere.

## Overestimation of geopolitics and hard power

Geopolitics has assumed an ever more prominent role in global affairs. Power projection matters. The balance of power remains an influential concept. And the notion of spheres of influence is implicit in the actions of the United States, China, Russia and even Europe. However, geopolitics is only part of a much bigger picture. US-China rivalry has for many become the defining issue of our time. Yet other threats and challenges – climate change, pandemic disease, global poverty – have had a considerably greater impact on the world, whether measured in loss of life, economic cost, political instability or social dislocation.

The exaggerated importance given to geopolitics stems from the realist misconception of a world centred on great power confrontation, leading in turn to an overestimation of the value of hard power. Thus, many in Washington regard China's military modernization as the greatest threat to US primacy, to Western interests and values, and to global order. Accordingly, they call for the US military to be bigger and better than ever, with new-generation nuclear weapons, enhanced missile defence, expanded strike capabilities, and conspicuous displays of power projection in the Indo-Pacific. All this comes under the Cold War rubric of "peace through strength".[8]

But such proposals are based on a false premise. The role of military power in China's rise has been minimal; Beijing has not fought a war since 1979, when it launched a brief unsuccessful invasion of northern Vietnam. Rather, it is China's economic and social transformation that has made it a global force. The real tools of Chinese power projection are trade, economic investment and the scientific revolution.[9] The Belt and Road Initiative (BRI), Huawei[10] and DeepSeek[11] are the flagships of Chinese foreign policy, not its three aircraft carriers (two of which are already obsolescent),[12] one overseas military base in Djibouti, petty naval harassment in the South China Sea, or sabre-rattling over Taiwan.

This is not to say that Chinese military activities have no importance, for they may lead to a conflict with disastrous, if unintended consequences. But the greatest threat China poses to Western interests and influence is through its soft power, primarily in winning hearts and minds across the Global South. If Western policy-makers fail to act on this reality, no amount of hard power will compensate for the deterioration of America's – and the West's – position in the world.

The shortcomings of hard power have been underlined by its overuse and the resultant self-harm. The long-running fiascos in Afghanistan and Iraq began with convincing demonstrations of US military might. But in the long run they had a devastating effect on America's international standing. Conversely, what has made the United States one of the most successful nations in history is its human capital, openness to innovation, and dynamism. These have been instrumental in delivering the power and prosperity that are so envied by other countries.

The United States is not alone in paying the penalty for its excessive reliance on military power. Putin's invasion of Ukraine has not only made Russia a pariah in Europe, but also strategically and economically dependent on China. Beijing, too, has misjudged the value of hard power. For decades, China benefited hugely from Western-led markets, investment and technology. But its threatening behaviour over Taiwan and in the South China Sea and its "wolf-warrior" rhetoric have awakened Western anxieties to the point that the "China opportunity" has mutated into the "China threat".

It is true, as Joseph Nye noted, that soft power often needs to be complemented by credible hard power.[13] But the natural balance between the two has been upset. Geopolitics and hard power are being over-emphasized at a time when their limitations are starkly evident. This disconnect is all the more striking for being out of kilter with public attitudes. While many political leaders continue to view global order through a twentieth-century, predominantly competitive prism, their peoples have more pressing concerns, from falling living standards to climate change.[14]

## Reconceptualizing self-interest

The foundation of any international order is self-interest. From the Pax Romana two thousand years ago to the US-led order of the post-Cold War era, it has played a decisive role in shaping and sustaining order. Today, this is truer than ever. It makes little sense, therefore, to speak about transcending self-interest. No international order has ever managed this, and it defies logic to suppose that such a feat might be possible in the current political climate.

However, it is feasible to reconceptualize and channel self-interest in more constructive ways. And it is vital that we do so. Self-interest is a pre-requisite of global problem solving. It drives international cooperation and constrains conflict. But often the opposite is the case. During the Covid-19 pandemic, narrow national interests crippled the responses of governments to the greatest public health emergency in a century. A more cooperative, internationalist and, yes, self-interested approach could have saved millions of lives. Similarly, the reluctance of countries to cooperate in combating climate change is not only a moral failure and threat to human security, but threatens to have a devastating impact on economic growth. According to one estimate, by 2050 global average incomes could drop by nearly a fifth on present trends.[15] Rich countries tend to regard global poverty as a problem of developing nations. Yet its consequences play out on a daily basis in the form of mass migration, encouraging political extremism and social instability in those very countries that believed "third world" penury was an issue of tangential concern to them. It has undermined Western societies far more effectively than the rise of China or Putin's invasion of Ukraine.

But if the self-interest of governments and societies should converge in theory, why has it proved so divisive in practice? And what can be done to make it a catalyst for revitalizing international order instead of a generator of interstate conflict? Three elements are critical here: recognizing the interconnectedness of our interests; a proper grasp of time; and practical empathy.

### Recognizing the interconnectedness of things

In the wake of the 2008 financial crisis, we have seen a growing backlash against internationalism and globalization, and the reassertion of national egoism and identity politics in regimes of all types. The response to Covid-19 highlighted how far the sense of being part of a global community has been eroded, a trend exacerbated by growing North–South divisions over the Russian invasion of Ukraine and the conflict in Gaza. International society is visibly fragmenting. At the same time, the world has never been more interconnected – not just economically, but politically, technologically, culturally and informationally.[16] We live in a time of hyper-globalization or multiple globalizations, while many of the threats and challenges facing us are universal.

The contradiction between insular attitudes and the reality of a world that is more interdependent than ever is a source of endless disruption and confrontation. Any attempt to rebuild international order is consequently contingent on recognizing the interconnectedness of our interests. To do so, means tackling two of the banes of the modern era: the de-globalization fallacy and narrow nationalism.

The de-globalization fallacy is based on a number of false premises. In the first place, the fragmentation of international society is *not* the same as de-globalization. Global order may be unravelling, with no consensus about its rules, but we belong nonetheless to one world. Developments thousands of miles away have a direct impact on our own lives. Thus, a pandemic that originated in China in 2020 killed millions of people around the world over the next two years. Russia's invasion of Ukraine disrupted the post-Covid recovery of the world economy. The carbon emissions of China and the United States have contributed significantly to global warming, as has the deforestation of the Amazon jungle. On a more positive note, global trade feeds and clothes the world, and provides the energy, infrastructure and goods that enable most people to live more comfortably. The development of Covid-19 vaccines relied on scientific expertise from many countries, international supply chains, as well as production in several overseas centres.

Globalization is about much more than the circulation of goods, services, technology and (liberal democratic) norms. It encompasses the full range of human activity. The character of globalization is also in flux. Compared to the Western-dominated model of the past half century, the contemporary version is more diverse and contested. As Ian Bremmer has observed, "it is less coordinated, deliberate and efficient than before".[17] Globalization is an organic process that takes place often irrespective of the will of even the most powerful nations. Whether it is the activity of multi-national corporations, Big Tech, non-governmental organizations, the explosion of information and disinformation on social media, or the large-scale movement of people and ideas, globalization is becoming more anarchic.

In these circumstances, it is perhaps understandable that there should be a backlash in the West against globalization, with many regarding it as antithetical to national interests. But globalization is neither intrinsically good nor bad. It is what it is: the "increased interconnectedness and interdependence of peoples and countries".[18] *It is also here to stay.* Universal threats such as climate change and pandemic disease belie the myth that we can cordon ourselves from "malign actors". Instead of wishing away reality, we should concentrate on adapting to globalization's challenges. The future will belong to those who are best able to do this.

It is no surprise at a time of global disorder that narrow nationalism should feature so prominently. Leaders, democratic as well as authoritarian, routinely resort to cultural and racist tropes for populist ends. Such toxic nationalism has little to do with national self-interest, but reflects the agendas of particular individuals and interest groups. Regrettably, though, it has proved highly influential. It has had a debilitating effect on the will and capacity of governments to cooperate in meeting transnational threats. It encourages short horizons and foments intolerance. And it corrodes international order.

The escalation of US-China tensions during the first Trump presidency (2017–21) illustrated the harmful consequences of nationalism. Policy disagreements between Washington and Beijing on matters ranging from trade and human rights to Taiwan and freedom of navigation in the South China Sea were stoked by nationalist and civilizational posturing on both sides. In this fraught atmosphere, already difficult problems became intractable, with a heightened risk of conflict. In the United Kingdom, the manipulation of xenophobic sentiments by the Conservative government of Boris Johnson following the 2016 Brexit referendum inflicted lasting harm on Britain's relations with the European Union, by far its largest trading partner (accounting for more than 40 per cent of total UK trade[19]).

One might suppose that politicians are invariably hostage to special interests and the lure of populism. But things don't have to be that way. It is indicative that the slight thaw in US-China relations that occurred during the last two years of the Biden administration coincided with a dialling-down of nationalist rhetoric.

There was movement in some areas, such as military-to-military dialogue, climate cooperation, and clamping down on the chemical precursors to fentanyl. On many issues, the substantive differences between Washington and Beijing remained as large as ever, but there was an appreciation that US-China interdependence and the interests of both sides necessitated a more pragmatic, less visceral approach.

## *A grasp of time*

It is often said that authoritarian leaders have the luxury of thinking long-term since they are not accountable to a fickle public, whereas democratic politicians must prioritize short-term goals if they are to remain in office. However, this proposition is tenuous. When one thinks of transformative leaders in history, many of them have been democratic – Abraham Lincoln (the emancipation of slaves), Franklin D. Roosevelt (New Deal), Nelson Mandela (post-apartheid nationhood) and Clement Attlee (British welfare state). Conversely, many authoritarian figures have not taken advantage of their longevity to effect positive change in society or in their country's international fortunes. Vladimir Putin (25 years and counting) has presided over an ultra-personalized system whose overriding raison d'être is the consolidation of power for its own sake. And because authoritarian leaders operate within a small bubble, they are susceptible to committing egregious blunders, such as the invasion of Ukraine.

One crucial quality that distinguished Lincoln, FDR and Mandela from the common run of leaders was their ability to think in more than one time-scale. They were immensely skilful tacticians, highly pragmatic and even ruthless. But they also saw the bigger picture. They recognized that the purpose of power was not power itself but to bring about far-reaching change.[20] Our political leaders (and those of future generations) face a similar challenge: how to balance the demands of politics with the imperatives of policy-making in the national interest. Unfortunately, it is a test most fail. And a key reason for this is that they have a poor grasp of time.

There are a couple of aspects to this problem. The first is the artificial separation of priorities between immediate (or "urgent") and long-term ("non-urgent"). Inevitably, those in the latter category assume secondary or peripheral importance. Climate policy in many countries suffers from this perception. Governments acknowledge the need to meet the threat of global warming. But in practice, reasons always crop up to delay or dilute action: protecting jobs in obsolescent carbon-intensive industries, the allegedly higher cost of renewables (often untrue), maintaining "energy security", boosting GDP by all available means. This procrastination reflects an underlying assumption that there is time enough to take action, which is why net-zero targets have been set far into the future (2050–70). By then, some hope, technology may have come up with a variety of solutions – converting natural gas into "green" hydrogen, recycling emissions through mass carbon capture and storage (CCS), geo-engineering, and so on.

But in reality there is very little time. Climate change represents a long-term threat, but it is also one whose consequences are with us already – in the accelerated melting of the Arctic sea ice to subsistence communities suffering drought and famine in the Sahel region of Africa; from the floods that inundated one third of Pakistan in 2022, to city dwellers in developed countries experiencing record heatwaves. Climate change directly affects hundreds of millions of people across the globe. A 2021 study estimated 5 million excess deaths a year in the period 2000–19 from temperature-related causes.[21] The WHO forecasts that climate change between 2030 and 2050 will cause an additional 250,000 deaths per year from malnutrition, malaria, diarrhoea and heat stress alone.[22] The impact of the climate crisis has been hardest on the developing world. But the Global North has been far from immune. In the summer of 2022 more than 60,000 people died in Europe from heat-related causes.[23]

The inability of policy-makers to recognize that a threat can be simultaneously long-term *and* immediate is compounded by their lack of perseverance in addressing it. There are no quick fixes. A successful approach to climate change, for example, is contingent on global cooperation sustained over decades. Even then, the outcomes may be underwhelming, such as only a modest slowdown in the rate of global warming. That makes climate policy a hard sell. Yet the alternatives – passivity, delay, resignation – promise almost unimaginably bad outcomes: not only increased mortality and a significant reduction of global GDP, but also the inundation of major coastal cities such as Shanghai and Mumbai, widespread desertification leading to large-scale food and water scarcities, terminal damage to eco-systems, and the extinction of many species. Confronting the threat of climate change is about self-interest in its most physical form, but it requires decision-makers to see the bigger picture, including retooling national economies for the low-carbon global economy of the future.

This raises a point in relation to international order more generally, which is that its credibility depends on its participants being in it for the long haul. That is why the visible erosion of Western support for Ukraine has been so damaging. For this advertises to Russia, and other would-be disruptors, that the advocates of international order are not truly committed to it, but will be constantly distracted or deflected by other priorities. The issue goes way beyond individual personalities, such as the current US president. Western leaders need to back up their lofty pronouncements with concrete actions. To say they will support Ukraine "for as long as it takes", with "ironclad" commitments, and then fail to provide meaningful security guarantees and real economic integration is to abuse the very idea of international order. In the case of European nations, it is also to sabotage their own direct security.

*Practical empathy*

Empathy is critical to the effective pursuit of self-interest. This statement seems counter-intuitive; many dictionaries define self-interest as promoting one's own interest while disregarding that of others. Yet self-interest in international politics requires a true understanding of the thinking, not just of allies and partners, but also of rivals, enemies and the uncommitted. It is vital to know who you're dealing with, for better or worse. What are their fears and aspirations? What attracts or repels them? What can be done to get them on board?

In recent years empathy has been in short supply. Key players have been so focused on their own goals and interests that they often seem to conduct policy in a vacuum. Thus, Western governments showed little grasp of the post-Soviet trauma of the Russian ruling elite during the 1990s, assuming instead that it would be forced to adjust to the new and permanent reality of a Western-dominated world. The stages of suicidal statecraft that marked the unravelling of the liberal order were not simply failures of execution, but also of perception. The George W. Bush administration scarcely cared that much of the world, including many allies, opposed the 2003 invasion of Iraq. America's self-interest was all-transcending and everyone else would have to live with it. During his first presidency, Donald Trump acted on the basis that his personal self-interest was America's, and that the views and preferences of allies were of negligible importance. His second presidency has only doubled down on these instincts.

The lack of understanding or even interest in the perspectives and priorities of others is a common failing of leaders, regardless of political hue. Xi Jinping has managed simultaneously to aggravate tensions with Washington, alienate once well-disposed European governments, and encourage many of China's Indo-Pacific neighbours to gravitate further towards the United States. Putin's expectation of a quick victory over Ukraine was fuelled by his mistaken belief that the Russian-speaking population in eastern Ukraine would welcome the invading forces as their own. Lack of empathy skewed the Kremlin's strategic calculus, with catastrophic results.

Although they are often conflated, empathy does not imply agreement. To state that Washington underestimated Moscow's opposition to NATO is in no way to argue that enlargement should not have happened. As noted in Chapter 1, exclusion of the former Warsaw Pact countries from the alliance would have created a dangerous security void at the heart of Europe. However, Western policymakers should have grasped that an imperial mentality would continue to shape the Kremlin's worldview. Recognizing this would have checked the wishful thinking underpinning much of Western policy towards Russia, exemplified by Germany's *Wandel durch Handel* ("change through trade") and the naïve belief of successive American presidents that they could "fix" or "park" Russia.

Understanding alternative – and often unpalatable – perspectives is more critical than ever. It is key to achieving the right mix of competition and coopera-tion in the West's relations with China. And it is no less vital in engaging with the Global South. It does little good for Western leaders to deplore the refusal of many non-Western countries to condemn Putin over Ukraine. They need to put themselves in their shoes. They might find it easier to comprehend, then, why the Global South is so resentful of the West while going easy on China, Russia and other authoritarian regimes. The eagerness of the West to whitewash its colonial past; its moralizing tone and casual double standards; the disjunction between lavish promises of investment and underwhelming outcomes; and an unsubtle instrumentalism that views developing countries as little more than pawns of great power competition – all these add up to an empathy deficit that is incompatible with self-interest.

## Prioritizing representativeness and inclusiveness

If self-interest is the foundation of a viable international order, then representa-tiveness and inclusiveness are indispensable to its functioning. The much-cited opposition between representativeness and efficacy is specious. In the twenty-first-century world, an unrepresentative order is a contradiction in terms. By ignoring the self-interest of the many, it sets itself up to fail, inviting obstruction and disruption at every turn.

The obstacles to building a representative international order are numer-ous. They include the self-entitlement and exclusivism of the major powers; the constant intrusion of geopolitical rivalries; the ossification of the UN Security Council; sundry jealousies between states at all levels; narrow self-interest; and the challenge of reconciling multiple competing demands. Nevertheless, as great as the difficulties are, leaders have a responsibility to try to overcome them. Because the status quo is untenable.

### Rectifying the under-representation of the Global South

It is no coincidence that since the Russian invasion of Ukraine, the Global South has capitalized on its enhanced profile and influence to obtain important conces-sions. In September 2023, the African Union was finally granted a permanent seat in the G-20 – nearly 15 years after the latter was created. A year earlier, Joe Biden hosted a US-Africa leaders' summit in Washington, a move that would have been improbable before the war.

US anxieties about Chinese and Russian influence in Africa were instrumental in shifting the dial. But a fluid global context also helped concentrate minds in Washington on the importance of Africa, and of the Global South more broadly. Nations that were previously ignored, marginalized or patronized now matter in global as well as regional terms.

Faced with a newly empowered and assertive Global South, Western decision-makers face a critical choice. They can aim to stay ahead of the game by actively supporting efforts to build a more representative international order. Or they can jealously guard their privileges in multilateral institutions, paying lip-service to the principle of a fair and equitable order, in which case they are liable to find themselves overtaken by events. It is not enough for a once dominant West to throw the Global South an occasional bone whenever it needs its cooperation – as we have seen over the war in Ukraine and in relation to China. Global South countries are getting better at leveraging engagement to gain a greater voice.

This trend is still in its infancy, and it is tempting to believe that the Global South comprises such a disparate group of countries that their capacity to organize effectively will not last. But that looks an unsafe bet. The present era is quite unlike that of the 1950s and early 1960s, when the Non-Aligned Movement was prominent. Power today is more diffuse. The rules are uncertain. The world is more globalized and interconnected than it has ever been. And international society is increasingly disorderly. Under such conditions, the Global South will have more, not fewer, opportunities to maximize its heft.

*A question of priorities*

Representativeness is not just a matter of increasing Global South numbers in international organizations. It also means rethinking the twenty-first-century policy agenda so that greater attention is devoted to issues of existential importance to developing countries, such as mitigating the consequences of climate change and alleviating their debt burden.

The contemporary global agenda reflects the relativities of power, and will continue to be shaped by major power perceptions of what is important. This means, among other things, that geopolitical competition will dominate international politics for some decades yet.

But change is afoot. As their reaction to the war in Ukraine has shown, Global South nations reject the presumption that Western priorities should invariably be theirs. They resent that the West's emphasis on geopolitics – containing China, countering Russia – takes the focus away from issues of primary interest to them. They also dislike the fact that not all conflicts receive due, much less equal, consideration. Whereas Western governments assign epic significance to Ukraine, no less destructive wars in Ethiopia and Sudan have been almost invisible. It is symptomatic that the civil war in Yemen and consequent humanitarian disaster – the worst in the world – were largely ignored until Houthi rebels started targeting commercial shipping in the Red Sea in late 2023. Overnight, a sideshow became the main event because it directly affected Western interests.

In a more representative and inclusive order, human development priorities and climate change would have as much band-width as US-China rivalry. That will not happen soon.[24] But Western policy-makers should have a care. It is in their collective self-interest to embrace a more representative agenda before the pressures for change become irresistible and the consequences (such as migration) become unmanageable.

## The importance of flexibility

In thinking about international order, it is natural to want to invest general principles with precise content. After all, one of the failings of the "rules-based international order" is that its precepts and norms have degenerated into a series of platitudes that can mean anything and nothing. There is, however, an equal and opposite danger – that of being overly prescriptive.

The only viable international order is one able to accommodate, and moderate, substantial differences in viewpoints, values and interests. Easy to say, but hard to do. We live in a world where rivals and opponents are routinely demonized. It has become much harder to build bridges or glide over disagreements. Politics, domestic and international, has become intensely polarized. Dogmatism rules.

These are hardly new problems. But they have got a lot worse. During the Cold War, the United States and the Soviet Union were locked in a global strategic and ideological confrontation. Nevertheless, following the scare of the Cuban Missile Crisis, they were able to keep this within certain bounds. They maintained reliable channels of communication, avoided direct conflict with each other, and concluded a number of bilateral and multilateral agreements, such as the SALT (Strategic Arms Limitations Talks) and SALT II treaties and the 1975 Helsinki Accords. In the process, they demonstrated that it was possible to co-exist, and engage constructively, with even the most committed foe. The world, it turned out, was big enough for two superpowers.

It should therefore be possible to build an international order that tolerates even the largest of differences and most intense of rivalries. But to do so means encouraging flexibility and accepting diversity.


## Norms over values

A flexible order would dispense with the illusion of "universal" values, and recognize instead the existence of multiple and often contradictory value systems. The overriding emphasis would be on the protection of core international norms. States would be left to get on with the business of governing themselves, *however they chose*, in return for observing certain basic principles of behaviour, such as refraining from "the threat or use of force against the territorial integrity or political independence of any state" (Article 2.4 of the UN Charter).

With governments having licence to behave badly within their own borders, the domestic outcomes would be unedifying or worse in many cases. Yet for international order to work, whether as a force for stability or foundation of problem solving, requires prioritizing the sovereign rights of nations and the principle of non-interference. States are more likely to cooperate with each other if they feel secure in their sovereignty, free from the pressure to conform to some "objective" standard of governance. Addressing challenges such as climate change will require all hands to the pump, regardless of political and ideological allegiances.

Such a normative shift would be challenging for Western policy-makers still loyal to the liberal tradition. But there is no sensible alternative. Decades of lecturing foreign governments about their human rights records have proved fruitless. Liberal interventionism has been thoroughly counter-productive. And democracy-building in general has been marked by moral inconsistency, poor judgement, and hubris. The sad fact is that the values of liberal humanism are not universal; indeed, they have been in steady retreat for nearly two decades, and are being eroded even within liberal democracies.[25]

None of this is to suggest that political repression and the violation of human rights do not matter. Rather, it is to recognize the limits of external action. If Western governments are unwilling to exercise influence over authoritarian allies such as Saudi Arabia and Egypt or, worse still, are bent on undermining democratic checks and balances in their own countries (Trumpian America), then what hope – or moral claim – do they have in complaining about abuses in, say, China?

There is a larger practical point as well. What matters most in terms of global order is not the type of regime in a given country, but how that country behaves towards others. In this connection, the common claim that authoritarian regimes are more disposed than democracies to foreign aggression does not bear serious scrutiny. The experience of the post-Cold War period demonstrates there is no automatic correlation. For example, although Putin's Russia has fought several wars, China's last foreign conflict was nearly half a century ago. Over the same period, the United States and other leading Western democracies (the United Kingdom and France) have initiated or actively participated in multiple wars.

We should engage with countries on the basis of their external actions, not their political systems. Accordingly, the high-handed behaviour of the People's Liberation Army (PLA) navy in the South China Sea is far more consequential for international order than Beijing's repression of the Uighurs, as deplorable as that is. The primary importance of foreign policy behaviour is also why Russia represents a greater menace than China. The latter is a revisionist power, but operates mostly within accepted parameters to achieve its goals. Putin, by contrast, is an "arsonist of the international system".[26] He thrives on anarchy; the more disorderly the world, the better.

### Rethinking global order

The post-Cold War "rules-based international order" – the liberal international order – is over and cannot be revived. This was the product of an extraordinary concatenation of power, vision and will. From the end of the Cold War to the start of its invasion of Iraq, the United States enjoyed a multi-dimensional dominance unprecedented in history. At the same time, it committed itself to implementing a sweeping vision of global order. Those conditions have ceased to exist. The United States no longer has the capacity, the self-belief or the drive to build a global Pax Americana. And Western liberal norms and values have lost their former pre-eminence.

As the world changes, so must the nature and shape of order itself. A new order needs to reflect a global context in which power has become much more diffuse, and be representative in ways that the US-led, Western-dominated order never has been, and a great power Concert never could be. It needs to be capacious enough to tolerate considerable normative, cultural and strategic diversity. It would involve much more substantial roles for China and India, but also for a host of middle powers – Brazil, Türkiye, South Africa, Indonesia, Nigeria, Saudi Arabia, Australia, among others – as well as significantly greater participation from across the Global South. Such an order would also have to find ways of managing a super-rogue Russia and a chronically disruptive North Korea and Iran. Non-state actors would exert a growing influence, and multilateral organizations would be central to international problem solving.

Decision-making in such an order would be complicated and chaotic. The world is pulled apart by opposing forces, it is often irrational, and it is generally resistant to order. Many inequities, real and perceived, will endure. Thus, the UN Security Council will remain with its antiquated procedures and privileges. Global South interests will continue to be under-represented in forums such as the G-20 and the COP (Conference of the Parties). And major powers will regularly flout international norms, much as they have always done.

To acknowledge these realities, however, does not mean surrendering to fatalism. We are not obliged to accept the current, acutely dysfunctional state of world disorder as "normal". It is past time to abandon long-held preconceptions, and to embrace instead a practical vision that emphasizes our collective responsibility for problem solving. The order that emerges would be flawed and fragile. But it would represent a signal improvement on what we have today. Its inclusiveness and flexibility would appeal to a critical mass of state and non-state actors, and offer some sort of foundation on which to tackle the mounting threats and challenges facing the world.

## 4

# THE UNITED STATES, CHINA AND THE MAKING OF A TWENTY-FIRST-CENTURY RELATIONSHIP

The post-Cold War "rules-based" international order may no longer be sustainable, but there will be many continuities from the recent past. Contrary to common perception, the United States is not in decline, and remains the pre-eminent power. It will play an outsize role in global affairs, regardless of who sits in the White House. Equally, China is not about to rule the world[1]; the description, "fragile superpower", is even more apposite today than when it was coined back in 2007.[2] China faces a prolonged struggle just to avoid falling further behind America. And despite apparently irreconcilable differences, much talk of decoupling, and predictions of impending conflict, some level of cooperative engagement between Washington and Beijing will remain critical to both sides and to international order.

In thinking about the United States, China, and their roles in global governance, we need to consider three central challenges. The first is adapting US primacy and leadership to a post-unipolar, post-liberal world. The task here is both substantive and presentational – America recasting itself as a driver of positive change rather than treating leadership as a historical entitlement or viewing the world through the social Darwinist lens of "survival of the fittest". The second big challenge is China's transformation from an essentially opportunistic power, absorbed by narrow self-interest, into a leading contributor to global governance. The third, and perhaps most difficult task, is to place US-China interaction on a stable footing, so that it stands as one of the foundations of international order instead of being a prime source of escalating disorder.

## American leadership in a post-unipolar world

The position of the United States is unenviable in many respects. As the world's strongest power, it is a ready target for the jealousies of others. Many countries rely on it for their security and economic welfare, yet resent this dependence.

Despite its generosity over several decades, the United States has often received little thanks for the vital support it provides. While its actions have been driven by self-interest, and have sometimes had disastrous outcomes, the ledger of US foreign policy remains largely positive.

A viable international order is contingent on the United States playing a leading role. However, it has become plain that the former, top-down model of US leadership is no longer appropriate. This asks too much of Washington; it is resisted by allies and partners, as well as by enemies and the non-aligned; and it is having the unintended consequence of weakening American influence around the world. Tellingly, there is growing pushback in the United States itself. During the 2024 presidential campaign, Donald Trump's focus on domestic priorities resonated strongly with the American public.

But if Washington needs to rethink its approach to global leadership, what would this actually entail and what are the chances of necessary change coming to pass? We can start with what the United States should *not* do. Any attempt to implement Trump's dystopian vision of world order (see Chapter 2) will rebound against American interests across the board. Already his actions have significantly strengthened China's global standing, discredited the transatlantic alliance, alienated much of the Global South, and given a growing number of countries every reason to diversify ties *away* from the United States. Today, the notion of American moral leadership appears ludicrous, as the Trump White House guts US democratic institutions and wreaks further havoc in the international system.

It is all too easy to lose hope of reversing these negative trends. The Republican Party is in thrall to the cult of Trump, while the Democratic Party appears to be suffering post-traumatic shock following Kamala Harris's defeat in the presidential election. Nevertheless, it is important to see beyond Trump – after all, he will be 82 at the end of his current presidential term in 2029 – and at least think about how the United States might reinvent itself for a post-unipolar world.

There are several elements that should form part of a revised American foreign policy. They include greater devolution of responsibilities to allies and a relaxed attitude towards European strategic autonomy; the shift to a more pragmatic, less ideological mindset; flexible multilateral engagement; a nuanced position on globalization; and better messaging.

## A smarter internationalism

A major failing of US foreign policy for much of the post-Cold War era has been an almost pathological compulsion to lead. As the only true global power, it has acted as if it must be the primary actor on every major issue. But *the United States does not always have to lead.* On some issues and in certain multilateral frameworks, it can and should play a secondary, supporting role. Self-interest, as always, should determine the degree of its involvement, not a messianic vision of America's special role as the world's saviour.[3] A smarter approach to international order would be selective. It would focus on priorities that matter most to American interests. It would share responsibility with others. And it would not feel the need to ram home the message that America is the "greatest nation on earth"[4] and "the leading force for good in the world".[5]

The acid test of a new type of US internationalism is the transatlantic alliance, specifically NATO. Successive US administrations – Democratic and Republican – have long complained about the Europeans not pulling their weight. The charge is a fair one – to a point. Since the foundation of the alliance in 1949, European member states have effectively contracted out their security to Washington, a dependency that if anything has increased since the end of the Cold War.

This situation is unhealthy and unsustainable. The Europeans clearly need to spend more on defence. Yet that is not the main issue. For decades, the United States, backed by the United Kingdom, has opposed European efforts to develop a distinct security and defence identity, for example, through the now defunct Western European Union (WEU) and the European Union's Common Security and Defence Policy. Washington has set itself against the very principle of European strategic autonomy, as promoted by French President Emmanuel Macron. It has done so to preserve America's security leadership in Europe through NATO. But the practical effect has been to reinforce European dependence on the United States.

US interests would be better served by a less intrusive approach. Extracting promises of increased defence spending is just scratching the surface of the problem.[6] What is really required is a change of mindset. Washington should welcome the desire of some European leaders to exercise greater initiative and, in certain areas, to act more autonomously. If they are to take responsibility for their own security, they should be allowed to get on with it as they see fit. As long as America attempts to micro-manage its allies, they will remain trapped in a culture of dependence, however much their defence budgets may expand.

Conversely, Washington should avoid lurching to the other extreme – downgrading its participation in NATO and European security, as Trump is doing. The single greatest advantage that the United States possesses over China is the support of multiple allies and partners around the world, nowhere more so than in Europe. It would be strategically negligent to discard these assets out of pique, myopia or small-mindedness. Even a modest show of respect towards the sensibilities of NATO member states would go a long way to keeping them onside.

Washington should also rethink the wisdom of pressuring European governments to play a more active role in the Indo-Pacific region, notably in containing China. In recent years, there has emerged an implicit – and sometimes explicit – threat that if they do not contribute more in the Indo-Pacific then the United States will downsize its role in safeguarding European security.[7] This position is counter-productive, as are crude attempts to force Berlin and Paris, in particular, to toe the US line on China and reduce economic ties with Beijing.[8] If Washington wants the Europeans to invest more in their own defence and rely less on America, it is illogical for them to expend precious resources in a theatre far away from their primary interests. Not only do they face a clear and present threat from Russia, but their contributions to Indo-Pacific security would be symbolic, too insignificant to make a difference. The best added value that European members can bring to the transatlantic alliance is to do a much better job of looking after their own security. That would free Washington to devote more resources to its own primary priorities in the Indo-Pacific.

## Less ideology, more pragmatism

Since the end of the Second World War, US presidents have consistently emphasized America's role as leader of the "free world". That mission has passed its use-by date and no longer serves any worthwhile purpose. Indeed, the Trump administration's attacks on European liberal democracy, and direct interference in the 2025 German federal election, point to an ever-widening transatlantic values-gap. No less importantly, the pretence of ideological convergence is ill-suited to managing relations with Asia, the Middle East, Africa and Latin America.

It is time for Washington to dial down the ideology – whether liberal or national populist – and adopt a more businesslike yet still ethical stance. There are three clear ways to go about this. The first, highlighted in the previous chapter, is to prioritize international norms and rules of conduct. This is something nearly all states can get behind since it is in their self-interest that there should be respect for national sovereignty and territorial integrity. The United States has an excellent opportunity to promote itself as the protector of international norms. But not if it reserves the right to change borders unilaterally, as in Trump's claims to the Panama Canal, Greenland and even Canada. Nor by dividing countries between "good" and "bad", or demanding that they choose between America and China.

The second path to a more effective US approach comes from the power of example. This idea, pursued by presidents from John F. Kennedy to Joe Biden, has become devalued over the course of the post-Cold War era. In its ill-judged efforts to "promote democracy" in Iraq, Afghanistan and Libya, the United States became complacent about the state of its own democracy and civil society. If it is serious about being a model for others, then it must start at home. For the rest of the world, seeing is believing. And what it sees in the United States is vicious political polarization and persecution, maladministration, skewing of the judiciary, systematic disinformation alongside a clampdown on free expression, and multiple cultural and identity fault-lines. Rather than preach to the world, the United States needs to get its own house in order, and reestablish the connection between democracy and good governance.

The third route to a reinvigorated framework for US foreign policy is a generosity of spirit. This requires devoting greater attention to priorities such as global poverty, food security and human development. Washington should recognize that few countries in the Global South are interested in the rights and wrongs of US-China rivalry. Their concerns are more prosaic: better access to public health, effective vaccines, decent sanitation, potable water, and financing for climate adaptation.

The US (and Western) response to these needs has been woefully inadequate. During the Biden years, Washington condemned Beijing's "debt-trap diplomacy", and criticized its loans for their lack of political conditionality. But such remonstrations fell on deaf ears. Although few in the Global South harbour illusions about Chinese benevolence, the West's own performance has been so dismal as to make China look good by comparison. The Belt and Road Initiative may have failed to deliver on many of its commitments, but it has at least delivered on some.[9] In stark contrast, the G-7's promised $600 billion investment from its Partnership for Global Infrastructure and Investment shows no sign of materializing,[10] while Biden's Indo-Pacific Economic Partnership was a dud due to the American refusal to open up market access to partner countries.[11]

More recently, the Trump administration's decision to drastically cut overseas aid and close down the United States Agency for International Development (USAID) is projecting an image of an ugly, mean-spirited America. The damage is not just reputational; there are geopolitical and economic consequences as well. If the United States wants to out-compete China in the Global South, including in adjoining regions such as Latin America,[12] it needs to demonstrate that it has more to offer by way of debt relief, trade access, and infrastructure investment. So far, however, it has shown no sign of drawing the correct conclusions; Trump's partiality to tariffs and resort to sundry forms of intimidation are strengthening Beijing's influence among many developing nations.

*Flexible multilateral engagement*

Global primacy and multilateralism are uneasy bedfellows at the best of times. Although the United States was the driving force behind the creation of the

United Nations, it has always found it dfficult to manage multiple parties with diverse and conflicting agendas. This has led it to favour two formats above all others. The first is an alliance system where its leadership is uncontested and its policy preferences are generally (although not always) respected. NATO is the prime example of this. The second format is minilateralism, as highlighted by the development of the Quad (United States, United Kingdom, Australia, India), AUKUS (Australia, United Kingdom, United States), the United States-Japan-Republic of Korea trilateral pact and the "Squad" (same membership as the Quad, except with the Philippines instead of India). The common denominator between these variants of multilateralism is that the United States is not merely a first among equals, but a colossus that dwarfs all other parties.

Conversely, Washington dislikes frameworks where its leadership is challenged and US policy goals are often frustrated. The UN Security Council is its biggest bugbear, but there has long been irritation with a number of other structures – the World Trade Organization (WTO), the World Health Organization (WHO) and the Conference of the Parties (COP) on Climate Change, to name just a few. Additionally, there is the historic problem of US Congressional opposition to multilateral commitments. That is why, for example, the United States has yet to ratify the UN Convention on the Law of the Sea (UNCLOS), although it abides by its provisions.

US scepticism towards multilateral diplomacy is notably more pronounced under a Republican administration; before Trump there was George W. Bush. It is unrealistic, therefore, to expect a more positive approach from Washington anytime soon. One of the least surprising moves of the second Trump presidency was to pull the United States out of the WHO and the Paris climate agreement (again). Such political demonstrations are nevertheless ill-advised. Withdrawal is more damaging to American influence than it is to the functioning of those organizations. Thus, Trump's 2017 decision to suspend US participation in the Paris agreement painted America as an international delinquent, but had minimal impact on the COP process. Similarly, leaving the Trans-Pacific Partnership turned out to be a blessing in disguise for other countries in the region. Japan led subsequent efforts to develop a much improved version of the partnership in the form of the Comprehensive and Progressive Agreement on Trans-Pacific Partnership (CPTPP). It is revealing that Beijing has since taken advantage of the US absence to lobby for Chinese membership. Inevitably, as the Trump administration downsizes its engagement with multilateral institutions, China and others are looking to fill the ensuing vacuum.

Just taking part is one way to sharpen up America's approach to multilateralism. Another is to act with more foresight within international organizations. Blocking the appointment of judges to the WTO's Appellate Body since 2017 has not only paralyzed the organization's operations,[13] it has undermined the reputation of the United States at a time when it is trying to make the case that China engages in unfair trade practices. Likewise, Washington's continuing failure to address the issue of inequitable voting shares in the World Bank and IMF – specifically the under-representation of developing countries – is at odds with its goal of countering the advance of Chinese influence across the Global South.

### Appreciating globalization

Since the Second World War, the United States has dominated globalization processes. But in recent years, the increasingly anarchic nature of globalization has encouraged the view that the United States is losing out, and not simply to spontaneous and impersonal forces, but to China. Globalization has become another front in their strategic and ideological confrontation.

The irony in all this is that the United States remains globalizer-in-chief. No other country comes close – whether in terms of military projection, economic and financial power, technological and informational reach, or cultural influence. US policy-makers believe that China benefits unfairly from globalization. But regardless of whether this is true, it is a perverse way of looking at the problem. The question should be: *who gains most from globalization?* An America that has shown an unparalleled capacity to attract the world's talent and to project hard and soft power, or a China labouring under a repressive political system, whose economic outlook is uncertain, which faces a long-term demographic crisis, and which has problematic relations with several of its neighbours? The answer is self-evident. The fact, too, that China is embedded in Western systems gives Washington lasting leverage. Chinese banks, for example, have been reluctant to do business with Russia following Putin's invasion of Ukraine for fear of incurring secondary sanctions. Although Beijing is conducting more of its business in local currency (renminbi), China will remain heavily dependent on the dollar and the SWIFT system for some years yet. And even as it reduces its US-dollar holdings, it faces the difficulty that other major currencies (such as the euro and the yen) are held by US allies.[14]

Far from losing out from globalization, the United States is better placed than any other country to continue enjoying its benefits. To do so, however, means supporting rather than persecuting America's world-leading universities.[15] It means abandoning extravagant illusions about decoupling and onshoring. It also entails a more nuanced tariff policy. The logic behind the Trump administration's imposition of swingeing tariffs across the board is straightforward – to revive American industry by insulating it against "unfair" competition and obtaining greater market access for manufacturing exports. But this approach is flawed. Tariffs are blunt instruments that often miss their targets while harming the very people they are intended to protect. The biggest loser from Trump's tariffs will not be China, which has long anticipated them and is already adapting,[16] but the American consumer (and voter) who will suffer inflated prices for goods and services.[17] Within the first few months of Trump 2.0, the White House's erratic actions had already spooked Wall Street and raised the spectre of domestic recession.[18]

There are also strategic costs to anti-globalization and the protectionist sentiments it promotes. A relentlessly self-centred approach to the world risks alienating close allies and partners.[19] However well-disposed (or apprehensive) they may be towards America, the stream of menaces emanating from Washington reinforces the case for exploring alternative options. The notion of "de-risking" – reducing supply chain and other economic vulnerabilities – applies not only in relation to China, but also to an extortionist (and vindictive) America.

Washington has no need to go down this path. Rather than fearing Chinese (or other) competition, it should make better use of the many tools it possesses to demonstrate that the United States has much more to offer a globalized world. Openness has been, and can continue to be, America's friend. Similarly, Washington will obtain far greater cooperation from partners in Europe and Asia, and across much of the Global South, if it seeks common ground ("practical empathy") with them rather than resorting to intimidation and blackmail. As Robert Keohane and Joseph Nye have observed, "Trump has focused so much on the costs of free-riding by allies that he neglects the fact that the United States gets to drive the bus – and thus pick the destination and the route".[20]

### Better messaging

In an age of mass information, good communication is vital. And the United States is ideally placed to reach a global audience. So why is it losing the battle of narratives in many parts of the world? Moreover, to countries such as China and Russia, whose own public diplomacy is hardly stellar.

Much of this comes down to a problem of expectations. The United States is not only the leading power in the world, it has also set itself up as the exemplar and arbiter of virtue in international relations. When it falls below its publicly declared standards, other countries are quick to point this out and, to borrow from Teddy Roosevelt, show "how the doer of deeds could have done them better".[21] By contrast, few expect the international behaviour of China and Russia to be anything other than self-interested.

But even allowing that the United States offers a ready target, there is much it could do to improve its communication. One way is to moderate the judgemental tone of its pronouncements. In the past, the endless reiteration of formulaic phrases – "rules-based international order", "the right side of history", "malign actors" – has been self-defeating. Such judgementalism is a major reason why Biden's democracy/autocracy divide resonated so poorly beyond the West.

Equally, Washington should eschew the unrestrained arrogance that has characterized US foreign policy since Trump's return to the presidency. At the time of writing, it is unclear how serious he is about acquiring the Panama Canal, Greenland or making Canada America's 51st state. What is evident, though, is that his public statements, including the refusal to rule out the use of force, broadcast an image of the United States as a global lout unfettered by international law.

The problem of poor messaging is not just about PR. No less harmful is the disjunction between rhetoric and action. When Barack Obama failed to act on his 2012 "red line" against the Assad regime's use of chemical weapons in the Syrian civil war, he made the United States look irresolute and weak. It signalled a lack of seriousness in standing up for principle and opened the way for Russia's subsequent military intervention. The Biden White House's communication on Ukraine was more disastrous still. It pledged to support Ukraine "for as long as it takes", but the tale of US (and Western) military assistance to Kyiv was one of too little, too slow, too late. This disconnect undermined Ukrainian morale, emboldened the Kremlin, and eroded US credibility.

Trump's renewed mission to "Make America Great Again" (MAGA) aims to position the United States as a self-confident superpower beholden to no-one. Such an America nevertheless needs effective, well-calibrated communication, whether to induce cooperation from others, deter enemies, or simply to convey its intentions reliably. One source of concern is that other governments may call Trump's bluff, in the belief that his trademark bluster will not be backed up by real action. That could be disastrous in a deteriorating international environment. It is not hard to envisage a situation whereby a crisis, say over Taiwan or in eastern Europe, develops in such a way as to leave him caught between two very bad choices: either having to climb down and admit American incapacity (or lack of will), or undertaking drastic action for which he is ill-prepared. Clarity of message is therefore crucial.

## China and its role in global governance

The challenge for China with global order is the opposite to that facing the United States. If the latter needs to tailor its international leadership for a post-unipolar age, then for Beijing the prime task is to upgrade its capacity to meet the responsibilities of global governance. Notwithstanding China's spectacular domestic transformation, its role in the international order remains relatively modest. It may be the world's second economic power, but geopolitically it is a predominantly regional actor. Although the 2022 US National Security Strategy described China as "the only competitor with both the intent to reshape the international order and, increasingly, the economic, diplomatic, military, and technological power to do it",[22] Beijing is a long way off from consummating such ambitions.

China remains markedly inferior to the United States by every significant measure of power. Despite a recent expansion, its nuclear inventory is more than 10 times smaller than that of Russia and the United States.[23] Its conventional capabilities, although much improved, are inferior in key respects to America's. Economic growth has fallen to its lowest point since 1990,[24] and may plateau at 2–3 per cent per annum in coming decades.[25] This, in turn, owes much to an acute demographic crisis. By the middle of the century, over-65s will make up more than a quarter of a shrinking population.[26] Far from China being ready to supplant the United States, the gap between them may widen.[27]

Xi has spoken of China becoming a global leader by 2050,[28] but even meeting this generous timeline faces significant hurdles. Many countries, not only in the West, fear that a global China would abuse its power to coerce others. This perception is doubly unfortunate – not just for Beijing's ability to realize its strategic aims, but also because the world needs China to play an active part in global problem solving. There will be no meaningful progress in mitigating climate change, alleviating the debt burden of developing countries, or building security in the Indo-Pacific without Chinese cooperation.

How, then, does Beijing go about balancing an independent foreign policy and the pursuit of Chinese interests with good international citizenship? One answer is that it won't. Xi will focus single-mindedly on advancing Chinese goals to the detriment of all others, aggravating confrontation with the United States and, very possibly, bringing about a major war. Yet another course is feasible, comprising better management of territorial disputes, a more generous approach to global problems, and greater care in public diplomacy.

*Managing territorial disputes*

In much of its neighbourhood, China is viewed as a threat. Part of this is a natural reaction to the impressive build-up of its "comprehensive national power".[29] But it also stems from Beijing's assertive and sometimes threatening behaviour on territorial questions. China is in dispute with countries the length and breadth of the Indo-Pacific, from Japan and South Korea in the north, to India in the southwest, to the Philippines, Vietnam, Malaysia and Brunei in the South China

Sea. And then there is the Taiwan question, on which Beijing's position has hardened considerably.

Although territorial disputes are a functional hazard of a country with multiple borders and neighbours, the Chinese handling of these disputes has been unconscionable and inept. Under Xi, Beijing revived the once dormant quarrel with Tokyo over the Senkaku/Diaoyu islands. Chinese breaches of the Line of Actual Control (LAC) with India in the Himalayas became more frequent, culminating in a major incursion and bloody skirmish in May 2020. The PLA navy has become more aggressive in the Western Pacific, harassing Philippine re-supply and fishing vessels around the Spratly islands. Beijing has also upped the ante in relation to Taiwan, conducting live-fire exercises, regularly entering its Air Defence Identification Zone, and crossing the median line between Taiwan and the mainland.

This intimidatory behaviour has proved highly counter-productive. Far from cowing its neighbours, it has driven some of them towards the United States. It has encouraged a view of China as a norm-busting bully, ready at any moment to threaten the sovereign rights of smaller states. It has pushed Washington to strengthen America's strategic presence in the Indo-Pacific – the very opposite of what Beijing wants. It has consolidated an anti-Beijing consensus in Washington. And it has increased the prospects of direct conflict between the United States and China. All this is happening at a time when Xi faces growing domestic headwinds.

There is little likelihood that any of China's numerous territorial disputes will be resolved soon. What is achievable, though, is their relative stabilization. And indeed this is what Xi has started trying to do, belatedly appreciating the self-harm caused by past Chinese actions. In October 2024, Beijing and New Delhi agreed joint patrols along the LAC, and Xi and Modi held their first bilateral meeting for five years at the margins of the BRICS summit in Kazan, Russia. But such moves will have only limited effect if they are seen as merely tactical responses to China's vulnerabilities. Beijing needs to demonstrate that it is committed to negotiated solutions. It has to prove that "win-win" is more than a slogan, and that it retains some respect for basic international norms. In practical terms, that means undertaking a series of confidence-building measures: refraining from naval harassment in the South China Sea; suspending joint air patrols with Russia near the Senkaku/Diaoyu islands; moderating PLA activity around Taiwan; expanding border management mechanisms with India along the full extent of the LAC; and refraining from provocative demonstrations of power projection, such as the PLA Navy's circumnavigation of Australia in March 2025.

Much of this goes against the grain. But Xi finds himself at a crossroads. He can either go about recovering some of the ground lost as a result of Beijing's excesses, or he can escalate tensions with neighbours and ensure the consolidation of an anti-China (if not necessarily pro-US) consensus throughout the Indo-Pacific and beyond. More than half a century ago, Mao Zedong faced an analogous choice. With the People's Republic surrounded by enemies near and far, he made the pragmatic decision to take up Richard Nixon's offer of cooperative engagement. This not only ushered in an era of strategic accommodation with the United States, it significantly enhanced China's security and facilitated the normalization of relations with key US allies such as Japan. Although the world is very different today, one lesson still holds true: China benefits far more from a stable regional environment than one that is fluid and uncertain and in which it is widely regarded as the main disruptive actor. Defusing territorial disputes would do more than anything to accomplish this.

## Generosity and self-interest

Although Beijing was once uncomfortable with the term "Global South", these days it pitches China as a leader in this "family of emerging markets and developing countries".[30] This raises a central question. Is China a global power, second only to the United States, or is it a developing country? Or both? For the most part, China has exploited this duality quite skilfully – gaining for itself the status of a global power without incurring the concomitant obligations.

But the contradiction is becoming harder to reconcile. A leading Brazilian scholar has observed that, "as China grows more powerful, it increasingly treats other countries not as a partner might, but as a great power would".[31] There are two particular problem areas. The first is debt. Belying its claims to be a developing economy, China has become the largest creditor nation in the world, accounting for more than 20 per cent of total IMF lending in the past decade.[32] It has taken a consistently tough line in debt negotiations, and been slow to grant relief except on a bilateral transactional basis. Until now, Beijing's stance has been mainly a source of irritation to Western governments, but with more than a hundred developing countries now struggling to service their debt repayments, the narrative of China as champion of the Global South looks fragile.[33]

The second area of vulnerability is the tension between China's position as the world's largest carbon emitter (double the volume of the United States) and its refusal to accept any financial liability for the consequent physical and economic damage to developing countries. Aided by the miserliness of rich Western nations over climate financing, Beijing has yet to suffer significant reputational consequences in the Global South. But as the world heats up and the fallout from climate change becomes more pronounced, principally in Africa and Asia, China will find it more difficult to sustain the pretence that it is a mere "developing country" with no responsibilities to others.[34]

A fluid and volatile international context adds further layers of complexity. As noted in Chapter 2, the Global South has become a prized constituency with a heightened sense of its own leverage. So the pressure will mount on China, as well as on the United States and the wider West, to be more generous. If Beijing is wise, it will respond by developing a more flexible and forward-thinking approach. If not, it risks losing ground to others, including aspiring candidates to Global South leadership, such as India and Brazil.[35]

## Mending public diplomacy

The weakest part of Chinese foreign policy is its public diplomacy. Nothing has had a more alienating effect on other countries than an often strident rhetoric that combines ultra-defensiveness, arrogance and a striking lack of empathy. Although this has been categorized under the ubiquitous label "wolf-warrior" from the 2017 film of the same name, the problems date back further, to Xi's ascension in 2012 and even to the aftermath of the 2008 global financial crisis. With China emerging as the world's number two power, its leadership saw diminishing reason to follow Deng Xiaoping's advice to stay modest.

To be sure, China's expanding ambitions, however artfully packaged, would have provoked a negative reaction in some quarters. But Beijing has made things much harder than they needed to be. Publicly mocking the West's handling of the Covid-19 pandemic[36]; blaming NATO for Putin's invasion of Ukraine; and clumsy attempts to divide the Europeans from America and from each other – these are just a few lowlights of recent Chinese diplomacy. Beijing's misjudgements are not limited to interaction with the West, but also undermine its relations with neighbours and in the Global South. In Africa, Chinese officials and companies have shown little interest in engaging with local communities. In the Indo-Pacific, Beijing's over-assertiveness on territorial issues is aggravated by gratuitous personal criticisms of foreign leaders.[37]

Then there is the discrepancy between words and actions when it comes to national sovereignty and territorial integrity. On paper, there is no greater defender of these principles than China. But this commitment is highly selective. Quite apart from an arbitrary approach to its own territorial disputes, it has also indulged the norm-breaking behaviour of close partners, such as Russia. Not only has Beijing failed to offer even the mildest or most oblique criticism of the 2022 invasion of Ukraine, it has increasingly sided with Moscow as the conflict has gone on. Chinese logistical and economic support has significantly boosted Russia's fortunes – and weakened its own bona fides.

An improvement in Chinese public diplomacy will not miraculously transform relations with the United States, which will be very difficult under virtually any scenario (see below). Nor is it likely to convince the world to believe in the notion of a benign China. But it would go some way to loosening the wider anti-Beijing consensus that has taken hold in the West. Fortunately from Beijing's perspective, the excesses of Trump 2.0 have given it a wonderful opportunity. As Trump follows through on his threats to impose worldwide tariffs and dilute America's security partnerships, China can win big as the leading advocate of positive-sum globalization, multilateral cooperation, and collective problem solving. But it will have to be cleverer. Rather than belabour the obvious short-comings of the Trump administration, rejoice in the breakdown of the West, or take liberties with China's neighbours, Beijing should concentrate on improving its own performance at home and abroad. The emphasis should be on demon-strating what China has to offer the world, not on crude opportunism or cheap shots against America and the West.

## Stabilizing the US-China relationship

Such has been the crisis of US-China relations that talk of a new Cold War has become commonplace. The more important question, however, is whether the two countries are heading for something much worse: a new hot war.[38] To some observers, US-China conflict has become a matter of when, not if, with sugges-tions that it may happen imminently.[39] If this transpires, then all bets about the future of global governance would be off. For although the United States and China lack the capacity to establish a new bipolar world order, they are certainly capable of wrecking the international system.

The problems of US-China interaction are essentially threefold. In the first place, the mutual animus is intense. Notwithstanding a slight softening of rheto-ric during the last two years of the Biden administration, this is an unequivocally adversarial relationship. The issue goes beyond substantive policy differences to a fundamental divergence over character and status. In Washington, there is a bipartisan consensus that China is a "malign actor", whose unchecked ambition poses an existential threat to US primacy and global order. Chinese attitudes towards the United States are no less hostile. America is the enemy that seeks to sabotage its growth, prosperity and stability by all available means – stra-tegic containment, punitive tariffs, denial of technology, disinformation and subversion.[40]

Second, US-China confrontation is taking place on multiple fronts. Washington's lengthy charge-sheet against Beijing includes the PLA's dangerous actions against Taiwan and in the South China Sea; its active support for Putin's war in Ukraine; Chinese involvement in the importation of fentanyl into the United States; Beijing's cyber operations against US and Western targets[41]; its unfair trade practices; theft of technology; persecution of the Uighurs (described as "genocide"); lack of transparency over the origins of Covid-19; and secretiveness over the expansion of its strategic nuclear arsenal and development of hypersonic missiles.

For their part, the Chinese have condemned Washington's support for Taipei, US Freedom of Navigation Operations (FONOPs) and missile defence plans, and the American alliance system with particular reference to the Quad and AUKUS. Beijing has accused the United States of provoking Putin's invasion of Ukraine and "giving the green light" to the slaughter of Palestinian civilians in Gaza.[42] It bitterly resents the pressure that Washington is exerting on allies to follow its lead on Taiwan, economic decoupling, and restricting Chinese access to Western technology. And, lately, it has condemned the imposition of tariffs against Chinese goods either coming directly to the United States or through third countries.

Third, potential flash-points for a US-China conflict have grown in number and volatility. Taiwan is the most immediate concern, but there is plenty of scope for trouble elsewhere – over FONOPs, in the South China Sea, on the Korean peninsula, in the Arctic, and collateral damage from territorial disputes between China and various US allies and partners.

Re-establishing some kind of normality in the US-China relationship will be immensely challenging, since the strategic goals of the two sides appear irreconcilable. To get a sense of how difficult the task will be, one needs only to recall the circumstances of the original normalization under Nixon and Mao over half a century ago. Although the two countries were poles apart politically and ideologically, there was at least a shared conviction that a better relationship was both necessary and possible. Today, by contrast, the almost unanimous expectation in Washington and Beijing is that their rivalry will intensify. More worryingly still, some welcome the prospect.[43]

Any attempt to stabilize the relationship must proceed from the recognition that the United States and China will be strategic rivals for many decades yet. If some kind of "normality" is to be reached, it will look nothing like that of the 1990s and 2000s. The circumstances of the relationship have changed drastically. Under virtually any president, US policy towards China will be fiercely competitive and sometimes confrontational. Much the same is true of attitudes in Beijing. Even in the improbable scenario of political liberalization, China will continue to assert itself on the global stage, strive to be the leading power in the Indo-Pacific, and remain committed to reunifying Taiwan with the mainland.

Given this unpromising context, what can be done to avoid worst-case outcomes? As it happens, there is a pathway to a modus vivendi. The key elements of this include improved channels of communication, acceptance of minimum "rules of the road", and selective cooperation.

*Channels of communication*

The most pressing priority is to improve deconfliction channels and procedures. Following the Biden-Xi bilateral at the San Francisco APEC summit in
November 2023, military-to-military dialogue has resumed. This modest step
was essential to minimize the likelihood of an accidental clash and consequent
military escalation. It serves the interests of both sides to have a system of safeguards – or "guardrails" – similar to that which kept the original Cold War from
becoming hot.

But crisis prevention and management are not enough. It is important to
develop a more comprehensive dialogue, lacking since Trump suspended the
Strategic and Economic Dialogue back in 2017. Although some in Washington
would regard such a move as a free concession to Beijing, communication should
never be confused with approbation or endorsement; its primary purposes are
to convey and receive messages, and to clarify intentions. Given the differences
and tensions between the United States and China, they cannot afford *not* to
talk to each other.

One way of finessing the optics would be to keep dialogue mechanisms relatively loose and informal, at least to begin with. This would enable both sides to
develop a degree of understanding on a range of critical issues, from deconfliction to technology. In the spirit of pragmatism, Beijing should also desist from
the unhelpful practice of suspending official contacts to signal its displeasure at
American actions – as occurred with climate and military talks following the
visit to Taiwan by House Speaker Nancy Pelosi in August 2022. Such gestures
are not merely futile, they serve to harden American attitudes towards China.

Whatever mechanisms are used, clear messaging is key, especially when
it comes to the potential use or threat of force.[44] Although the United States
has maintained a policy of "strategic ambiguity" over the defence of Taiwan,
that approach looks problematic following the Russian invasion of Ukraine.
Ambiguity is supposed to have a deterrent effect by keeping Beijing guessing
about America's response. But the danger is that it may suggest confusion or a
lack of resolve. Given Trump's remarks that the United States might not defend
the island in the event of an invasion from the mainland,[45] there is ample potential for a misunderstanding, with disastrous consequences. If Washington is
serious about protecting Taiwan, it needs to leave Beijing in no doubt that it
would intervene militarily in the event of an assault on the island. Equally, if it is
no longer committed to Taiwan's defence, it should say so. Strategic ambiguity
can be maintained as a formal public position, but it must be underpinned by
strategic clarity about US intentions, communicated through backchannels.[46]
Anything else is an accident waiting to happen.

## Minimum "rules of the road"

A sober US-China relationship is contingent on underplaying ideological and political differences. These are so stark that they hardly need restating. They are also unbridgeable for the foreseeable future. Washington and Beijing need to find ways of managing their many policy disagreements, free from extraneous considerations.

Like international rules, the notion of "rules of the road" is malleable, and there are a lot of grey areas. It seems simple enough to say that the United States and China should refrain from provocative actions, but how does one judge what is provocative? Just in the context of the South China Sea, Washington regards the escalation of PLA activity as reckless, while Beijing holds similarly jaundiced views about FONOPs and visits to Taiwan by senior US law-makers.

That said, there are certain rules or principles that both sides could usefully follow. The most important is to refrain from the direct use of force, not only against each other, but in the Indo-Pacific generally. This restraint would be complemented by deconfliction and confidence-building measures, such as prior notice of significant military movements, exercises and weapons tests.

At the political level, Washington would adhere to the "One China" policy, while Beijing would undertake, privately, not to attack or blockade Taiwan. China would exercise greater discretion in its foreign intelligence and influence activities in the West, while the United States would refrain from loose talk about strategic and technological containment. Ideally, both governments would focus on policy substance, pick their quarrels, and moderate the urge to score debating points.

All this is easier said than done, which raises the question of what to do when red lines or "rules of the road" are broken. In recent years, the default response has been to indulge in loud recriminations, which have only aggravated matters. While some of this may be unavoidable, particularly in response to a clash at sea, there is much that can be done through backchannels. The model here would be the resolution of the 2001 EP-3 plane incident near Hainan island, in which public grandstanding was counterbalanced by quiet diplomacy, thereby limiting damage to the wider relationship.[47] Today's international environment is much less forgiving than it was then, but the precedent remains useful nonetheless. This brings us back to the importance of regular and multifaceted communication. The more Washington and Beijing talk, the better the chances are of successful crisis management and a more stable relationship.

*Selective cooperation*

The United States and China are at loggerheads on so many levels – security, political, economic, technological and normative – that it is hard to see how the situation can improve. I have suggested that better communication and some sort of agreement on rules of the road could help stabilize the relationship. But this is pretty meagre fare. It might put the brakes on a further deterioration, but it is unlikely to be enough to reverse it.

There is one area, however, that could be a game-changer, and that is enhanced cooperation in problem solving. For all their differences, the United States and China do share an interest in a generally peaceful world – something that sets them apart from openly disruptive actors such as Russia, Iran and North Korea. To achieve that they have to work together, much as they might dislike doing so.

The modest cooperation of the late Biden era offers a clue as to how things could unfold. Before its suspension following the Pelosi visit, the climate dialogue had been cordial and relatively productive, boosted by the personal rapport between the respective climate envoys, John Kerry and Xie Zhenhua. When it was eventually resumed, the two sides agreed specific commitments to reduce methane emissions and accelerate the development of renewable energy.[48] This limited cooperation has since been scuppered by a Republican administration that is openly denialist about climate change. Nevertheless, while the focus of US-China bilateral cooperation may change, depending on who sits in the White House, the principle of active engagement need not. For example, instead of climate cooperation the emphasis could shift to managing the threat of narcotics trafficking and other forms of transnational crime. Or the two sides might develop a dedicated technological forum that would engage on AI and cyber governance. This could contribute to confidence-building in what will be one of the most testing areas of the relationship going forward.

Inevitably, too, Washington and Beijing will have to find a way of working together on economic issues. Despite the US emphasis on decoupling and a drop-off in bilateral trade since 2022,[49] the two economies – by far the largest in the world – remain closely tied.[50] Trump's infatuation with tariffs threatens this relationship, but it is uncertain how far, and for how long, he will be prepared to risk major ructions in the global economy and recession at home as the price for damaging Chinese interests. Among other things, the functioning of major US industries, including defence, depends heavily on the importation of Chinese rare earth elements.[51] Although Beijing has reacted angrily to US (and European) tariffs, its actions have been relatively restrained to date.[52] In time, the Chinese leadership could become more responsive to US concerns over the balance of trade. There may be scope for some sort of accommodation, one sufficiently attractive to a US president who fancies himself as a deal-maker.[53]

The United States and China may also look to establish a broader arrangement on security. In addition to instituting deconfliction procedures, they will have to address the issue of nuclear arms control at some stage. Until recently, the Chinese government had rebuffed American efforts to get it to engage in the process,[54] and it remains strongly averse to suggestions that it should curb the expansion of its nuclear arsenal. But this position will become harder to sustain. Pressure will come not just from Washington, but also from Moscow and even the Global South, irritated by the nuclear powers' disregard of Article VI of the Non-Proliferation Treaty (NPT).[55]

## Towards a better future: the US-China relationship and global order

Even in a flatter world where power is more diffuse than ever, the United States and China will continue to exert a primary influence on global affairs. They can make the difference in salvaging some sort of international order or, alternatively, ensure that the current world disorder degenerates into major power conflict. More than that, the United States and China, in often very different ways, will be crucial to our collective capacity to address global challenges from climate change to technological transformation.

The greatest gift Washington and Beijing can give the world is to restore some measure of predictability and stability to their relationship. That means abandoning unrealistic hopes of "victory", moderating expectations of each other, and making their interaction as businesslike as possible. If this were to happen, US-China political and security interaction might come to resemble that of the United States and the Soviet Union after the Cuban Missile Crisis. There would be no illusions that they were anything other than strategic foes, but their rivalry would be contained within reasonable bounds. It would amount to what former Australian Prime Minister (and Sinologist) Kevin Rudd has termed "managed strategic competition".[56]

In this scenario, Washington would recognize that the key to US global primacy is not through *mano a mano* confrontation with its closest rival, but by consistently outperforming it at home and internationally. Beijing would remain committed to reunification of Taiwan with the mainland and to projecting Chinese power in the Indo-Pacific and beyond, but would appreciate that the best way to achieve its ends is through persuasion, co-option and strategic patience. And the United States and China would move on from a reductive reasoning that views global order principally through the prism of their rivalry, and instead act as engines of constructive change and effective problem solving.

## 5

# POWERS IN FLUX: ADAPTING TO CHANGE

It is fashionable to view international politics in binary terms: the United States versus China; the rules-based order against "might is right"; the democracy/autocracy divide; a declining West and rising East; and even good versus evil. Much of this reflects our yearning for clarity amidst so much chaos and uncertainty.

However, real life defies such simplicities. The world is not binary, let alone bipolar. The United States and China, notwithstanding their central importance, are not hegemons bestriding the earth. The rules-based order is only rules-based in Western eyes, while a new authoritarian order remains a mirage. Countries do not divide neatly between democracies and autocracies. And a collective "West" is not about to be displaced by a collective "East".

The complexity of the contemporary world is nowhere more evident than in the diffusion of power among multiple players. Lately, discussion has revolved around the rise of so-called middle powers, determined "to be at the table and not on the menu".[1] But the cast of actors extends well beyond this undoubtedly influential category. It also includes powers in decline, such as Russia, Britain and France; would-be global players like India; countries that have never been associated with the notion of power at all, as in much of the Global South; and non-state actors of various kinds.

This chapter is about "powers in flux" – significant state actors whose influence is either declining, rising or experiencing some form of transition. The members of this amorphous lot could hardly be more different in many respects. But they have three things in common.

The first is ambition. Powers in flux are intent on maximizing their influence and status within the international system. Traditional powers reject the narrative (and reality) of decline by reaffirming their "greatness" at every opportunity, while middle or emerging powers seek to convert regional weight into global heft.

The second common denominator of powers in flux is an abiding belief in their own "special-ness". This is reflected in strenuous efforts to preserve a distinct sovereign identity and to assert the principle – or myth – of an independent foreign policy.

The third characteristic shared by many countries is the most problematic: the gulf between a sense of entitlement and actual contributions to international problem solving. Powers in flux demand respect and sometimes deference, but remain reluctant to take on the burdens of global governance. Parochialism defines and constrains their approach to the world.

The combination of these elements – driving ambition, excessive self-regard, and serial underperformance – has proved antithetical to global order, especially against the backdrop of major power rivalry and weakening international norms and institutions. For all their potential, powers in flux have been an individual and collective disappointment, frequently aggravating rather than alleviating problems. This perhaps explains why ideas of great power accommodation have made something of a comeback. We place our hopes in the restoration of "pragmatism" and good sense in Washington, Beijing and other leading capitals.

But in reality the task of revitalizing international order cannot be left to a notional US-China accommodation or "Concert" of great powers. It requires the active participation of many nations. The challenge, of course, is to make this happen. For it is not enough that powers in flux should identify a stake in order-building or that their overall weight has grown, they have to step up and deliver. With influence comes responsibility. The future of global governance hinges on their capacity and will to translate individual aspirations into collective outcomes. Powers in flux can make a real difference, but only if they are able to break the cycle of over-entitlement and under-achievement.

### Adapting to decline

Adapting to decline is exceptionally difficult for any major power. Typically, adjustment occurs only when that power has no choice in the matter, following crushing and irreversible defeat, as with Germany and Japan after the Second World War. There is the occasional, partial exception to the rule, such as Britain's retreat in the face of its own imperial exhaustion and the global rise of America. But generally speaking, the natural response of major powers to decline is denial.

#### *Russia*

Post-Soviet Russia exemplifies this. First under Boris Yeltsin, and particularly during the long rule of Vladimir Putin, it has shown no readiness to adapt to decline or re-invent itself as a modern, post-imperial state. There are many reasons why, but the most important is that the ruling elite simply do not regard Russia as a declining power. They continue to believe in its great power destiny, all the more so when the US-led, post-Cold War international order has imploded.

Integral to this worldview is an abiding faith in the tenets of classical realism: the centrality of geopolitics and security; the superiority of hard power and especially military might; and the dominance of international politics by the great powers. Moreover, Putin and other policy-makers see no advantage in Russia trying to become a "modern" kind of power, but believe it should play to its traditional military and geopolitical strengths. For them, Russia's democratic era of the 1990s – a time of economic crisis and strategic retrenchment – proved that following Western rules is a sure path to weakness and irrelevance.

The Kremlin's denial of Russian decline is constantly buttressed by military action – in Georgia 2008, Crimea and the Donbass 2014–15, Syria post-2015, and the 2022 invasion of Ukraine. Putin is explicit in his ambition to recover Russia's "historic lands". He does not care that such neo-imperialism contravenes the core UN principle of respecting the territorial integrity of other nations. Given the neutral stance of much of the Global South, the support of China, and the flakiness of Trumpian America, he judges that any reputational damage to Russia is far less important than the ability to intimidate its enemies.

As long as this mindset prevails, Russia will constitute a serious obstacle to international order. For if Putin cannot have the order he desires – a great power-centred system in which Russia enjoys similar status to the United States and China – then his preference is for anarchy. Indeed, he revels in being an agent of chaos. This is both low-maintenance and highly effective in ensuring that Russia remains on everyone's radar. Moscow's disruptive influence extends from Latin America to the Sahel, from the Middle East to the Korean peninsula. It feeds off corruption, dysfunction and division; it is skilful in exploiting Western policy shortcomings; and it profits from a disorderly global context. The return of Donald Trump is a godsend in this respect. Moscow has scarcely been able to contain its joy at the turn of events – America's distancing from Ukraine, the upending of NATO, the ructions in transatlantic relations, and the unravelling of a unitary West.

The challenge for other nations is to manage, circumvent or minimize the impact of a rogue Russia. But this will not be easy. Some observers put their faith in Putin's mortality (age 73 in 2025) and hope that a successor will prove more amenable. But despite much speculation about his health, Putin has shown no sign of leaving. Besides, many in the Russian political establishment share his views about world order. Putin has been able to tap into deep wells of resentment, articulating a national-populist message that resonates strongly across the elite and society. A successor could turn out to be no less imperialist and even more aggressive. Another hope some cling to is that Russia's accumulated failings will become so critical as to force a rethink of its place and mission in the world. However, the Ukraine war has highlighted Russia's resilience as well as weaknesses, and reinforced Putin's conviction that he will prevail.

All this raises the question of how foreign, and especially Western, governments should engage with Moscow. They can start by recognizing the limits of their influence on Russian decision-making. From the outset of the post-Soviet period, efforts to advise, pressure or punish the Kremlin have been almost uniformly futile. If Russia is to adapt to the twenty-first-century world, it will have to find its own way. It will not follow a Western, or for that matter Chinese, template of "normality", but will act according to its own lights.

What Western governments can do, however, is to up their own game. Sustained, this could have the cumulative effect of persuading Moscow, over time, to rethink its ideas of self-interest. But the key lies in doing, not talking – with the West demonstrating by example that it has the more compelling arguments. This was the secret to its success during the Cold War, and it will be essential to interaction with Russia in the future.

Ukraine is a litmus test. If Western support for Kyiv collapses, it will not just be the Ukrainian people who lose out. The principle itself of an international order would be eviscerated as Putin's brand of great power revanchism is vindicated. He would have licence to keep behaving badly, threatening neighbours and destabilizing European security. Conversely, if Western governments provide Ukraine with proper security guarantees and integrate it within European structures (NATO and the EU), they may regain some of the credibility they have leaked in recent years. Developing a meaningful deterrent against future Russian aggression will be both expensive and risky. But the alternatives – appeasement, half-measures, the fond hope that the Kremlin will be content with its winnings so far – are more dangerous still.[2]

Paradoxically, Russia could end up as a major beneficiary from an equitable peace in Ukraine. This might facilitate a gradual transition from being a predominantly military power, fixated on its neighbourhood, into a more versatile and globally influential player. Eventually, Russia could emerge as a hybrid transcontinental power, retaining elements of its historical identity as an empire but complementing these with the agility of a middle power. Its foreign policy might then resemble India's "multi-aligned" approach (discussed below), in which it maintains advantageous but flexible relations with a diverse range of countries and international institutions. Such a course is counter-intuitive but would represent the surest route to the strategic independence the Kremlin has sought to regain ever since the fall of the USSR. Russia would neither be as reliant on the West as it was in the 1990s, nor on China as it is today.

This is a long-term vision, and the way ahead will be torrid. Russia, whether under Putin or a successor, will pose a major challenge to international order for years to come. In the short to medium term, the "new Cold War" feared by many may turn out to be the least bad outcome. For this would hold out hope of a relative stability and predictability, whereby Russia mostly operates within the international system rather than giving full rein to its destructive instincts. Such a Russia could still be a significant contributor to the global commons, notably in strategic and other forms of arms control.

## The United Kingdom, France and the European Union

Leading European powers such as the United Kingdom and France appear better than most to have weathered the transition from empires to modern nation-states. Yet they, too, have struggled to come to terms with their diminishing status and influence. Although they see themselves as global players, their impact on contemporary international politics and the world economy is secondary. Despite possessing nuclear weapons and being permanent members of the UN Security Council, they are not fully sovereign actors with independent foreign policies. And for much of the post-Cold War era their strategic footprint has been receding.

*British foreign policy* has long laboured under two major failings. The first, common among former global powers, is an enduring sense of superiority and entitlement. The second is a lack of appreciation of where the United Kingdom's true strengths lie. These failings have ensured that it has badly underperformed.

The problems go beyond individual policy misjudgements. The Brexit imbroglio was a massive distraction that marginalized the United Kingdom on many regional and global issues. It caused – and continues to inflict – serious damage to the British economy.[3] And it has reinforced a dismal image of a Little Britain consumed by narrow-mindedness. But Brexit was a manifestation of deeper flaws. It confirmed a consistent pattern of delusional thinking about the United Kingdom's importance in the world. In reality, it is a declining power, whose governance under Conservative Party rule (2010–24) plumbed new depths of incompetence and venality. Even the pride of British foreign policy – the so-called "special relationship" with America – is much more special to London than to Washington, for whom it is just one of many important relationships. The popular notion that the United Kingdom can be a bridge between America and Europe is a conceit, as is the strange hankering for the label of "superpower" (in connection with AI, defence, development, etc.).

Lack of self-awareness is compounded by an unreconstructed understanding of power and influence in the modern world. If Britain is to be a twenty-first-century force, it will not be by rigidly adhering to conventional metrics, such as military might and geopolitical projection. Britain's comparative advantages do not lie in hard power. Four SSBNs (nuclear ballistic missile submarines), a couple of aircraft carriers, a modest-sized army and a smattering of overseas bases do not a great power make. Sending an aircraft carrier through the South China Sea or ramping up defence spending will do nothing to alter this. Nor will hugging the United States ever tighter.

To exercise significant influence, the United Kingdom must recast itself as a different kind of power. Although it needs to bolster its defence capabilities, it should build on its comparative advantages in other areas. That means expanding its world-class scientific and technological research capabilities, including in AI; consolidating its position as a global provider of tertiary education; disseminating British culture through outlets such as the BBC; setting the pace in the transition from fossil fuels to renewable energy; and being generous with humanitarian assistance to developing countries.

London also needs to rethink its major relationships. The transatlantic alliance will remain important to British foreign and defence policy. However, it is imprudent to be over-reliant on the United States or NATO, especially given Trump's recasting of American foreign policy. Strategic flexibility is imperative in a world of unstable loyalties. That entails much closer ties with the European Union; strengthening relationships with leading European players, such as France and Germany; and committing seriously to engagement with Asia, especially with China, India and Japan. Strategic flexibility also involves expanding participation in various multilateral institutions, rather than simply doubling up on Western bodies like NATO and the G-7.

In several respects, *French foreign policy* is markedly different from Britain's. Paris has adopted a more independent stance vis-à-vis Washington and in its overall conduct of international relations. Nevertheless, in its quest to carve out a distinct role in the twenty-first-century global order, France faces similar challenges. The most demanding is to calibrate goals to capabilities. President Emmanuel Macron promotes France as a global player, but its real level is that of a regional-plus actor. It is the leading power in continental Europe, but its influence in Asia, the Middle East, and the Americas is peripheral. It maintains a substantial presence in Africa and Oceania, but even in those regions it is being displaced – as highlighted by the 2022 withdrawal of French forces from Mali, the growing Russian military presence across the Sahel, and China's expanding footprint in the Pacific.

Macron has sought to mitigate French decline by reinvigorating the narrative of strategic autonomy, distancing himself from Washington's hard line over China, and reasserting leadership over Europe. But these efforts have encountered significant obstacles. The war in Ukraine has highlighted the extent of Europe's dependence on the US security umbrella. Paris's relative dovishness towards Beijing has led to sharp tensions with Washington. And, following the 2024 French legislative elections, Macron's domestic position has been severely weakened, limiting what he can do in foreign policy.

Macron's mercurial approach to diplomacy is also an issue. His penchant for the dramatic – variously describing NATO as "brain-dead",[4] proposing peace negotiations with Putin in 2022, and unilaterally broaching the possible deployment of NATO ground troops in Ukraine (2024) – annoys and worries other European leaders. He is right to emphasize the importance of common European positions, notably on Ukraine. Yet his frequent failure to consult adequately provokes mistrust about Paris's motives.

A less showy, more guileful approach by Paris might massage some of these sensitivities, and improve the chances of pan-European cooperation on substantive priorities. In this connection, the sea-change in US foreign policy offers France real opportunities. Almost overnight, European strategic autonomy has been transformed from a contentious idea into an inescapable necessity. European nations now have no option but to become more independent of America. In this new environment, France is uniquely placed to reinvent itself as a twenty-first-century power – by strengthening European political unity and resilience; building up European defence capabilities supported by French (and British) nuclear weapons; holding the line against American tariffs and Chinese dumping; and leading the way in the development of renewable energy and on AI governance.

But Paris has to be careful. France has toiled for decades to reconcile its heritage as a great imperial power with a post-imperial emphasis on a broader European identity. With strategic autonomy back in vogue, there is an obvious danger of giving in to delusions of grandeur. The opportunities that have opened up as a result of Trump's actions could easily close again. France can be a leading player in an emerging international order, but only if it thinks and acts collectively. Its national self-interest is intimately bound to that of others, and to its capacity to translate individual ambition into wider positive-sum outcomes.

The *European Union* is the most successful example of multilateral cooperation in history, measured by impact, longevity, and the benefits to its member states. It has grown into the biggest trading bloc in the world, and forged a remarkable degree of political and moral consensus over an expanse of territory that was the scene of mass slaughter in two world wars. The close relationship between France and Germany, in conflict for much of the previous two centuries, is a singular feat.

But past achievements do not guarantee a healthy future. The EU is under mounting pressure, especially from within. It has been weakened by the departure of the United Kingdom, the consolidation of illiberal democracy in Hungary, and the rise of populist nationalism across the continent. During the Chancellorship of Angela Merkel's successor, Olaf Scholz (2021–25), the de facto Franco-German condominium at the heart of the European project frayed badly.[5]

The EU is struggling to develop a coherent vision of what and where it wants to be in the twenty-first-century world. The grand project of the 1992 Maastricht Treaty – "an ever closer union among the peoples of Europe", with a "common foreign and security policy"[6] – is dead in the water. Instead, there are multiple fissures: between individual member states and the European Commission, fiscal conservatives and liberals, Berlin and Paris, and between diehard Atlanticists and those who believe Europe must pursue greater strategic autonomy. Disagreements over policy towards China, Russia and Ukraine have become acrimonious. The liberal values that once defined "European-ness" are under attack from all sides.

European Commission President Ursula von der Leyen promotes the EU as a major player on the world stage. But although it remains a formidable economic actor, its international weight is shrinking. The war in Ukraine has highlighted Europe's vulnerabilities, and weakened its internal cohesion. Notwithstanding an impressive level of integration, the EU is not a unitary actor, but a collection of 27 sovereign states of widely varying capabilities and sometimes competing interests.

The EU's strengths lie in soft power, and it should aim to maximize these rather than pursue unrealistic geopolitical aims. Relatedly, it should beware the perils of overreach. The Maastricht vision of comprehensive European integration underestimated the yen for national sovereignty, and unwittingly weakened the European project. An analogous danger exists today. By attempting to be a geopolitical actor in its own right rather than a framework for member state action, the EU may end up diluting its core strengths without acquiring new ones.

Brussels can learn other useful lessons. One is the need for better messaging. The EU should promote its achievements as the world's largest contributor to international development assistance and climate finance. At the same time, it should lose the smugness that permeates many of its statements about democracy, the rule of law, and international order.[7] The EU also needs to deliver on its promises. The Global Gateway programme, which aims to mobilize €300 billion in investment over the period 2021–27, has been a disappointment. Far from rivalling China's BRI, it has led to criticism of "paternalistic" attitudes and excessive bureaucracy, and of being poorly targeted.[8]

Looking ahead, it will be vital for European nations to preserve autonomous decision-making. They cannot afford to allow themselves to be bullied by Washington over China, tariffs or digital policy, or by Beijing over trade dumping, cyber interference and Taiwan. Autonomy, however, necessitates a more collective mindset, not for the sake of abstractions like a "single Europe", but in pursuit of concrete shared interests. There is a natural inclination in some capitals, notably London, to place their hopes in individual preferential treatment from Washington. But this is misguided, inviting outsiders to exploit European division and shortsightedness. Attempting to appease Trump, in particular, is a form of Stockholm syndrome that has only encouraged the White House to ride roughshod over European interests, as exemplified by the deeply flawed US-EU trade deal of July 2025.[9]

Despite evident limitations, the United Kingdom, France, the EU and, perhaps now Germany (under new Chancellor Friedrich Merz) can be important contributors to global governance. But only if they play to their strengths, and pursue a more flexible and diversified approach to the world. The pull of the United States remains powerful, and European leaders will continue to be drawn towards Washington. However, they cannot allow sentimentality and tradition to cloud their judgement of where their true national and continental interests lie – whether on Ukraine and European security, climate policy, technology regulation, or countering disinformation. Europeans should recognize that the old dependencies are no longer practicable, and question lazy assumptions about shared transatlantic values and interests.[10] A failure to adjust to new realities is to accept not just a diminished role in the world, but also a loss of sovereignty on the European continent itself. In that event, Europe would once again become a major source of international disorder, less a model than an anti-model of rules-based behaviour.

## Managing rise

History is replete with examples of great powers suffering post-imperial trauma and struggling to adjust to decline. Rising powers, on the other hand, appear to have everything going for them: a feeling of empowerment, confidence, momentum. From their perspective, what's not to like?

As it happens, quite a lot. The rise of new powers (or return of the old) almost invariably encounters stiff resistance. The ongoing American backlash against China is a vivid but by no means unique example. In the 1970s and 1980s, the United States reacted viscerally to Japan's emergence as an economic powerhouse. Such rivalry often transcends ideology. Although China under Xi Jinping is an authoritarian state, Japan half a century ago was a democracy whose political and economic development had been shaped by Washington.

Another problem rising powers face is that of expectations. Again, China stands out. As its economy grew in the 1990s and 2000s, so did American demands that it contribute more to the international order. Deputy Secretary of State Robert Zoellick famously called on China to become a "responsible stakeholder". Crucially, Zoellick envisaged that it "would work with us to sustain the international system that has enabled its success".[11] In other words, China would not be an independent stakeholder so much as America's loyal lieutenant in upholding the global economy. It soon became evident that Beijing's understanding of the terms of its engagement with the international system diverged sharply from Washington's.

### *The opportunities and pitfalls of success: the case of India*

India's situation exemplifies these tensions. In important respects, its fortunes appear ascendant. In June 2024, Prime Minister Narendra Modi was re-elected to his third term in office. The Indian economy is one of the fastest growing in the world (6–7 per cent annually). The population is young, dynamic and outward-looking. New Delhi's foreign policy of "multi-alignment" has proved generally successful.[12] India is a favoured partner of several Western governments, yet has retained its identity as an independent centre of power. It has substantially increased its influence within the Global South, maintained close ties with Russia, and improved relations with China. Its multilateral profile is higher than it has ever been. It is prominent in the G-20 and the BRICS, and is a candidate for permanent membership of the UN Security Council.

India is clearly a rising power, with the potential to become a multi-dimensional global power. Yet it is a long way from achieving this goal. Indeed, there are signs that Indian policy-makers, flushed with success, have overestimated its chances and underestimated the challenges ahead. Several obstacles could slow or derail India's ascent.

The most fundamental issue is domestic instability. Although Modi's Bharatiya Janata Party (BJP) won the most seats in the 2024 Indian parliamentary election, it did not gain the absolute majority that most pundits forecast. The election results underlined the huge divisions in Indian society – between the majority Hindu population and the estimated 200 million Muslims (around 15 per cent of the total population); between rich and poor; between the cities and countryside; and between north and south.[13] Modi's attempts to clamp down on the opposition, the independent media, and state rights have exacerbated economic and social tensions as well as political and ethnic fault-lines.[14]

The second major challenge India faces is a difficult regional environment. Fulfilling its global aspirations is complicated by geopolitical rivalry and territorial disputes with China, a decades-long confrontation with Pakistan, and the resistance of assorted neighbours to Indian dominance.[15]

Third, India possesses nothing like the financial resources of China. Its GDP is five times smaller; its population is already larger; and its territory is a third the size of China's. There is nothing inevitable about India's transition into a developed economy by the middle of the century.[16] This matters for its foreign policy because the effectiveness of New Delhi's outreach to the Global South will hang on whether it can deliver tangible benefits to developing countries. Thus far, its loans and investments in Africa and Asia are a fraction of Beijing's; an Indian BRI appears an unlikely prospect.

Fourth, there is a gulf between India's global ambition and its ability and willingness to contribute to international problem solving. It has offered little on conflict mediation in relation to Ukraine and Gaza. It is a sometimes obstructive presence in the WTO, where it has stalled negotiations on agriculture.[17] On climate policy, India is more part of the problem than the solution. It is already the world's third largest carbon emitter, it continues to invest heavily in coal production,[18] and its net-zero timeline is a long way off (2070). The suggestion that India, as a developing country, should be allowed greater leeway when it comes to emissions will become harder to square with its rising international profile and the destruction wrought by climate change in many Global South countries.

Finally, despite its past success, New Delhi's multi-alignment policy may be tough to sustain. As India grows into a global role, will it remain an independent centre of power, or align itself with America to "sustain the international system" (as per Zoellick's vision with China)? Washington has long cultivated India as a strategic counterweight to China. But Modi has been wary of being too closely associated with America and the West, since this is hardly compatible with his aspirations to lead the Global South and pursue an autonomous foreign policy.[19] While previous US presidents tolerated the ambiguity of New Delhi's "multi-aligned" stance, under Trump it has come to be regarded as disloyal. The result is the worst crisis of US-India relations in a generation.[20]

India's rise, then, will not be easy, and may turn out to be less impressive than many anticipate. The historian Ramachandra Guha believes that India is "likely to remain what it is today: a middling power with a vibrant entrepreneurial culture and mostly fair elections alongside malfunctioning public institutions and persisting cleavages of religion, gender, caste, and region".[21] To some extent, the outcome is out of its hands. There is only so much that India can do to defuse security and geopolitical tensions in a volatile neighbourhood. Even in a best-case scenario it will take decades to catch up economically to China, let alone the United States. And it will inevitably be affected by the vagaries of US foreign policy.[22]

Nevertheless, there are steps India can take to improve its chances of shaping the international order. Mainly, it is a case of avoiding some of the errors, misjudgements and vices of other leading powers – American exceptionalism, Chinese triumphalism, Europe's misplaced sense of superiority. Rather than obsessing about status,[23] India should concentrate on building up its capabilities. China's contrasting experiences under Deng Xiaoping and Xi Jinping are instructive in this regard. During the Deng era, China consistently played down its strengths, and was able to grow rapidly with the help of the United States and the Western-led global economy. Under Xi, however, Beijing's assertive and sometimes confrontational approach has aggravated the backlash against China.

If India is to be a new type of power, as many hope, it needs to tailor its approach accordingly. Demanding permanent membership of the UN Security Council as a right, loudly asserting leadership of the Global South, promoting itself as a Hindu "civilization-state"[24] – all point to an old-fashioned culture of entitlement and messianism. Instead, the emphasis should be on what India can bring to global governance and the global commons, not on what the world allegedly owes India.

Most of all, India needs to look to itself. One of the themes of this book is that domestic weaknesses have foreign policy implications. America's stature in the world has been critically undermined by misgovernment and corruption at home. Modi may feel that he can act with impunity, secure in the belief that foreign governments will support him no matter what. But experience has demonstrated that New Delhi can ill afford such hubris. Repression at home and arrogance abroad encourage political resistance, inhibit economic growth, and provoke international blowback.[25]

### The era of middle powers?

The concept of middle powers elicits more questions than answers. According to the World Economic Forum (WEF), middle powers sit below great powers (which are described misleadingly as "countries that exert economic, political and military dominance over the world"), but are nevertheless "states with extensive diplomatic, economic, multilateral, and sometimes military, clout". The WEF acknowledges, however, that the term is "imprecise and contested" and that the influence of middle powers is hard to measure.[26]

Part of the problem is that middle powers differ substantially in terms of influence, outlook and priorities, with some definitions encompassing countries as disparate as India and Norway.[27] We sometimes think of middle powers as regional or continental leaders, like Nigeria or Indonesia. But several of them, including Brazil, Saudi Arabia and Türkiye, aspire also to exert global influence.[28]

Some middle powers act fairly independently, while others, such as Australia and Canada, have been among America's closest allies.

That said, we should not get too hung up on definitional questions. What matters is whether this diverse group of state actors can, individually and collectively, help address the crisis of international order. The answer is a qualified "yes". But much is contingent on the specific circumstances and issues at hand. Even then, the influence of middle powers will be partial and conditional. It will require them to think beyond their immediate self-interest. They will have to work with major powers, with each other, and through multilateral institutions. And they will need to accept burdensome obligations as the price of enhanced status and influence.

Three issue-areas offer particular opportunities for middle powers to play a significant role in global governance: conflict resolution and management; strategic balancing; and climate policy.

## Conflict resolution and management

The decades since the end of the Second World War are commonly described as the Long Peace. In fact, this expression is deceptive. Since 1945, there have been literally hundreds of armed conflicts around the world, many of them extremely bloody, resulting in the killing of millions of soldiers and civilians, and inflicting enormous physical destruction and economic damage. "Long Peace" is therefore a relative term, reflecting the absence of *global* conflict. (The Korean War, which saw direct intervention by UN forces as well as by the United States, the Soviet Union and the People's Republic of China, was nevertheless a limited war fought over a small amount of territory.)

Given the regional nature of modern wars, it is logical that middle powers should play active roles in defusing and, ideally, resolving them. The need for them to do so is all the more compelling given the evident shortcomings of the major powers. The United States, despite its unrivalled strength, has struggled to manage conflict in the Middle East. Indeed, it has often instigated or escalated it, notably in Iraq and Afghanistan. The war in Gaza exposed the Biden administration's inability to act as an honest broker or moderate the actions of Israel. This ineffectualness has since carried over into active collusion between Trump and Netanyahu, especially evident in the June 2025 attacks on Iran's nuclear facilities.[29] Similarly, China promotes itself as a disinterested mediator in the conflict in Ukraine,[30] but its support of the Russian war effort and the closeness of Sino-Russian ties preclude it from being able to fulfil this role. Its aggressive pursuit of territorial and maritime claims further undermines its credibility as a would-be peacemaker.

By contrast, the credentials of middle powers are boosted by the occasional success. In the first three years of the war in Ukraine, the one negotiated outcome was the June 2022 agreement secured by Turkish President Recep Erdoğan, ensuring the safe passage of Ukrainian (and Russian) grain exports through the Black Sea. Although this arrangement broke down after a year, it was vital both in providing Ukraine with an economic lifeline and in stabilizing global grain prices, crucial to the food security of many developing countries. Another, less publicized example of effective regional diplomacy was the African Union's (AU) intervention in the Ethiopian civil war, a conflict almost as destructive as the war in Ukraine. The participation of middle powers such as South Africa, Nigeria and Kenya was instrumental in halting the bloodshed, at least for the time being.[31]

Looking ahead, the prospects for peace in Ukraine hinge on whether Putin is prepared to settle for the gains Russia has made since the start of the invasion in February 2022, or whether he will try for more: emasculation of Ukraine as a sovereign state, degradation of the NATO alliance, and overthrowing the post-Cold War order in Europe. To date, all the indications are that he will pursue the second course of action, in which case the war is likely to grind on for some time.

But if there is to be a negotiated solution, it will certainly require the involvement of other parties. Although the common assumption is that European powers, such as Britain and France, will play leading roles, the pivotal player could be Türkiye. Although a member of NATO, it is in most respects a non-aligned power, maintaining close political and economic ties with Russia and adopting a neutral position on the war. Its security influence is significant and growing. And it has form in brokering and implementing agreements.

Regional powers will be similarly critical to managing conflicts in the Middle East. Egypt and Qatar have played a prominent role in US-led efforts to achieve a ceasefire agreement in Gaza, but in the longer run the key peacemaker may turn out to be Saudi Arabia. Although a US ally, Riyadh has been pursuing an increasingly independent foreign policy. It maintains functional ties with Jerusalem, while Saudi-Iranian relations have also thawed somewhat. It helps, too, that Crown Prince Mohammed bin Salman (MBS) is keen to make his mark as a peacemaker, seeing it as a way of promoting Saudi Arabia as a major power in its own right.

## Strategic balancing

When CIA Director William Burns referred to the "hedging middle" in his 2023 Ditchley lecture (see Introduction), he was describing the propensity of middle powers to balance between great powers "in order to expand their strategic autonomy and maximize their options". Burns viewed this in a negative light, observing that rivalries between middle powers "have often been the match that ignited collisions between major powers".[32]

There is another way to view middle-power hedging, however, and that is as a corrective to the excessive emphasis on geopolitical balancing and ideological schisms in international politics. For that to happen, middle powers need to think beyond "playing" the major powers to extract short-term gains (such as advantageous commercial and security deals), and instead conceive of self-interest in larger, more constructive terms.

Middle powers can maximize their international weight in various ways. India and Türkiye promote themselves as independent powers, explicitly rejecting the binarism of great power geopolitics – New Delhi through its multi-aligned policy, and Ankara by combining NATO membership with close cooperation with Russia. Another, relatively friction-free approach is to participate actively in intra-regional organizations where shared economic interests outweigh geopolitical considerations. The best example of this is the Comprehensive and Progressive Agreement on Trans-Pacific Partnership (CPTPP), which has thrived in the absence of the world's two leading economies.

Far from igniting collisions between the major powers, as Burns warned, the hedging middle may help to forestall confrontation. Several ASEAN member states are in dispute with Beijing over South China Sea territoriality. Yet if anything this has increased their desire for cooperative ties with China, and given them a real stake in efforts to contain US-China rivalry. With their asymmetrical hedging – leaning to Washington for security and to Beijing for trade – middle powers like Indonesia, Malaysia, Vietnam and Singapore constitute a de facto "peace lobby" in the region. While they have little direct input into American and Chinese decision-making, the very presence of this sizeable "hedging middle", with its reluctance to commit to one side over the other, constitutes an important brake on potential conflict.

## Climate policy

Arguably the issue where middle powers possess the greatest leverage is climate change. Their capacity to make a difference is at once considerable, multifaceted and under-utilized. The universality of the threat of climate change, and the fact that it will be with us for many decades yet, practically ensure a key role for middle powers. This is even before factoring in a Trump administration whose denialism means that it has no interest in addressing the threat.

It is unclear, though, whether the influence of middle powers will be predominantly positive – facilitating climate mitigation – or negative, obstructing the transition to a post-carbon future. The signals are mixed. Saudi Arabia has led efforts by oil and gas exporting nations to oppose the phase-out of fossil fuels, disrupting successive COP summits in the process.[33] Yet it is also planning a major expansion of solar and nuclear energy capacity, and is investing in renewable energy projects overseas.[34] Oil and gas underpin Saudi Arabia's prosperity and its ability to project power. But Riyadh is conscious that in a post-industrial and post-carbon world, fossil fuels could become a wasting strategic asset. MBS's Vision 2030 is predicated on transitioning to a less carbon-dependent future. And if Saudi Arabia is to become a leader of the Global South, it will need to be more responsive to developing country concerns over climate change.

Brazil faces similar conundrums in juggling comparative economic advantages, strategic ambition, and reputational considerations. The country is the world's largest exporter of beef, an industry that is a prime source of methane emissions (whose warming power is 80 times that of carbon dioxide). For decades, but especially under former President Jair Bolsonaro (2019–22), Brazil presided over the mass deforestation of the Amazon basin, one of the world's largest carbon sinks. Much of this was done in order to expand the production of soya beans, of which Brazil is the world's largest exporter.

Since President Lula da Silva's return to office in January 2023, the rate of deforestation has slowed. Nevertheless, this continues to be a huge problem; an estimated one million trees are cut down or burned every day in the Amazon basin.[35] The Lula administration is expanding agricultural exports to meet rising external demand, principally from China, and the Brazilian economy is more carbon- and methane-intensive than ever, fuelled (literally) by the discovery of significant new oil reserves. Lula portrays himself as the champion of international efforts to tackle climate change,[36] but his practical commitment to this goal is equivocal.[37]

The cases of Saudi Arabia and Brazil illustrate what might be called a middle-power trap. MBS and Lula envision their countries as more than regional powers; their horizons are global. Yet their foreign policies are conditioned and constrained by parochial views of the national interest.

Thus, Riyadh has allowed itself to become a scapegoat for the world's failure to slow global warming, when a little more flexibility over language at COP summits could have positioned it as a mediator of compromise solutions. Its rigid approach reflects an insecurity common among middle powers: the fear they may be railroaded into unwanted courses of action unless they show "toughness" at every juncture. Paradoxically, it is exactly this type of reflexive response that limits their options, damages their reputations, and stymies their global aspirations.

Lula promotes Brazil as a leader of the Global South, an image he hopes to burnish by hosting the COP30 summit in Belem in November 2025.[38] But such recognition must be earned by adopting more forward-looking policies. Brazil can stick to its current high-emission economic model, in which case it is just another country following its own path. Or it can set a template for responsible – and advantageous – middle-power behaviour. What it can't do is have it both ways: pursue a self-centred approach to global agenda issues like climate change *and* gain support for its claims to Global South leadership.

## Going back to first principles

One of the most significant consequences of the diffusion of power over the past two decades has been the growing number of influential actors. As Fareed Zakaria pointed out back in 2009, this process is less a matter of American decline than of the "rise of the rest".[39] Since then, the trend has only accelerated. Democracy may be retreating in many countries, but international order – or rather disorder – has become more "democratic". Unfortunately, the diffusion of power has not resulted in better governance.

It is tempting to explain away such disruption as part of the natural transition from one order to the next, the implication being that normal service – an order of some kind – will eventually be restored. However, such determinism (and complacency) is unwarranted. There is nothing to suggest that powers in flux, and middle powers in particular, will become less important over time. On the contrary, today's disorder could become more anarchic. It makes sense, therefore, to harness the ambition of these disparate actors to the benefit of international order while this is still possible.

The three core principles of a new internationalism set out in Chapter 3 – a reconceptualized self-interest; greater representativeness and inclusiveness; and flexibility – apply to all types of actors. But they are especially pertinent to middle powers. The first priority is to persuade this group to take a broader view of self-interest. Most middle powers are unaccustomed to wielding significant influence in international affairs, and so lack the maturity to think beyond narrow, short-term goals. Getting them to see the bigger picture, and to use their power for the greater good as well as their own immediate agendas, is critical but undeniably difficult.

What could make a difference, however, is applying the second principle of the new internationalism: integrating middle powers more effectively in multilateral decision-making. Empowering them in international institutions would give them a greater sense of ownership and responsibility. Ideally, such integration would involve reforming existing global organizations, such as the UN Security

Council, the IMF, and the World Bank, in order to make them more representative. But given the impediments to reform (see next chapter), regional bodies and frameworks (the AU, the CPTPP) and Global South groups (such as the G-77 in climate policy) may be more promising vehicles of middle-power influence.

Nothing comes for free. Whatever the format, middle powers will need to subordinate or manage their own rivalries, work more closely together, and concentrate on maximizing their collective clout. They must seize the moment. With the breakdown of international rules, major power relations in limbo if not crisis, an obsessively self-absorbed American president, and acute divisions between North and South, middle powers will rarely have a better opportunity to make their mark, to be initiators of change and leaders in problem solving.

That brings us to the third principle of internationalism, namely flexibility. Without this, states are more likely to be agents of disorder rather than order, obstructing solutions and escalating conflicts. Flexibility, by definition, is a loose and imprecise notion. In the context of middle-power influence, however, it is principally about compartmentalization – delinking action on selected issues from larger concerns about the behaviour of states. Saudi Arabia's military intervention in Yemen led to one of the worst humanitarian disasters of recent times. But its cooperation is essential to conflict management elsewhere in the Middle East, especially Israel/Palestine and now Iran, as well as in areas such as climate action. Much as we might deplore some of Riyadh's actions, it is vital to focus on where it can make a positive difference. Generally speaking, we need to take cooperation whenever and from whomever it is forthcoming. Which is why it is necessary to maintain regular communication with even the worst of regimes, for example Putin's Russia.

Some middle powers will continue to behave selfishly and even destructively. But others may take longer views and recognize that their interests are best served by a functioning international society that they have a major role in shaping. After all, it is not as if the alternative – a spiralling global disorder – offers them any better prospects. There are plenty of obstacles on the road ahead, and no guarantees. But if the commitment of middle powers to effective governance should begin to match the level of their ambition, they could end up being among the biggest winners in an emergent international order.

# 6

# FLEXIBLE MULTILATERALISM

One of the most visible manifestations of the current world disorder is the worsening crisis of multilateralism. At a time when humanity faces exceptional challenges, international institutions have never been more necessary. Yet as they have proliferated, many have become unfit for purpose, and confidence in multilateralism has sunk to historic lows.

In part, this reflects the distemper of our age, marked by intensifying strategic rivalries, sharp ideological differences, and deep pessimism about the future. But there are other, more basic problems as well. Multilateral institutions have become notorious not just for their inefficiency but also their inequity, something that is becoming harder to tolerate with the diffusion of international power. The five permanent members (P-5) of the UN Security Council have not changed since 1945. The voting shares of rising powers such as China and India in the IMF and World Bank remain disproportionately small, while those of developing nations are derisory. Then there is the matter of countries skewing multilateral agencies to favour their individual agendas – as China has done with the UN Human Rights Council over the plight of the Uighurs, and with the World Health Organization (WHO) over the origins of the Covid-19 pandemic.

We are trapped in a vicious cycle. As governments lose faith in established global institutions, they become more inclined to go their own way or pursue alternative arrangements involving an exclusive circle of allies and close partners. The ideal of an overarching, inclusive international community is giving way to tribalism and fragmentation. From being synonymous with international cooperation (however flawed), multilateralism is, more than ever, a mechanism for power projection and an arena for competing world-views.

The practical consequences of multilateralism's struggles have been acute. During the Covid-19 pandemic, the undermining of the WHO by the United States and China weakened the international response to the spread of the virus and contributed to the extraordinary death toll. The dysfunctionality of the Conference of the Parties (COP) process is a significant constraint in addressing the threat of climate change. And gridlock within the UN Security Council has crippled its capacity to manage, much less prevent, conflicts around the world.

It is evident that any functioning international order needs effective multilateral institutions. The difficulty is getting there. It is not simply a matter of reforming the governance of existing organizations or setting up new structures. The biggest challenge is to persuade state and non-state actors to buy into an innately imperfect approach to problem solving. For there is no getting away from the fact that multilateral outcomes are often unsatisfactory, the product of grubby compromises, in which selfish national interests outweigh the greater good.

The question, then, is not whether we can "fix" multilateralism, but whether we can improve on what we have. In this chapter, I argue this is not only achievable, but essential. The key lies in flexibility – recognizing the virtues of choice and making use of the full range of multilateral instruments from the global to the minilateral. For what ultimately matters is the act of cooperation rather than the precise form it takes. Legitimacy and credibility come from performance.

### Reform: constraints and possibilities

More than any single institution, the United Nations has become identified with the shortcomings of multilateralism. However, many of the criticisms levelled against it are unjustified. For one thing, the United Nations is not monolithic; it comprises several bodies (including the Security Council and the General Assembly), many specialized agencies, and sundry committees. Some of these have performed poorly, but others have made critical contributions to human welfare and development. Our attention is inevitably drawn to high-profile failures, notably the Security Council, while we take for granted the achievements of the International Civil Aviation Organization (ICAO) and the UN Convention on the Law of the Sea, and the vital work of agencies such as the Office of the United Nations High Commissioner for Refugees (UNHCR). Furthermore, many of the problems of the United Nations are due to factors beyond its control, such as inadequate funding, lack of cooperation (or worse) from member states, or the enormity of the challenge – for example, achieving peace in Israel/ Palestine. As has been pointed out, "the UN is a framework, an instrument, a tool; by itself, it is not an agent of action".[1]

The United Nations Security Council is simultaneously the most prominent and least functional of all multilateral institutions. It is obvious that it needs to be drastically reformed. Equally obviously, there is no chance of this happening in the foreseeable future. The main reason is that the Security Council is primarily a status-affirming institution. For the P-5, membership formalizes their great power credentials. Although in principle they recognize the need for reform, in practice they have favoured the status quo as the least bad outcome. That equates to ensuring their own membership in perpetuity and allowing no dilution of their veto-wielding power. For decades, there was also a de facto consensus on limiting the size of the Security Council, although during his presidency Joe Biden started to press for expansion.

The difficulties do not end there. If there is to be an increase in the number of permanent members, who should be chosen? China opposes permanent membership for India and Japan. Italy and Spain object to Germany. Argentina and Mexico resist Brazil's claims. And Nigeria, South Africa, Egypt, Algeria, Ethiopia and Senegal are vying over who might represent Africa. Meanwhile, the current P-5 believe that any new permanent members should not receive the same veto-wielding privileges as them, in effect supporting the creation of two classes of permanent membership.[2]

There appears no way out of this mess of special interests, extreme status-consciousness, and deep mistrust. Security Council reform has been constantly mooted, but to minimal effect.[3] The lack of progress has been evident even when the West's relations with China and Russia have been relatively smooth. But today, when US-China relations and Russia-West engagement are so problematic, the prospects are negligible.

How, then, do we break through the cycle of hopelessness and frustration? The first priority is to focus reform efforts in areas where they can make a real difference. We should stop fetishizing the Security Council, which barely operates as a policy-making body. The various proposals for its expansion would do little to remedy the problems of ineffectiveness and unrepresentativeness; they would merely enlarge the gilded elite of world politics.

Rather than trying to reform the unreformable, we ought to prioritize more practical and achievable objectives. Improving the work of UN specialized agencies – from the IMF and World Bank to the WHO – is especially important. Compared to the Security Council, these bodies have considerably greater impact on people's lives across the globe. But their utility, too, is declining, as they become increasingly inequitable and dysfunctional.[4]

The biggest challenge is to address the issue of (un)representativeness. The Global South's paltry voting shares in the IMF and the World Bank are an international scandal. Kristalina Georgieva, head of the IMF, has acknowledged that the fund should "reflect the economic realities of today's world, not that of the last century".[5] But there has been no tangible movement towards righting the injustice of existing arrangements. The leading European powers – the United Kingdom, France and Germany – have resisted redistribution of their disproportionately large shares, while the United States refuses to consider any increase in China's quota.[6] Reform has fallen victim to zero-sum calculus and the escalation of US-China rivalry.

Redistributing voting shares is not simply a question of natural justice. It is also key to more effective policy-making. Changes in the running of the IMF and World Bank would sharpen up multilateral approaches to the problem of indebtedness in the Global South, and improve the prospects of meaningful debt relief.[7] Reforms are also necessary to facilitate financing to developing countries for renewable energy projects, thereby helping to mitigate climate change.[8]

It would be idle to pretend that the Western powers will readily surrender their dominant position in the Bretton Woods system. The United States, in particular, will not give up its de facto (and sole) power of veto. Indeed, given the Trump administration's loathing of UN institutions and of multilateralism in general, Washington will become more unyielding over the next few years.

In the longer term, though, the West faces a critical choice. If it continues to block major changes to the functioning of the IMF and World Bank, developing nations will shop around for alternatives to the Bretton Woods system, which risks becoming marginalized. The multilateral menu is more extensive than it has ever been. Almost inevitably, the biggest beneficiary of Western shortsightedness would be Beijing, with its Belt and Road Initiative and lending institutions such as the Asian Infrastructure Investment Bank (AIIB).

The self-defeating nature of much of Western policy-making in multilateral institutions is evident also in a penny-pinching attitude towards *funding*. Belying the managerialist credo of "doing more with less", in the real world reduced funding invariably results in worse performance. Such has been the experience of the WHO.

The WHO was much praised for its role in combating the SARS pandemic in 2003, but was later condemned for its response to Covid-19. What changed? Most of all, the international context. The WHO suffered, in particular, from the deterioration of US-China relations. One consequence was a substantial reduction in the funds available to the organization. When Covid-19 hit the world in early 2020, the WHO's annual operating budget was a measly $2 billion – less than that of many American university hospitals.[9] With only minimal core funding, it became excessively reliant on powerful member states, both for financing and access. The WHO may have given the Chinese government an easy ride over the latter's lack of transparency on the origins of the coronavirus, but it was in an impossible position; it had neither the muscle nor the budget to put Beijing under any serious pressure.

The experience of the WHO during Covid-19 highlights a more general problem. A lack of trust in multilateral institutions means that member states do not invest enough in them, resulting in a downward spiral of worsening performance and a further decline in confidence. Some Western governments – the United States principally – have made the provision of funding conditional on reforms to governance. But who should determine the principles of good institutional practice, or decide whether they have been properly implemented? The issue here is a microcosm of the much broader debate about who sets the rules of international order. Western liberal democracies assess good institutional governance according to what they regard as universally applicable standards of efficiency, accountability and transparency. But for many nations, equitable representation, inclusiveness and democratic decision-making are more important considerations.

Reconciling these opposing perspectives is challenging enough by itself, without factoring in geopolitical rivalry and ideological differences. Nevertheless, all countries have an interest in developing a reasonable framework for cooperation. A functioning WHO is indispensable to the world's ability to adapt to future pandemics.[10] More money will not transform it into an efficient organization overnight; reforms to its governance are needed as well.[11] But without adequate funding, the WHO will never be the multilateral institution that (most) Western governments hope for. All sides have to give a little in order to gain a lot.

### The search for alternatives

The sheer difficulty of reforming traditional, UN-based institutions has led states to look for ways of supplementing or circumventing them. The thinking here is that global multilateral cooperation remains essential, but that other structures and mechanisms are required if there is to be actual progress. This view cuts across political and ideological lines; disappointment with global multilateralism and the UN system is near-universal. Unfortunately, none of the alternatives have had much success so far, with a pronounced gap between extravagant claims and underwhelming outcomes.

The 2022 Russian invasion of Ukraine raised the profile of the *G-7*, which had been in decline for some years. The G-7 is cohesive to the extent that its members are Western democracies that pledge allegiance to the "rules-based international order". But it suffers from two major problems. First, it has little moral or political authority outside the West. John Ikenberry has previously suggested that the G-7's "most elevated role … is to speak for the community of nations, defend the core principles of the UN Charter, and make the case for the great modern-era project of building a cooperative world order with a glimmering of decency and justice".[12] But few (if any) non-Western nations share this view; they see the G-7 instead as a vehicle of Western self-interest and self-aggrandizement. The optics of its summits only reinforce this impression – the world's richest nations coming together to pontificate on global order and governance. The G-7's stature has been further diminished by Donald Trump's transparent contempt for the notion of a rules-based order – and for the G-7 itself. His calls for an unrepent-ant Russia to be re-admitted to the group[13] threaten to put it out of business altogether.

The other defect of the G-7 is that, despite efforts to impart greater substance to its proceedings, it remains a glorified talking-shop whose declarations rarely translate into tangible results. Its inadequacies were highlighted during the global financial crisis, when it became necessary to establish the G-20. More recently, the ongoing failure of the Partnership for Global Infrastructure and Investment (PGII) has exposed the G-7's limitations, and further damaged its credibility with Global South nations.[14]

Two things need to happen if the G-7 is to become more than a cosy and largely irrelevant Western club. One is to expand its membership beyond the original seven members. The group has flirted with this idea, for example inviting selected leaders from other major democracies to attend its summits. Regular outside attendees include India, Australia, Brazil, South Korea and South Africa. But this "plus" formula does not address the basic problem that the G-7 is a quasi-Concert of Western powers. External invitees are guests, not full participants.[15] That needs to change if the group wishes to broaden its appeal and influence.[16]

The second change is even more important. The G-7 has to show that it can produce measurable results. In this connection, the story of the PGII highlights *what not to do*. It is counter-productive to talk about "mobilizing" massive private investments when there is no clear idea how this will be done. Such vague gener-alities are uncomfortably reminiscent of analogous Western "commitments" to provide climate financing to poor countries under the Paris Agreement, and no less reputation-shredding. The G-7 would be far better off promising less, and actually delivering.

Once upon a time, the *G-20* was the great hope of multilateral cooperation. Its creation in 2008 acted on the realization that global problems required global approaches. The G-20's emergency measures in response to the financial cri-sis staved off global economic collapse. This action was made possible because agreement was not limited to the West alone, but included China, India, Russia and prominent Global South countries such as Brazil, Saudi Arabia, South Africa and Türkiye.

Since that initial promise, however, the G-20 has lost momentum. The con-sensus of 2008 seems in retrospect to have been a one-off, time-limited response to an extraordinary event. Subsequent developments offer little encouragement that the solidarity of that time can be replicated. The Common Framework on Debt, established in 2020, has been a failure. And the G-20 response to Covid-19 was paralyzed by disunity and acrimony. The likely intensification of US-China rivalry and Trump's hostility towards multilateralism suggest a grim outlook.

Yet perhaps there is a path forward. The 2023 decision to grant Africa a second permanent seat was not just important symbolically – belated recognition for the fastest developing continent after Asia[17] – but also because it hinted that the G-20 might give growing attention to the UN's Sustainable Development Goals (SDGs).[18] In this spirit, Brazilian President Lula da Silva used the 2024 summit in Rio de Janeiro to launch a "Global Alliance against Hunger and Poverty", promising to "eradicate world hunger by 2030".[19] While this latter goal is aspirational rather than realistic, it reflects the shift towards a more inclusive agenda, building on the human development focus of the 2022 and 2023 summits in Bali and New Delhi, respectively. That said, there is a long way to go in converting noble intentions into concrete outcomes. Much will hinge on middle powers, in particular, being able to sustain the policy momentum.

The profile of the *BRICS* has risen substantially in recent times. Regrettably, though, this framework is defined more by what it opposes than what it stands for. The BRICS has become a kind of anti-G7, in much the same way that the "multipolar order" is frequently counterposed against the "rules-based international order".

Even more than the G-7, the BRICS suffers from the disparity between hype and performance. Although there have been sporadic attempts to make it a more purposeful entity, these have been largely unsuccessful. The New Development Bank (NDB) was established in 2014, ostensibly to fund infrastructural projects, but in reality to dilute the dominance of the Bretton Woods institutions. More than a decade later, the NDB's impact remains limited.[20] It is symptomatic of the bank's weakness that it suspended all Russia-based projects in response to the American threat of sanctions over Putin's invasion of Ukraine. In October 2024, Putin used the Kazan BRICS summit to call for a new international payments framework (the "BRICS bridge") as an alternative to the US-dominated financial system. But the idea fell flat. The other BRICs members depend heavily on the US dollar in their trade and economic transactions, while the speculative nature of the Russian proposals inspired little confidence.[21]

The BRICS is hampered by a seemingly insoluble conundrum. Russia (in particular) and China see the forum as a geopolitical and normative counterpoint to the West. Accordingly, they are keen to expand the size and scope of the BRICS; the bigger the membership, the more credible the challenge. However, things have not worked out as they hoped. Even in its long-established form (Brazil, Russia, India, China and later South Africa), the disparateness of the BRICS prevented it from articulating, let alone implementing, a common vision of global governance. The decision at the 2023 summit to offer membership to Iran, Egypt, Ethiopia, the United Arab Emirates, Argentina (which later declined) and Saudi Arabia (which has yet to accept) makes this more difficult still. Egypt and the UAE have close political and security ties with the United States. Strategic tensions between China and India remain significant. And Brazil and India are anxious to ensure that the BRICS does not acquire an overtly anti-Western character.

Prospects for the BRICS will be limited as long as these contradictions are unresolved. Some observers point to the impending further expansion of its membership and believe that the framework "will shape the future of the international order".[22] Yet it will not do so on its present, essentially negative trajectory. The BRICS can either be broad-based or anti-Western, but it cannot be both. Just as many countries have resisted US calls to take sides against China and Russia, so they are averse to joining a grand coalition against the West.

There may be a future for the BRICS, but it will depend on two variables. First, if Global South countries lose hope of meaningful reform in the Bretton Woods system, they may come to see the BRICS as a potential alternative (among many). Second, if the BRICS can shift towards a more businesslike agenda, centred on economic and human development priorities, it may be well-placed to meet this institutional demand. However, this will require a fundamental change of mindset in Moscow and Beijing, namely, de-prioritizing geopolitics and great power balancing. On present trends, that seems improbable.

## Lessons from the regional

The most successful type of multilateral cooperation is regional. This comes in various forms. At one end of the spectrum are tightly knit and regulated institutions like the EU and NATO. They are bound together by myriad rules and specific obligations, and shared historical and cultural experience. They strive to present united positions on international issues, even if they sometimes fall short.

In stark contrast are looser organizations, such as ASEAN (Association of Southeast Asian Nations) and the SCO (Shanghai Cooperation Organization). Their "rules" are highly flexible, policy unity is not imperative, and differences between members are glossed over. One critical distinction from the EU is that ASEAN and SCO members rarely concern themselves with the domestic affairs of others in the group. For them, the principle of non-interference outweighs virtually all other considerations.

A third category of regional multilateralism is issues-based, comprising specialized trade groupings like the Comprehensive and Progressive Agreement on Trans-Pacific Partnership (CPTPP) and the Regional Comprehensive Economic Partnership (RCEP). The members of these bodies are politically and ideologically diverse, but identify convergent practical interests.

The common denominator among these very different regional organizations is that they are all successful in their own way. As such, they offer valuable lessons about how multilateralism can work, even under the most testing of conditions.

## The primacy of self-interest

The most prized quality of regional organizations is the ability to meet the requirements of their constituents. The EU has transformed the economies of its member states, and strengthened their position in the world. There is no doubt they would be worse off outside than inside the Union. (Post-Brexit, the United Kingdom is discovering this to its cost.) It is revealing that Hungary, despite its complaints about Brussels and open rejection of liberal values, shows no desire to leave the Union. The EU's lasting allure is also reflected in the queue of countries keen to become members.[23]

If the EU has been the exemplar of regional multilateralism, then NATO can claim to be the model of a political-military alliance. Since its foundation in 1949, it has been central to an enduring transatlantic relationship that has benefited both Europeans and Americans. More than any other single actor, NATO has consummated the idea of the West. And its power of attraction remains compelling. Far from the alliance being driven by a lust for expansion, as is often alleged, it is the other way around: countries, most recently Ukraine, strive to partake in its promise of shared security.

Self-interest is also key to the popularity of trade-related groupings, such as the CPTPP and the RCEP. They focus on priorities that are directly relevant to members – market access, tariffs, and trade rules and standards – and that transcend ideological differences. Thus, the CPTPP comprises mainly democracies, but also Vietnam (a one-party Communist state) and Brunei (an absolute monarchy). The RCEP is centred mainly on ASEAN, but includes China, Japan, South Korea, Australia and New Zealand.

ASEAN is regarded by some Western observers as the epitome of ineffectual multilateralism.[24] Unlike the EU, it is not backed up by a strong bureaucracy. Substantive policy coordination is minimal, and ASEAN unity is more notional than real. For example, it has never been able to come up with a common position on South China Sea territoriality although several of its members are in dispute with China. (The presence within ASEAN of Laos and Cambodia, de facto Chinese client-states, as well as Myanmar, precludes this.) Nevertheless, ASEAN has definite strengths, the most important of which is to give its members a sense of security that comes from being in numbers. This is not enough on its own, which is why different ASEAN nations also maintain close defence and security ties with the United States or China. But being among friends and neighbours counts for a lot, and is appreciated for what it brings.

## Political culture

Successful regional bodies reflect their particular political, cultural and temporal context. The emphasis in the EU and NATO on democracy and the rule of law emanates from a tradition of liberal humanism dating back to the Enlightenment. For these organizations, and their member states, values are truly interests. In the aftermath of the Cold War and the demise of the Soviet system, it was logical that they should embrace the states of Central and Eastern Europe. Authoritarianism was out, freedom was triumphant – or so it appeared.

The thicket of laws and regulations embodied by the EU's Acquis Communautaire has worked precisely because member states are accustomed to the rule of law and strong institutions in their own national governance. So while they chafe against the long reach of Brussels, and jealously preserve sovereign prerogatives, they implicitly recognize the legitimacy and normality of (some) supranational regulation. They believe – rightly – that they can continue to act as sovereign states while benefiting from being part of the largest economic-political bloc in the world. Political culture is buttressed by a keen sense of self-interest.

By contrast, ASEAN's loose brand of multilateralism works for its members because it is not prescriptive, does not impinge in any way on their sovereignty, and allows them to pursue flexible relations with a wide range of partners. It has never been the "ASEAN way" to take tough positions and make committal or principled choices. It could scarcely be otherwise. In Asia, national sovereignty is a paramount principle, institutions are weak, the practice of democracy and the rule of law is patchy, and there is no precedent for an economic bloc like the EU, let alone a political-military alliance along the lines of NATO.[25] Viewed from a Western perspective, these are serious flaws that prevent effective policy-making. But for many in Asia, the fluidity of ASEAN is natural and advantageous. As the former Singaporean diplomat and scholar Kishore Mahbubani has noted, "ASEAN's greatest strength, paradoxically, is its relative weakness and heterogeneity, which ensures that no power sees it as threatening".[26]

The significance of political culture is apparent if we try to imagine the EU and ASEAN switching places. The institutional and policy discipline of the former would be anathema to ASEAN members, never mind the emphasis on shared values and the running commentary on failures of governance in individual countries. Conversely, the lack of policy content, split loyalties, and dilettantism of ASEAN would drive EU members mad. Yet in their own habitat each organization has survived, and often thrived, for more than half a century.

## Democratic decision-making

The most effective regional bodies tend to be democratic and relatively egalitarian in their internal modus operandi. This not only gives them legitimacy, but also empowers member states by involving them in decision-making. Of course, this comes with its frustrations. Hungary has been a consistently disruptive presence within the EU, while Türkiye delayed the NATO accession of Finland and Sweden in an effort to leverage bilateral concessions from Helsinki and Stockholm.

Nevertheless, the advantages of a democratic and generally consensual approach outweigh its disadvantages. The long-term credibility of NATO, for example, rests on it being genuinely multilateral, rather than just an extension of US policy and power (central though that is). Take away that collective spirit, and the alliance would be severely, perhaps fatally, weakened. The benefits of collegial decision-making are especially evident in "flatter" frameworks like the CPTPP. The absence of the United States and China has allowed it to evolve into a cooperative trans-Pacific mechanism. In the RCEP, the presence of major economies such as Japan (fourth largest in the world), South Korea and Australia, ensures that it is much more than a China-plus arrangement. This internal balance distinguishes the CPTPP and RCEP from other institutions, notably the AIIB, where China's dominance is manifest and the bank's operations are potentially hostage to Beijing's foreign and trade policy agenda.[27]

The virtues of democratic multilateralism are magnified if we consider the alternatives. Russian efforts to promote the Collective Security Treaty Organization (CSTO) and the Eurasian Economic Union (EAEU) as multilateral structures in the post-Soviet space have been hindered from the start by the fact that they are multilateral in name, but unilateral in substance. They are rooted in a retrograde vision of a lost empire, whose revival is desired by few beyond the Kremlin.[28]

The SCO is a bona fide multilateral mechanism, but one whose development has been inhibited by its origins and by the disproportionate influence exercised by China and Russia. Beginning life in 1996 as the Shanghai Five (China, Russia, Kazakhstan, Kyrgyzstan, Tajikistan), its original remit was to develop security confidence-building along the old Sino-Soviet border. In 2001, it morphed into the SCO, with a more ambitious regional security agenda. The new organization was a by-product of improved Sino-Russian relations, and was useful in neutralizing nascent tensions between Moscow and Beijing as a result of China's expanding footprint in Central Asia. But this also meant that the SCO became more an adjunct of their partnership than a properly functioning multilateral framework.

Beijing and Moscow are cognizant of the problem and have consequently broadened the organization's membership. However, this has created new complications. The accession of India and Pakistan in 2017 made the SCO more inclusive and representative – more "democratic". But it also imported significant security tensions and accentuated regional divisions. Today, the SCO remains a structure in search of a mission. It exists, but to no clear purpose.

## The importance of adaptability

Institutions, like empires, are susceptible to overreach. Contrary to conventional wisdom, the main danger is not geographical overreach – extending membership to too many countries – so much as functional overload, trying to do too much. As we saw in the previous chapter, the EU's Maastricht project of a close political union and a common foreign and security policy proved too much for member states to swallow. And now there is the risk that in the desire to spread its geopolitical wings the EU may end up eroding its basic strengths as a trade bloc.

But for the most part the EU has found – or stumbled into – a reasonable balance of priorities. Member states have curbed the Commission's political ambitions, and the limitations of the EU's hard power have prevented it from being taken seriously as a geopolitical actor. Almost by default, the EU has been forced to concentrate on its core mission as an economic powerhouse.

There is, however, a danger of being *too* conservative. The international landscape is constantly evolving, and often in harmful and unpredictable ways. The very qualities and characteristics that have sustained regional organizations in the past may not work as well – or at all – in the future. For example, ASEAN faces mounting pressures from a fraught security environment in the Indo-Pacific. Its innate conservatism carries the risk of it becoming sidelined by events and increasingly marginal to the interests of member states.[29] As regional tensions escalate, countries may look to alternative bilateral and multilateral arrangements.[30]

It is NATO, however, that faces the biggest tests. Following years of drift, Putin's 2022 invasion of Ukraine re-energized the alliance, giving it fresh purpose, or at least reviving the old Cold War rationale. But the return of a direct Russian threat has exposed major uncertainties, especially over Article V of the North Atlantic Treaty – the provision of mutual support if one or more alliance members is attacked. For countries with good relations with Russia, such as Hungary, Slovakia and Türkiye, rendering such aid is no longer a given, while the commitment of several other members – Greece, Bulgaria, Cyprus – is also in doubt. Meanwhile, the rise of the far right across Europe could transform NATO's political character, with prominent figures (Hungarian Prime Minister Viktor Orban, Slovak Prime Minister Robert Fico, President of the French Rassemblement National Marine Le Pen, leader of Alternative für Deutschland Alice Weidel) seeing in Putin a kindred spirit. The founding character of NATO as an alliance of democracies "bound together by common values" is under mortal threat.[31]

The biggest worry for NATO is the new administration in Washington. During his first presidency, Trump repeatedly questioned the value of the alliance, and he has since reaffirmed his doubts about the applicability of Article V.[32] More importantly, America's strategic focus has shifted. Notwithstanding the bloody war in Ukraine, Washington's chief foreign policy priority is not safeguarding European security or countering Russian aggression. It is to beat back the multi-dimensional challenge of China.[33] Viewed from the Trump White House, if NATO cannot contribute meaningfully to this goal, then it has little value.

An American withdrawal from the alliance, or significant downsizing of its commitment, would require European members to step up – a real stretch given their ingrained US dependence. On Ukraine, it is unlikely that Washington will provide meaningful security guarantees to Kyiv or a proper backstop to support European peacekeepers (under the "coalition of the willing")[34] if they are attacked by Russian forces. In other words, the Europeans would be on their own. Article V of the North Atlantic Treaty would not apply, and the very basis of the transatlantic alliance would be in jeopardy.

The task of modernizing NATO for a new era goes well beyond the willingness of European governments to spend 5 per cent of GDP on defence and defence-related priorities, as promised at the 2025 summit in The Hague. Member states must re-examine core assumptions: about the overall purpose of the alliance, the nature and extent of America's role, the viability of Article V, and the range – geographical and functional – of NATO operations. The alliance faces major stress-tests of its cohesiveness and utility, with debates about its future likely to be deeply polarized.[35] Under these circumstances, the ability to adapt has become a matter of existential importance for NATO, not least because of the possibility that the formal alliance could give way over time to a patchwork of bespoke minilateral arrangements.

## The lure of minilateralism

Modern-day minilateralism stems from a mix of deep-seated frustration with the shortcomings of multilateralism, heightened threat perceptions, and a growing sense of urgency. Although the term is of recent derivation, the idea itself is not new. The nineteenth-century Concert of Europe was a minilateral framework. So was the US-led "coalition of the willing" in Iraq. And the G-7 might also be described as a minilateral forum.

What defines minilateralism is not only size, but spirit. Its basic premise is that it is more effective to work with a few like-minded partners than to try, generally in vain, to build a larger consensus. The Biden administration was an avid proponent of minilateralism, with its focus on the Quadrilateral Security Dialogue (the "Quad"), AUKUS, the "Squad", and the US-Japan-Republic of Korea trilateral pact.

Minilateralism has obvious attractions, especially when achieving agreement in larger formats is so difficult. It is undoubtedly a "nimble and adaptive framework",[36] and is consistent with US efforts to strengthen its security partnerships in the Indo-Pacific against the challenge of China. However, minilateralism comes with its own problems. The most evident is the lack of wider legitimacy. AUKUS is a de facto Anglosphere entente, while the Quad, despite past attempts to expand its agenda to include issues such as climate change, is driven by the logic of strategic containment. This is a concern not just for outsiders, but also for members. India, for example, is wary of being perceived as America's sidekick in the Indo-Pacific.[37] Despite its own anxieties about Chinese geopolitical and irredentist ambitions, it is uncomfortable with the idea of overt containment.

New Delhi's reservations point to a major drawback of minilateral mechanisms, namely, that they can become, or be seen as, instruments of unilateral ambition. This perception undercut the US-led coalition of the willing in Iraq. It has discredited Moscow's efforts to promote the CSTO and the EAEU. And it is likely to limit the effectiveness of the Quad and AUKUS looking ahead. Small may be "beautiful" in some eyes, but to others it is elitist, non-transparent and provocative.

Worse still, minilateralism may encourage the tribalization of the international system at a time when global cooperation is needed more than ever to address challenges ranging from climate change to technology governance. Its apparent simplicities promise a comforting ease of engagement, but reduce the incentive to reach out to opponents and to the unconverted. With its emphasis on political like-mindedness, minilateralism all but gives up on the ideal of an international community in favour of serving narrower geopolitical and security ends. Consequently, it can never be *the* answer to the challenge of multilateral cooperation, but at best only one of many tools.

### Making multilateralism work

The recent experience of multilateral institutions leads to a number of conclusions. First, the more "political" the institution the more flawed it tends to be. The most effective organizations and frameworks are those with practical functions, where performance is more important than status. That is one reason why ICAO and UNCLOS work much better than the Security Council, and why the CPTPP and RCEP are more productive than the BRICS or the G-7. Civil aviation, sea traffic and trade matter directly to all nations, which incentivizes governments to cooperate with one another. (Tellingly, the outright politicization of the WTO has almost entirely nullified its unity.)

The fortunes of international institutions are contingent on the behaviour of nation-states. The faults of multilateralism are principally those of national leaders and governments. Equally, the successes of multilateral diplomacy – the founding of the United Nations, the resolution of the Cuban Missile Crisis, the G-20 emergency response to the global financial crisis – occur when nations are committed to making it work.

Major powers are key to the future of multilateralism. US leadership has sustained NATO for three quarters of a century, but now Washington's antipathy towards Europe[38] threatens the alliance's continuing viability. By the same token, major power contestation almost invariably undermines multilateral bodies, the Security Council most of all. There is a fine balance here: multilateral institutions need major powers to be invested in them, while major powers need to moderate their natural instincts if such institutions are to function properly. Covid-19 exposed the limitations of the WHO, but more than that it highlighted the catastrophic consequences of zero-sum attitudes in Washington and Beijing. The WTO has likewise been a casualty of US-China rivalry.

This raises questions about the outlook for multilateralism, especially in light of the Trump administration's hostility towards it. In Chapter 4, I sketched out a minimalist approach that Washington might pursue to keep its options open. But in reality it will almost certainly maintain a negative and even destructive attitude towards international institutions. The rest of the world has to be prepared for this, and to stay in the game. It cannot afford to lose hope or allow itself to be held hostage by any one country, however powerful. Global cooperation on issues such as climate change, pandemic disease and international security is too important. Besides, there will come a time when the United States will want to re-engage with multilateral organizations and processes, especially if it feels that absence is diminishing its global influence relative to China. Such an about-turn has happened before, as recently as 2021 when Biden succeeded Trump as president, and it will happen again.

It is plausible to think of regionalism as the future of multilateralism. A streamlined approach involving a smaller cast of players holds definite appeal, and for many countries it represents their best chance of exercising influence. However, in a globalized world, regional organizations and mechanisms will not always be up to the task. The pandemic highlighted the importance of *global* cooperation in the face of a worldwide threat. Climate change requires policy responses that cut across regions and continents. And a global approach is indispensable in addressing a whole raft of other challenges, from transport to refugees and migration to food security.

Inclusiveness, far from being incompatible with effective multilateralism, is integral to it. Typically, the best performing institutions and frameworks are those that are genuinely representative of their constituencies. This is principally about legitimacy. The Security Council is a failure not just because of the P-5 animosities that sabotage its operation, but also because it is blatantly unrepresentative of the twenty-first-century world. The G-7's declarations about global infrastructural investment, climate change and human development have minimal resonance because they occur within a Western bubble with next to no input from the Global South. On the other hand, the EU, NATO and ASEAN have been successful because they serve the interests and reflect the mood of their members. Regional solidarity is hard to replicate on a global scale, where there are so many more players, all with their own agendas. Nevertheless, it is possible. The lessons of successful regionalism – self-interest, a feel for political culture, democratic decision-making, adaptability – apply to global multilateral cooperation as well.

The multilateral architecture of the future will be untidy, with overlapping and sometimes competing jurisdictions. The UN system will remain, largely unreformed and undermined by vested interests. Alongside it will sit political-military alliances such as NATO (in some form), regional bodies (the EU, ASEAN, the African Union), looser frameworks (G-20, the BRICS), trade-centred groupings like the CPTPP and the RCEP, and minilateral entities such as the Quad.

Such a smorgasbord of multilateral organizations may well exacerbate fragmentation of the international system. But better outcomes are possible. Countries, large and small, should avail themselves of the widest possible range of mechanisms, like India has done as part of its "multi-aligned" foreign policy. Institutional diversity – and competition – is healthy. Greater choice may also engender a process of "creative destruction", whereby multilateral structures that are no longer useful gradually wither away or are sidelined, while those that are left become more equitable and efficient.

In maximizing options – from global bodies to regional trade forums to single-issue groupings – flexible multilateralism should make it easier and more attractive for states to work together. That in itself is not a guarantee of success. But just by fostering a spirit of engagement, it would contribute to a more positive and inclusive approach to problem solving. Today, when the liberal vision of a rules-based order is discredited, when international rules are breaking down, and the moral authority of the major powers has sunk to new depths, multilateralism in all its variety has never been more essential to the rebuilding of international order.

# 7

# THINKING BEYOND THE STATE

Hedley Bull in *The Anarchical Society* asserted that "the starting point of international relations is the existence of states".[1] More than that, he defined international society as "a society of states".[2] This view of the world later came under attack for being excessively narrow and for failing to "recognise the extent to which the [international] system was moving decisively 'beyond Westphalia'". Writing in 2002 on the 25th anniversary of Bull's opus, Oxford Professor Andrew Hurrell argued that "any contemporary analysis of order and governance needs to place order within the state system against the other two arenas within which all social order needs to be understood ... civil society on the one hand ... and economic markets on the other".[3]

With the benefit of a further quarter of a century's hindsight, we can see that both these eminent scholars were right – and wrong. Hurrell was surely premature in announcing that the world was moving "decisively" beyond the system of states. Today, state actors continue to dominate the international system. Order and governance is primarily contingent on their relations with one another. And national sovereignty has become the supreme good for virtually all governments, regardless of political orientation. Any viable vision of global governance must start from the premise that state actors will remain, for the foreseeable future, the basic building blocks of international society – as Bull emphasized.

Nevertheless, Hurrell was right to home in on Bull's state-centrism. International society is much more than a society of states, central though they are to its functioning (and dysfunction). This was true in Bull's time, but it is especially so today. Non-state actors, from big business to independent media and non-governmental organizations (NGOs), are exerting a growing influence on the foreign policies of nations and on international order. Their impact is evident in the responses to some of the great challenges of the twenty-first century, such as climate change, technological transformation, and the information revolution.

In thinking about how to revitalize order, we therefore need to look beyond the nation-state. While national governments will remain the primary actors, to rely solely on them is self-limiting and self-defeating. The scale and complexity of the tasks facing humanity require all the resources at our disposal. Global challenges demand all-of-society responses. And while governments are instinctively averse to devolving decision-making, it is in their interest to do so. Real authority rests on the ability to deliver. But that will remain elusive unless non-state actors, and the public more broadly, are incorporated into problem solving. The failures of governance over the past two decades have underlined the bankruptcy of old-fashioned, top-down approaches. A change of direction is long overdue.

### Game-changers in an evolving world

Non-state actors have, at various times, played immensely important roles in foreign policy; suffice to recall the British East India Company's involvement in the conquest of India, and the Dutch East India Company's expansion into Southeast Asia. During the Cold War, leading firms were instrumental in promoting Western geopolitical and economic interests. The Anglo-Iranian Oil Company (later British Petroleum – BP), notoriously, was implicated in the 1953 CIA/MI6 coup against Iranian Prime Minister Mohammed Mossadegh. More generally, business enterprises have always lobbied governments to advance their commercial interests and shape the international environment in their favour.

So what's new? For one thing, non-state actors today are more influential than at any time in history. Companies such as Meta (Facebook), X (formerly Twitter), Amazon and Google (Alphabet) have global reach, touching the lives of billions. Compared to them, even the biggest commercial empires of the past were pygmies. The horizons of Big Tech and social media giants are limitless; they extend beyond influencing individual policies to dominating the global information space.[4] And this reach translates into a potentially decisive influence over political outcomes and the very character of governance.[5] Big Tech magnates such as Elon Musk and Peter Thiel contributed significantly to Donald Trump's victory in the 2024 US presidential election, a result with far-reaching implications for international order. Musk, with his "Department of Government Efficiency" (DOGE), was at the forefront of the White House's early efforts to dismantle the US federal bureaucracy.[6]

The second big difference from past eras is the number and diversity of non-state actors. They encompass not only big business and commercial lobbies, but also previously marginalized sectors. NGOs and civil society have far greater impact than when Bull was writing. Take climate change. The reason this is on the global agenda is almost entirely because of growing public awareness of the problem and the consequent bottom-up pressure on politicians to act. On this issue, governments have been followers, not leaders.[7]

Third, modern non-state actors are much more independent and "anarchic" than their predecessors. Unlike the British East India Company, which acted as a quasi-official arm of the British Empire, today's Big Tech companies operate in the service of no national interest; they are their own "nations" with their own distinct priorities.[8] While they work with government and desire its support, they have vigorously resisted attempts to regulate their activities. Freedom of action is the basis of their power, giving them a degree of autonomy greater than many nation-states.

Other non-state actors are more anarchic still. The most extreme examples are international terrorist organizations such as al-Qaeda and Islamic State/ Daesh, which reject the legitimacy of national governments and seek to destroy the system of states. For them, any rules-based international order is anathema. But there are also more moderate and law-abiding non-state actors whose common denominator is that they act separately from government. They include human rights organizations, international charities, climate action groups, and independent research institutes, think-tanks and universities. Nearly all of them pursue their aims peacefully, and few could be called revolutionary. Yet the cumulative effect of their activities is to erode the monopoly of states over the conduct of international relations. Purposefully or otherwise, they add to the disorderliness of international society.

Finally, on a more general level, there is unprecedented public scrutiny of foreign policy-making. This is no longer an elite preserve, determined only by a handful of leaders. The Brexit debate in the United Kingdom exemplified how far things have moved. In former times, Prime Minister David Cameron, a Remainer, might have hoped to manage the decision-making process. But he was overtaken by events. While he was not helped by Eurosceptic elements within his own Conservative Party, the single biggest variable was the close involvement of the public. Many were bored by the detail of the arguments, but nevertheless identified a personal stake in the outcomes, empathizing with the Leavers' slogan of "taking back control".

All this raises the question of whether the proliferation of non-state actors and their growing influence preclude a rules-based order. Not necessarily. But it is clear that we need to think more creatively about how to bring non-state actors and civil society into order-building. It is easy enough to mouth platitudes about collective decision-making and problem solving. It is far harder to put this into practice. But if we are to address twenty-first-century threats and challenges, we must find a way.


## Collective problem solving

As I foreshadowed in the Introduction to this book, there are two major challenges to integrating non-state actors into global governance. The first is to inject dynamism into decision-making while still ensuring proper accountability. Getting the balance right is vital. Lose sight of necessary safeguards – for example in AI governance or over social media content – and the likely outcome is escalating disorder or worse. Conversely, intrusive controls can stifle innovation and lead to political and intellectual stagnation when we can least afford it.

The second challenge is to develop productive relations between state and non-state actors. This is less obviously a problem in business-state ties, where there is a record of cooperation going back centuries. But it is a very different story when it comes to engagement between NGOs and government, which is often characterized by mutual mistrust, frustration and contempt. And the bigger the issue, the more difficult the interaction – as over climate policy.

There is a third challenge, which is incentivizing public participation in decision-making. Historically, leaders have sought either to instrumentalize, defuse or ignore popular opinion. They have seldom viewed the public as a genuine partner in problem solving. This is especially the case in foreign policy. "Ordinary" citizens are said to care little and to be poorly informed about what goes on in the world. Yet this perception is outdated. Ever larger numbers of people are working and travelling abroad.[9] Thanks to social media, the general public is more globally aware than it has ever been. The notion, then, that "the great and the good" can conduct international relations while taking the public for granted is untenable – as a complacent Cameron found to his cost over the Brexit referendum.

Greater public participation will not by itself bring about better governance. Popular attitudes may reflect xenophobia, parochialism, and political, religious and cultural intolerance. The public can also be fickle, its attention distracted by the latest subject *du jour* or personality politicians offering up snake-oil remedies, ready scapegoats, and conspiracy theories. The task, then, is to turn greater public involvement into a force for constructive change.

There is no part of the contemporary policy agenda that would not benefit from the active participation of non-state actors, and closer cooperation between government, business and civil society. But three issue-areas, in particular, lend themselves to non-state engagement: climate policy; technology and AI governance; and the information revolution.

## Climate policy

Climate change engages an eclectic cast of non-state actors. They include a worldwide scientific community that highlights the extent of the threat and works on technological solutions; corporate enterprises investing in renewable energy projects; independent media outlets disseminating information (and disinformation); local and regional administrations committed to ambitious carbon-reduction policies[10]; and NGOs holding governments to account.

The existence of such a diverse group of players is unsurprising. Climate change is the most universal of threats, affecting literally every person on the planet. Unfortunately, this universality has not been matched by a commensurate sense of urgency among governments. Although nearly 150 of them have committed to achieving net-zero emissions, the timelines lie far into the future – 2050 for the United States (pre-Trump 2.0) and the EU, 2060 for China, 2070 for India. More pertinently, existing commitments are being diluted amidst the continuing expansion of fossil fuels development.[11] We are witnessing the unravelling of the 2015 Paris agreement, whereby the Conference of the Parties (COP) agreed to limit global warming to less than 2 degrees centigrade above pre-industrial levels by 2100, while aiming for a rise of below 1.5 degrees. In a 2024 survey of climate scientists, 77 per cent estimated that the actual rate of increase would exceed 2.5 degrees, with 42 per cent forecasting an increase of above 3 degrees.[12] The UN Environment Programme (UNEP) believes the earth is currently on course for a temperature rise of up to 3.1 degrees by 2100.[13]

The annual COP summits have degenerated into vast jamborees, an opportunity for world leaders to flash their climate credentials and for oil and gas executives to tout new deals. Summit outcomes, such as they are, are invariably exaggerated. Follow-up is poor. Accountability is minimal as failings are whitewashed. And core tasks are either fudged or ignored altogether. These include the need for rich countries to take responsibility for historical emissions, compensate developing nations for the "loss-and-damage" resulting from climate change, and fulfil their obligations (under the Paris agreement) to help finance the energy transition of poor countries from fossil fuels to renewables.[14] The COP process has become an exercise in green-washing, enabling governments to promote the illusion that they are pursuing meaningful action to address the climate crisis, when the reality is that almost none of them regard this as a first-order priority.

It has become evident that governments alone are either unable or unwilling to tackle climate change in earnest. Non-state actors need to become much more involved in developing and implementing policy. But in an international system that remains heavily skewed towards states, how can this be achieved? What actions might give fresh impetus to the struggle against climate change?

*Rejecting doomism*

It is easiest to start with what we shouldn't do, namely, surrender to doom-ism. Climate scientists rightly highlight the consequences of runaway climate change, but this cannot be a counsel of despair. We do not have the luxury of being demoralized by the (admittedly many) negatives or to give in to the siren call of those who argue that it is too late to do anything about global warming. Christiana Figueres, who presided over the 2015 Paris COP,[15] puts it well: "A sense of despair ... robs us of our agency, makes us vulnerable to mis- and disin-formation, and prevents the radical collaboration we need". She adds that "we ... have the responsibility – and the opportunity – to shape the future differently. We must take stock of the science, triple down on our efforts *and* deploy the perspective of possibility".[16]

Equally, we should not obsess about targets. It is important to try to keep global warming below 2 degrees, and ideally below 1.5 degrees, as per the Paris agreement. But it is not the end of things if, as seems certain, the world fails to achieve this. As the head of UNEP has pointed out, "every fraction of a degree avoided counts in terms of lives saved, economies protected, damages avoided, biodiversity conserved and the ability to rapidly bring down any temperature overshoot".[17]

A viable response to the challenge of climate change should emphasize the benefits of taking action rather than belabour the sacrifices that have to be made. To date, the prevailing narrative has been more sackcloth-and-ashes than incen-tives, reflected in strictures not to eat meat, drive cars, fly abroad, and so on. This approach is counter-productive. When the picture is of unremitting doom and gloom, or of ceaseless abstinence, most politicians and a large part of the public tend to switch off or retreat into fatalism.

People need a positive vision. The cause of combating climate change would be immeasurably strengthened if it were more explicitly tied to outcomes that favour everyone, regardless of political orientation or economic status. These include superior air quality, cleaner drinking water, warmer homes in winter and cooler in summer, and better health. The accent should be on improving the quality of life – general and individual – rather than hectoring people about their shortcomings.

In fact, there are a number of positive trends: the rapid expansion of solar energy capacity and the recovery of the wind sector[18]; the reality that in many countries renewables are cheaper than oil, gas and coal[19]; the growing share of solar and wind in electricity generation; the creation of millions of new jobs in the green economy[20]; and the roll-out of electric vehicles (EVs) around the world.[21] It is as important to appreciate and publicize the successes of climate policy as it is to identify what still needs to be done.

*Engaging with the "enemy"*

The mechanics of climate cooperation are complicated, as is the role of non-state actors within it. How do you get governments, energy majors, NGOs, climate scientists and activists to engage usefully with each other at the same table? Trying to reconcile opposing perspectives and interests is hugely testing, as the experience of successive failed COP summits testifies. Just throwing people together is unlikely to lead to better results in the future.

The prominent climate scientist, Bill McGuire, proposes a leaner, more focused alternative to the COP process, revolving around several smaller bodies, each devoted to addressing a specific climate-related issue – energy, agriculture, deforestation, transport, loss-and-damage. These bodies would operate full-time, year-round. They would be properly representative of developed and developing countries, and include experts from academe and NGOs as well as government and the business sector. Much of the hard graft of negotiations would take place out of the public eye. And any agreements would be signed off by national governments. One can debate the specifics, but McGuire's essential point is persuasive: the COP process is too unwieldy and needs to be replaced by a less showy and more professional approach.[22]

However, fixing mechanisms of decision-making and consultation is insufficient without a sea-change in attitudes – not only from governments and energy companies, but also NGOs and activists. As long as climate change debates continue to be portrayed in binary and adversarial terms – pragmatic decision-makers versus impractical idealists; exploitative commercial interests against righteous climate action groups; moral and immoral – then the prospects of concerted action will remain poor. Instead, there needs to be a process of mutual learning between different parties. Over time, this can become the basis for long-term working relationships that facilitate solutions to common problems.[23]

Major energy companies such as BP, Shell and Saudi Aramco have a vital role to play in tackling climate change. That reality may be hard to accept, given their continuing commitment to fossil fuel development. Yet if these companies are a large part of the problem, they also possess critical technical expertise and the financial resources to invest heavily in renewable forms of energy. The challenge ahead will be to persuade them, through various economic and legal incentives, to reorient their primary activity away from fossil fuels to areas such as solar, wind and even nuclear. That will take considerable time and effort, and there will be many setbacks. Companies need to be confident that such a shift is in their commercial interest. Profit, not altruism, will be the main driver of energy transition.

The Biden administration's 2022 Inflation Reduction Act (IRA) shows us a way forward. The Act budgeted $394 billion in federal funding for clean energy projects over a period of 10 years, mainly in the form of tax credits to encourage private sector investment. The goal was to lower national carbon emissions while also improving commercial competitiveness, stimulating innovation, and boosting employment and productivity.[24] Importantly, the IRA's benefits cut across the political divide; most projects were located in Republican (and climate-sceptic) parts of the country.[25] Since returning to the presidency, Trump has committed himself to undoing the IRA. But even if he succeeds, it remains a useful template for business-centred climate action in the future. Government support will be essential to boost private investment in renewables.

It is a tragedy that climate policy has become mired in political and culture "wars". Much of the blame is fairly apportioned to populist nationalists who have seized on a hot-button topic they can exploit. But liberal and hard-left voices also deserve censure for allowing the issue to be hijacked by a wider radical agenda. Climate action needs to appeal beyond its core constituencies to conservatives as well.[26] In this connection, ideas such as "de-growth" are unhelpful in building consensus or raising public awareness. They reinforce a false dichotomy between environmental and economic goals. The development of renewable energy and other "green" policies should be viewed not only as virtuous in the general sense – safeguarding the environment for future generations – but as the rational *economic* course now: commercially profitable, reducing energy costs, opening up new employment possibilities, and alleviating the burden on public health services.[27]

### Smarter tactics

One of the challenges for any policy actor is finding the most effective methods to advance their objectives. Regrettably, climate action groups have not been good at this. The "direct action" of Extinction Rebellion and Just Stop Oil exemplifies an approach that favours short-term drama over longer-term effect – to the detriment of their cause. It is one thing to pressure governments and energy companies to fulfil their responsibilities. It is quite another to engage in juvenile stunts that alienate decision-makers and, more important still, the uncommitted public whose support is essential to any progress.

There are far better ways for NGOs and climate action groups to influence climate policy. One is to take legal action in response to the failure of governments and energy companies to meet their commitments to cut greenhouse gas emissions. In May 2024, the UK High Court ruled that the Conservative government's climate action plan was unlawful as there was insufficient evidence it would lead to reduced emissions. The judgement was in response to a joint suit by several climate action groups, including Friends of the Earth, ClientEarth and the Good Law Project. The High Court judgement put the onus on the government to come up with a revised climate plan.[28] Three years earlier, a court in the Netherlands ruled that Royal Dutch Shell had to reduce its carbon emissions by 45 per cent compared to 2019.[29] Such suits will not always be successful – in November 2024, Shell successfully appealed the judgement – but they have already had a greater impact on policy than the futile gestures favoured by radical activists.[30]

Another accessible way of shifting the dial on climate policy is through the political process. Compared to the rest of the population, younger people are considerably more exercised about climate change, and more committed to redressing the damage it causes.[31] They constitute a formidable mobilizable force whose potential for action will only grow, driven by two factors: the rising impact of climate change; and the expansion of social media. Until now, governments have tended to be complacent about the younger generation, counting on its disillusionment with party politics. But climate change could turn out to be an electoral game-changer, particularly if NGOs are able to coordinate their approaches – as in the lawsuits against the UK government and Shell.[32] More than any single thing, direct political engagement by the public would grab the attention of governments and energy companies, and improve the prospects of serious action to mitigate climate change.

## Technology and AI governance

Technological transformation is the most elusive and fast-moving challenge of our time. It touches almost every aspect of human existence – war and peace, economic growth and social development, public health, information and dis-information. If there is to be a rules-based order in the twenty-first century, it will be one shaped by technology. We are only just beginning to discover the possibilities of where it might take us, and are scarcely the wiser about the risks. Technology raises a host of complex political, strategic, ethical and regulatory issues. It is also a field where non-state actors – in the form of "Big Tech"[33] – are especially influential. More than any other issue-area, it calls into question the classical paradigm of international order as an order between states.

Policy responses to the challenges of technological transformation are still in their infancy, and nowhere more so than in Artificial Intelligence (AI). There is a rough consensus that some kind of rules-based regime is necessary, but very little on what it should look like, including within the West where America's laissez-faire, industry-led approach to regulation contrasts with the European Union's preference for tighter government controls. Joseph Nye noted that "history shows that societies take time to learn how to respond to major disruptive technological changes and to put in place rules that make the world safer from new dangers".[34] But time is exactly what is lacking; the pace of technological development is far outstripping the capacity of any regulatory framework to manage it. The risks are compounded in a disorderly international environment, marked by US-China rivalry, the breakdown of norms, and a lack of trust in multilateral regimes.

Ian Bremmer and Mustafa Suleyman write that "few powerful constituencies favor containing AI – and all incentives point toward continued inaction".[35] The picture, however, is mixed. There have been some signs of greater urgency in addressing the risks of unbridled AI development. In November 2023, 28 governments, including the United States and China, as well as the European Union, met at Bletchley Park in the United Kingdom and agreed a declaration on AI safety standards and safeguards.[36] As US President, Joe Biden issued an Executive Order on the development and use of AI.[37] The United States and the United Kingdom set up AI Safety Institutes. And the EU passed a comprehensive AI Act in July 2024, following the earlier introduction of a Digital Services Act in October 2022.[38]

Lately, Western governments have rowed back on some of these initiatives. The follow-up to Bletchley, the Paris AI summit in February 2025, saw a shift away from the previous emphasis on safety towards a much greater tolerance of risk in the name of innovation. US Vice President JD Vance attacked EU attempts to regulate the activities of American tech companies through its Digital Services Act.[39] British Prime Minister Keir Starmer did not attend in Paris, and Britain, along with the United States, refused to sign the summit declaration.

It is clear there can be no rules-based regime governing technology without significant involvement by Big Tech. These companies possess not only superior expertise, but also global reach and extraordinary financial power.[40] The trouble, however, is that they are averse to any external controls or oversight. They would like us to trust instead in their ability to manage risk through self-regulation. During the Biden years, they were prepared to go through the motions of AI safety, doing the minimum to ward off the threat of onerous government restrictions, but not allowing such concerns to slow the development and dissemination of their products. But under Trump they have ceased pretending to care, confident that the White House will allow them plenty of latitude and support them against European attempts to regulate their activities.

For the time being, then, any technology regime is likely to depend more on self-restraint than concrete rules. But this is a fragile and unsustainable basis for AI governance. As Suleyman has emphasized, the growth of AI technology is a generational challenge requiring a generational response.[41] Although governments need to resist the urge to over-regulate, they will have to become more involved, not least because of the national security implications of AI development.

For example, there will need to be state controls over the transfer of high-end technology with potentially military applications. Equally, Big Tech must overcome the temptation to foster a freewheeling environment where meaningful checks and balances are absent. It has a vested interest in working closely with civil society to allay concerns about personal privacy, workers' rights, and potentially harmful effects of AI.

If a broad-based public-private partnership emerges, technology could have the same largely positive impact on governance, the economy and society in the twenty-first century as the Industrial Revolution did in the eighteenth and nineteenth centuries, minus the latter's worst excesses. But if there is no such partnership, or technology governance degenerates into opaque arrangements between politicians and tech leaders, the fallout could be very damaging. The bromance between Trump and Musk, brief though it was, showed how plutocratic ties may subvert democratic norms and institutions and the rule of law.[42] There is a danger, too, that such collusion results in the further marginalization and alienation of large sections of society, with adverse consequences for political and social stability. An early warning sign here is the souring of public attitudes towards tech companies.[43]

## Technology and international norms

The difficulties of AI governance are multiplied at the international level. Technology is at the forefront of US-China rivalry, the twenty-first-century equivalent of the nuclear arms and space races during the Cold War.[44] Both sides view mastery over it as the foundation of other sources of power – geopolitical, security, economic, political and normative.[45] To update Halford Mackinder's well-known aphorism, who rules technology commands the world.[46] In this competitive spirit, Trump on the third day of his presidency announced the launch of Stargate, a \$500 billion venture "to build the largest AI infrastructure project by far in history".[47] Less than a week later, however, Chinese start-up DeepSeek launched a new AI model that roiled US (and European) financial markets, and briefly slashed the value of Nvidia, the world's most valuable company.[48]

An international rules-based regime for technology, and AI in particular, appears improbable anytime soon. Various ideas have been proposed, such as an advisory body along the lines of the UN Intergovernmental Panel on Climate Change and a crisis response mechanism like the Financial Stability Board.[49] But it is hard to see the two leading technological powers, the United States and China, agreeing on technological norms when they disagree over so much else. The dynamic between them is intensely competitive and often antagonistic. US efforts to deny China access to high-end chip technology and components have driven Beijing to accelerate indigenous production, weakening Washington's leverage in influencing a future regime for AI governance.[50]

There is a more fundamental problem, too: the normative gulf between America and China. Their approaches to technology governance are diametrically opposed. There is no ready way to square the libertarianism of Silicon Valley (and the Trump White House) with the intrusive oversight and control practised by the Chinese state. Another, essentially unbridgeable, difference is the relative position of tech companies in the two countries. In the United States, Big Tech enjoys a level of power, influence and freedom that Chinese counterparts – Alibaba, Baidu, ByteDance and Tencent – can only dream of.

It is likely, then, that any future technological order will be fragmented, with different norms applying in different parts of the world – ranging from comprehensive state control in China to a much lighter touch in America.[51] It may eventually be possible to establish a multi-level, flexible international regime based on certain minimum rules – a rough code of conduct rather than a formal charter. But even to get to that point will require at the very least a significant improvement in US-China interstate relations.

## The information revolution

Information in its various dimensions will be at the forefront of the twenty-first-century global agenda. We are only at the beginning of a "permanent revolution", breathtaking in its speed and scale. The accelerated development of AI will have enormous implications for the presentation and dissemination of information. Critical conundrums, such as the trade-off between freedom of speech and responsibility/accountability, will become more acute. And non-state actors, primarily but not only in the form of Big Tech, will be pivotal to the success or failure of attempts to counter disinformation and safeguard the integrity of political processes.

The information revolution is generally a positive phenomenon. It is wonderful to enjoy unparalleled access to news and entertainment, and nothing highlights more the interconnectedness of the world. But the downside of the mass availability of information is that it has become increasingly difficult to distinguish between truth and falsehood. The former American diplomat and Senator Daniel Moynihan once wrote that "you are entitled to your own opinion. But you are not entitled to your own facts". That view seems quaint today, when one person's truth is often another person's lie. We are living in a "post-truth" world, or at least a world with multiple "truths".

Of course, during the Cold War there were sharply contradictory narratives emanating from Washington and Moscow (not to mention Beijing). And disinformation and propaganda are as old as the hills. But there are several features that mark the current era as different. One is the sheer volume of information/disinformation. Another is that the number of actors has proliferated; never has the global information space been so fiercely contested by so many. This competition (or worse) extends beyond the conventional binaries of East versus West, North versus South, or the democracy/autocracy divide. Notwithstanding the monopolistic instincts of Big Tech oligarchs, information has become thoroughly disaggregated and ubiquitous. Social media is out-muscling traditional modes of communication in responding to an insatiable hunger for news, entertainment and networking.[52] At the same time, much of this new media is scarcely accountable for its product, and cares little for basic standards of journalism. The environment has become anarchic in the literal sense of the word – that is, with no controlling rules or principles to give order.

Predictably, governments in liberal democracies are floundering. Politicians speak of the need to counter disinformation, but are reticent about proposing specific remedies. Understandably so, since the whole area of disinformation is a political, ethical and legal minefield. Much of the public debate revolves around the principle of freedom of speech, as enshrined in the First Amendment of the American Constitution and the foundation documents of many other democracies. Yet the real issue is *power* – winning the battle of narratives and influencing public policy, whatever the cost to truth or stability.[53]

The primacy of power considerations helps explain the fluctuations in Big Tech's approach to disinformation in recent years. During his first presidency, Trump was able to send thousands of mendacious posts without being shut down.[54] Facebook only suspended his account following the storming of the US Congress by a far-right mob he had incited, and when he was about to leave office. In the Biden years, Big Tech leaders sought to allay administration concerns about the risks of unchecked AI and disinformation. Various high-profile meetings took place in the White House, and noises were made about the importance of safeguarding against disinformation.

Today, the dynamic could hardly be more different. Over the course of 2024, as a Trump victory in the US presidential election appeared increasingly likely, Big Tech leaders changed their tune. Elon Musk became very active in supporting the Trump campaign, both financially and in getting the message out to a mass audience. Amazon's Jeff Bezos, owner of the liberal *Washington Post*, blocked the paper from endorsing Kamala Harris. Following Trump's victory, other Big Tech leaders lost no time in ingratiating themselves with the president-elect. It was apt that they should stand directly behind his immediate family during the inauguration ceremony.[55] On a more substantive level, Mark Zuckerberg closed down Facebook's fact-checking programme on the specious grounds of returning to "our roots around free expression".[56] In fact, he was simply adapting to the changed political situation by removing a major irritant to the Republican Party and to Trump himself. The notion of an objective truth was jettisoned, a casualty of personal self-interest.[57]

All this reflects the reality that disinformation does not occur in a vacuum, but thrives in a polarized and/or corrupt political culture. To attempt to fix the former without addressing the latter is akin to treating the symptoms of a disease rather than its causes. Social media organizations are rightly criticized for failing to regulate some of the content on their platforms, and they need to tighten controls over flagrant cases of disinformation – such as vaccine conspiracy theories, racist posts, and various other forms of "hate" messaging. But guiltier still are the politicians who routinely peddle falsehoods, and who foster a climate in which "truth" and "fake news" are whatever they decide.

Against this backdrop, there are few straightforward prescriptions. It has been suggested that more money should be invested in public broadcasting and local news outlets, and that the regulatory framework needs to be tightened.[58] These ideas are sensible, but they do not address the main issue. What is really required is a transformation of the relationship between politics and information. The only viable approach to countering disinformation is one that is inclusive, whereby state and non-state actors keep each other relatively honest, and the general public is actively involved. That requires government decision-makers to embrace a vibrant public sphere (see below); media conglomerates to recognize the benefits of competition and at least some regulation; and a shift away from collusive oligarchic arrangements.

Bringing about such a revolution in attitudes and policies may appear impossible. But the situation is more fluid than it looks. For the most part, the relationship between government and Big Tech is driven by narrow (and short-term) opportunism rather than deeply-held convictions. As such, it is susceptible to changing events and circumstances. The Trump-Musk bromance, notably, was cut short by the inevitable clash between two super egos. There may come a point, even quite soon, when Big Tech's self-centred libertarianism comes into conflict with US national security imperatives. Or there are growing tensions between Big Tech and the populist base of the Republican Party.[59] In time, a future Democratic President would almost certainly look to restore some controls over disinformation, all the more so if Big Tech becomes too closely associated with the Republican Party.

We should not assume, too, that people will tamely acquiesce to a system in which they are habitually deceived and disempowered. The growing blowback against the dominating influence of Big Tech suggests otherwise. The kind of disorder that has seen a stream of incumbent leaders ejected from power (see Prologue) indicates that the public cannot be taken for granted, and that it is not averse to disorder as a means of ensuring democratic expression and accountability, or simply out of frustration. Much as some governments and media moguls might wish to be left to their own devices, they would be prudent to recognize the "anarchic" instincts of the public and the destabilizing consequences of an environment where disinformation is routinized.

## Regulating the global information space

Attempting to establish a uniform regime to regulate the global information space is neither feasible nor desirable. It is difficult enough to develop a consensus in a single country, let alone attempt to apply common standards across multiple borders. US-China antagonism, so evident over technology, is even more pronounced when it comes to information and disinformation. Beijing regards Big Tech-led social media as subversive, while Washington views Chinese-owned outlets in a similarly hostile light, as the controversy over the operation of TikTok has highlighted.[60] Meanwhile, transatlantic relations in this area are becoming fractious as Big Tech enlists the US government in efforts to dilute social media regulation in the European Union. JD Vance's remarks at the 2025 Paris AI summit and then at the Munich Security Conference point to a normative chasm between America and Europe.[61]

All that said, we should not exclude the eventual emergence of some limited "rules of the road". Big Tech companies could, for example, play a pivotal role in facilitating a future US-China accommodation. Their political and economic influence in America, and commercial ties with China,[62] make them better suited than most to be a backchannel on information and technology issues. Although the obstacles are formidable, establishing some kind of regular, if informal, dialogue would be useful in itself. Big Tech could act as a "transmission belt" between Washington and Beijing – not only for communication on sensitive subjects, such as AI and cyber-intelligence, but also in reaching informal understandings about the limits of disinformation activities.[63]

## Civil society

And what of the general public? Where does it stand in relation to international order and global governance? As noted earlier, governments tend to view the public more as a challenge than an aid to problem solving, a reluctant lumpen mass that needs to be managed or marginalized.

Yet since ancient Athens, history has shown that states which encourage people to be active citizens reap the benefits. The connection between government and people has been critical to the success of the United States, the world's only true superpower, just as it was vital to the British Empire's fortunes in the nineteenth century. Engagement by civil society[64] lends legitimacy and support to foreign policy goals, while acting as a check – sometimes – to egregious errors and misjudgements. Even the exceptions often prove the rule. Had Tony Blair heeded popular opposition to the 2003 invasion of Iraq, one of the worst debacles of British foreign policy might have been avoided.

Public participation in foreign policy is set to expand dramatically in coming decades, regardless of the wishes of state actors. The ubiquity of issues such as climate change, technological transformation and the information revolution will override attempts by governments to monopolize decision-making. Already, the choice is no longer about whether or not to involve the public, but about creating the conditions under which its participation can be most beneficial.

## Transparency

One path is through more transparent decision-making. Politicians often treat the public as irredeemably ignorant and incurious. This is reflected in a reluctance to take it into their confidence and properly explain and debate issues. During the Brexit campaign, the senior Conservative MP Michael Gove epitomized this dumbing-down approach, when he claimed that the British people "have had enough of experts".[65] But in fact it was the pro-Brexit camp that had no use for pesky economic realities. The public's subsequent reaction to Covid-19 revealed it had plenty of time for genuine expertise[66]; its trust of the scientists contrasted vividly with its contempt for self-entitled politicians and corrupt businesspeople profiteering from the pandemic.

What matters here is not just the accuracy of information, but also the way it is conveyed. The public can be deceived by disinformation, become frustrated by poor communication, or simply resent being taken for granted. During the Brexit campaign, the main problem was not the lies and half-truths of the Leavers; it was the failure of the Remain camp to make a compelling case for Britain's continued membership of the European Union. Its uninspiring message was that membership would be less bad and less risky than withdrawal. Not surprisingly, this proved a loser.

Transparency is not without risk. The democratization of foreign policy will not automatically generate positive outcomes. People can be spooked by irrational fears as well as have genuine concerns. However, more often than not, treating the public as a rational actor and responsible partner offers better chances of governments making good decisions. One idea in this connection is to develop the institution of citizens' assemblies so that they contribute directly to policy-making rather than being essentially symbolic forums.[67]

## Accountability

Global problem solving in the twenty-first century is contingent on revitalizing domestic governance through the restoration of public standards and accountability. But this will not come without strenuous effort. We may be lucky. Just as the international system has laboured under the worst set of leaders in a century, so the wheel may turn and bring a new generation that is dynamic, imaginative and public-spirited. Or it may not. Bad governance is about much more than the failings of individual politicians. It reflects a broader environment that allows and even facilitates the emergence of authoritarian "strongmen", populist charlatans and ultra-nationalist opportunists.

The adage that every nation gets the government it deserves may seem harsh, but the governed as well as the governing should be accountable. All of us have a duty to be interested and active citizens. That means, in the first instance, owning the decisions we make. The bare minimum is registering and showing up to vote. But it also involves taking the time to educate oneself about the policy choices that are out there. Most of all, it means putting pressure on our democratic representatives to perform, rather than resigning ourselves to the seeming inevitability of misgovernment.

At the same time, we need to retain realistic expectations. One of the defects of the political culture of states, including democracies, is that we put our leaders on a pedestal. We demand they solve immensely difficult problems, and pillory them when they fail. But many of these problems – such as climate change – are the legacy of decades of failed policies, and so will not be easily fixed. We are entitled to expect decision-makers to be committed and energetic in pursuing solutions, but not that they should be miracle workers.

Publics are also guilty of expecting policy measures to be largely cost-free. We demand action on climate change, but are unwilling to adjust our life-style. We call for better public services, but object to the tax increases necessary to fund these. (As Oliver Wendell Holmes famously said, "taxes are the price we pay for a civilized society".) We regard immigrants as freeloaders, yet overlook their vital role in sustaining the public services (such as health and social care) we take for granted. In these circumstances, it is hardly surprising that we have seen the proliferation of unprincipled "personality" politicians, the corruption of politics by special interests, and policy bankruptcy on a systemic scale. We do not have to accept such miserable outcomes. Through active engagement, we can help raise domestic political standards, and in the process contribute to a more humane and dynamic international society.

## The primacy and limitations of nation-states

Today, state actors are asserting themselves on the global stage more than at any time since the end of the Cold War. Earlier hopes of a world built on universal values have given way to a resurgent nationalism. Defying predictions of its impending demise, Westphalia is back with a vengeance.

The notion, then, that national governments might be willing to share, or devolve, decision-making powers to non-state actors looks far-fetched. And yet that is what must happen if there is to be any serious prospect of a functioning international order. For the truth is that states have rarely been less well-equipped to meet the challenges before them – from climate change to pandemics, from technological transformation to the information revolution. With few exceptions, their responses have ranged from the mediocre to the inept, marked along the way by serial negligence and buck-passing. Governments continue to covet and cling on to power, but know not how to convert this into effective policy-making.

This situation is unsustainable in terms of addressing the twenty-first-century global agenda. But it is also bad news for the legitimacy and credibility of national governments themselves. Deception, disinformation and repression may cloud the issue for a while, but not indefinitely. In democracies, a failure to perform is punished by being voted out of office. But even authoritarian regimes are under mounting pressure to deliver, as highlighted by Xi Jinping's struggles to boost Chinese economic growth. Counter-intuitive as it must seem, it is in the *self-interest* of governments of all types to adopt a more inclusive and collaborative approach to decision-making – to share power, in other words. At a time when their capacity for problem solving has never been more stretched, and the whole process of governing has become infinitely more complex, policy-makers need all the help they can get.

States will remain the primary actors in the international system. But a state-centred order cannot be maintained on the same basis as before – through top-down direction and management by national governments. Increasingly, its viability is contingent on multiple players – non-state actors and civil society, as well as political elites – identifying a direct stake in positive outcomes and working together to make them happen. If there is to be an international society in the future, it will not resemble the relatively narrow "society of states" described by Hedley Bull half a century ago. It will be a much broader and more diverse *society of peoples* linked by shared interests and aspirations.

# EPILOGUE: TOMORROW'S WORLD

We are wont to assign epic significance to shocking events, to see them as reflections or harbingers of extraordinary change. In a speech three days after the Russian invasion of Ukraine, German Chancellor Olaf Scholz thus spoke of a "watershed" – *Zeitenwende* – in the history of the continent. The world, he declared, would no longer be the same, it would be defined by the contest between power and law.[1] In similar vein, the return of Donald Trump to the White House has come to be viewed as a political earthquake, one that has not only shaken American democracy, but also overturned fundamental norms of international behaviour.

It is easy to lose perspective in the face of such happenings. Stunned by the outrageous or the spectacular, we underestimate historical continuities and succumb to recency bias. Just in the last 25 years, one can make a fair case for 9/11, China's accession to the WTO, the US-led invasion of Iraq, the global financial crisis, and Covid-19 all being transformative moments. Were these any less significant in their wider impact than Putin's armed aggression or Trump's shock-and-awe approach to international relations? Through overuse, the modish concept of "inflection points" risks becoming meaningless.

Nevertheless, the current era does feel especially consequential. The Long Peace that has endured since the end of the Second World War is under greater threat than at any time since the Cuban Missile Crisis. US-China tensions could translate into a kinetic war, all the more lethal for the multiplier effect of technology. Global order is visibly unravelling, giving way to a new age of chronic disorder and fragmentation.

The present historical juncture transcends the binary simplicities of democracy versus autocracy and great power rivalry. It reflects a multi-dimensional world, in which many disparate challenges have coalesced to create a perfect storm that threatens the very future of international society. The breadth and complexity of these challenges resist ready solutions. It is definitely not the case that "the old playbooks may work just fine".[2] Some US policy-makers advocate "defeating" China as a straightforward prescription to the problem of global order and disorder.[3] If only things were that simple. Even if it were feasible, a hypothetical US "victory" over China would get us no closer to addressing runaway climate change, global poverty, more frequent and powerful pandemics, loss of control over the use of AI, and mass disinformation. Hawkishness may make (some) people feel good. But it is a prospectless course, condemning us to a Hobbesian "state of nature" from which we might never escape.

The central argument of this book is that we can do much better. Not by harking back to a lost world where the great powers arranged international order and kept the peace. That is a fantasy. But by looking forward to a world of possibilities as well as risks. In times of crisis and anxiety, such as we are living through, it is normal to experience a sense of helplessness. And it would be foolish to underestimate the scale of the task before us. Yet the situation is far from hopeless, and certainly nothing is written. So in this final chapter, I want to set out how a revitalized international society might emerge, not as a utopian dream, but as a concrete reality.

### The re-emergence of international society

The world I picture is one where there is some kind of functioning global order, to which a healthy majority of state and non-state actors would be committed. Major powers such as the United States and China would play leading roles, but the instinct to dominate would be tempered by awareness of the limits of their authority, and by the counterbalancing influence of other actors. The general observance of basic international norms would improve. Multilateral engagement would be boosted by the proliferation of diverse and flexible mechanisms. Liberal democracies would regain some of their purpose but discover humility. Global South countries would play active roles in global governance. And non-state actors would make vital contributions to international problem solving.

There would still be serious conflicts, and some problems – such as climate change and large-scale disinformation – might remain unresolved (or worsen). Often, it would be a matter of achieving least bad outcomes. Global order would be a relative concept. No party would be completely satisfied, while there would be many malcontents, plus others who retained a vested interest in disorder. But despite some negative trends, the overall direction of travel would be positive. We would not merely talk about the great challenges of our time, but actively face up to them.

How might such an order transpire, and why would states, especially major powers, abide by international rules and norms when they have played fast and loose with them for decades? Donald Trump has made it abundantly clear that he has no intention of subordinating his view of American interests to a wider rules-based order, and a future Democratic president would scarcely be any less "America-first" in this respect. It is similarly difficult to imagine that Beijing, even under a leader less authoritarian than Xi Jinping, would compromise on Chinese national interests. Factor into the mix an array of disruptive state and non-state actors, rising security tensions, geopolitical competition, global economic strains and virulent nationalism, and the case for pessimism appears unchallengeable.

However, we should not be so quick to rule out the re-emergence of a viable international society. What looks improbable today could become reality under the pressure of changing circumstances, and surprisingly quickly. It would not be the first time that unexpected outcomes have materialized from the most unpromising of environments. Suffice to recall the speed of the Soviet demise and end of the Cold War, China's spectacular rise from the depths of the Cultural Revolution, and the emergence of Franco-German entente and a common European identity after the Second World War. Trump's actions have sparked fears of a catastrophic breakdown of world order. And that cannot be excluded. But his presidency could also have the unintended consequence of stimulating international cooperation, by demonstrating just how unattractive the alternatives are to engagement in an interdependent world.

*Pathways to change*

There are several possible pathways by which a new global order might arise. One is a growing appreciation by states, including the major powers, that there are threats larger and more consuming than the usual rivalries. An issue such as climate change is still viewed as a second-order priority by most governments. But over the next few decades, its consequences will become much more pronounced and harder to deny. As extreme climate events become the norm rather than the exception, there will be mounting popular pressure on all governments to take decisive action. As the economic calculus increasingly favours renewable sources of energy and zero- or low-carbon development, investment will shift away from fossil fuels and carbon-intensive industries. As the impact on public health and welfare becomes intolerable, the threat of mass protests will grow. Diminishing food and water security in many parts of the world will lead to population movements that dwarf the refugee crises of today. In short, the universality, extreme gravity and immediacy of such problems will push them to the top of the agenda. Driven by self-interest and the instinct for political survival, governments will have to find ways of working with each other, overriding their geopolitical and ideological differences.

A second pathway to a new rules-based order is even more painful. Under this scenario, state actors engage in various forms of confrontation, including major war, before settling on another "Long Peace". Thus, we might initially see a process of "de-globalization" or rather attempts to move in this direction. The world divides along normative, political and economic lines. Unsurprisingly, this proves hugely counter-productive, not least for the interests of the major players. In time, they come to accept that a condition of more or less constant confrontation is debilitating, with consequences that are unsustainable.

War would be a disaster and a tragedy, and nobody sane could wish it. We should recall, however, that the original rules-based global order arose out of the destruction of the Second World War. Faced with the task of rebuilding the world, governments joined together in a remarkable cooperative enterprise. They did so despite significant differences in political systems, levels of economic development, social culture and world-views, in turn magnified by Cold War confrontation. The nightmare possibility of total war, including nuclear destruction, concentrated disparate minds on the common and absolute need to establish some sort of order that would help safeguard their collective security, rebuild shattered economies, and restore a relative normality. This led to the founding of the United Nations.

A major war between the United States and China would wreak tremendous destruction. It would not only impact the combatants, but also throw the Indo-Pacific region into chaos, massively disrupt international trade flows, and inflict enormous harm on the global economy. At the same time, a war on this scale might create the conditions – and the demand – for a comprehensive rules-based framework. By exposing the inadequacy of the existing international system, and the perils of chronic lawlessness and conflict, it would underline the vital importance of building a more inclusive, equitable and stable world.

A much safer pathway to a new rules-based order is through a heightened consciousness of the classic security dilemma: the more one party seeks to strengthen its national security at the expense of others, the more they strive to counterbalance and compensate for this. The disproportionate emphasis on military power today is engendering a multi-fronted arms race – nuclear, conventional, space, cyber – with no end (or slowing-down) in sight. At some stage, one or more parties may judge that this is unaffordable, especially when there are so many pressing global challenges that affect them directly and that need to be addressed urgently.

### Forces of change

With the steady diffusion of power around the world, the prospects of a viable international order and society may improve. There would be two processes at work. At one level, the leading powers recognize the limits to which they are able to prosecute their individual agendas and impose their vision of global governance. In these circumstances, they may welcome sharing the burdens of problem solving with an assortment of other players. For example, although Trump has disparaged allies and partners, he may come to appreciate their utility as the shortcomings of his unilateral, "America-first" approach are relentlessly exposed. Equally, Beijing may learn that it cannot cherry-pick which international norms to observe and which ones to ignore, without incurring major costs to China's security and prosperity.

At another level, middle powers, regional states and non-state actors become more self-confident and assertive – as is already happening. In previous chapters, I have highlighted the growing role of middle powers in conflict management, and of non-state actors in AI governance and mass information. Over time, the influence of these players is likely to spread to other areas of activity, resulting in a more disputatious, but also more dynamic and ultimately more resilient global order. Meanwhile, civil society becomes empowered, even in non- or partially democratic countries. Politicians are subject to greater scrutiny and accountability, and the demands for competent government grow more vociferous and difficult to resist.

The final element of a new international order is the revival of multilateral institutions. In a positive scenario, they would perform several critical functions. Most directly, they would be a primary channel through which different actors shape regional and global governance. Rules, enshrined and implemented through the action of such institutions, would acquire greater legitimacy. There would be a tighter nexus between the ideal of a rules-based order and the practical dividends of multilateral action. The diversity of international institutions turns out to be a blessing, encouraging engagement even from the usually sceptical. Cooperation would be selective and imperfect, and there would still be a de facto hierarchy of states, reflecting the relativities of power. Grandstanding and point-scoring would continue to obstruct substantive progress. But there would be an implicit recognition that multilateralism and its institutions are invaluable in helping to keep order and limit conflict; in providing a framework for global economic development; and in fostering a sense of international community.

## Principles of a new order

Underpinning all this would be the core principles of the new internationalism set out in Chapter 3: self-interest, representativeness and inclusiveness and flexibility. Any international order lives or dies depending on whether its constituent elements, principally nation-states, see such an order as being in their interest. During the Cold War, the US-led liberal order thrived because the collective

West that comprised its primary membership benefited greatly from it. And this success carried over into the first decade of the post-Cold War era; for a brief period, a sufficient mass of the world's nations trusted in a unitary, rules-based international order. But when this order came to be seen as both unfair *and* vulnerable, it began to unravel.

The biggest obstacle to a return to the "rules-based international order" is not Donald Trump, the opposition of a few "malign actors" or an "axis of upheaval".[4] It is that most nations feel marginalized, exploited or undervalued by such an order. They have come to view it as a Western construct, managed by the West for the benefit of the West. While they may not actively seek to detonate it, unlike Putin or Trump, neither are they committed to defending its "rules". That will only happen when they are integrated as full participants in global decision-making.

A new international order will need to be more representative and inclusive than any in history, appealing to the broadest range of stakeholders. In a world that has never been so globalized or interconnected, anything less will not hold. Such an order would have to transcend – at least some of the time – strategic rivalries, ideological fault-lines, and economic and social inequalities. It would also have to be more than a society of states, reaching across peoples as well.

A future international order would be based on the consolidation of certain basic principles, such as the inviolability of national borders, respect for territorial integrity and the peaceful resolution of disputes. Beyond that, it is unhelpful to be overly prescriptive. The aim should be to reinforce minimum standards of international behaviour, not to promote the values of liberal humanism – values that are either poorly understood, ignored or rejected outright by much of the world. A shift to a more pragmatic and flexible mindset is long overdue, one that accepts the world as inherently flawed, and engages with its constituent states on the basis of specific interests and synergies. Difficult as it undoubtedly is, cooperation with rivals and enemies is no less essential than with allies and partners. This is not about holding hands and singing kumbaya; it is realism in the truest sense, facing up to uncomfortable truths and responding to them in the best way possible.

Revitalizing international order will require immense effort and good fortune. Failure is a real possibility. However, there is no sensible alternative to attempting the enterprise. The classical Western "rules-based" vision lacks wider legitimacy and credibility. The great power-centred model imagined by realist thinkers is profoundly unrealistic. The "multipolar order" is an aspiration without substance. The intense self-centredness of Trump's "America-first" messianism offers little or nothing to others. And the existing world disorder is a ticket to a future of escalating dangers, up to and including major wars.

Although the Covid-19 pandemic exposed the selfishness and narrow-mindedness of states, it confirmed one abiding reality: twenty-first-century problems are global, and so must be their solutions. There will be no effective action on climate change absent such an approach. Poverty and inequality in the Global South impact directly on the Global North. Technological transformation and the information revolution will not be managed without non-state actors and civil society playing substantial roles. Those countries that are unwilling to look beyond the parochial and the short term will be among the prime casualties of change. Genuine security is interdependent. In the end, we live and flourish by working together to meet common threats and challenges, or we go down divided.

## Rethinking liberalism for a "post-liberal" age

Our story began with the unravelling of the post-Cold War liberal order, so it feels appropriate to end by considering how liberal norms and values might fit into a twenty-first-century "post-liberal" world.

It is common these days to write off liberalism. It is not only Vladimir Putin who believes that it is "obsolete",[5] so, too, do many people in the West. And others go through the motions of subscribing to liberal principles – democracy, the rule of law, the separation of powers, transparency and accountability – but then casually disregard them. At a time when liberalism is in depression around the world, it may therefore seem absurd to speak about its revival.

Nevertheless, there are reasons for cautious optimism. For one thing, the game is still afoot. The cause of liberalism has suffered a number of body blows, but it still enjoys a substantial lead in popularity over other value systems. Authoritarianism may be on the rise in some parts of the world, but it offers no coherent ideology, let alone one commanding broad support. The desire of countries for Chinese trade and investment should not be misconstrued as endorsement of a mythical "China model" or "Beijing consensus". This is a business transaction; governments seek Chinese funds, not Chinese values. Indeed, authoritarianism has rarely looked less fit for purpose as a basis for global governance. The excesses of Trump 2.0 have only underlined the incompatibility of the rule of self-styled "strong-men" with a functioning international society.

Liberal norms and institutions will continue to influence international order and society well into the current century. The question is how much. The decisive variable will be the extent to which their benefits are shared at home and abroad. Liberalism cannot afford to be identified with a brutish capitalism, whereby large parts of society are marginalized or abandoned. It needs to *reestablish the link between liberal values and good governance*. It must show itself to be humane and equitable as well as efficient; for the latter is hardly possible without the former. And just as the viability of contemporary liberalism depends on righting the imbalance between economic growth and social justice, so its prospects internationally are contingent on the West regaining a global conscience.

Liberalism has no automatic right to respect. Its values and norms are not *self-evidently* superior. Lecturing others about their shortcomings while behaving badly oneself has tarnished the notion of an international order founded on liberal principles. The task facing liberalism is therefore similar to that of the West in its Cold War struggle with the Soviet Union. It needs to outperform the competition, rather than whining about an uneven playing field or the unfair tactics of its opponents. Liberalism retains crucial advantages. The democracies of the West still count among the wealthiest and most technologically advanced countries in the world. Their political, economic, normative and cultural ties remain strong, enabling them to coordinate their actions closely. They have the soft power – resources and structures – to shape the global economy and to deliver trade, investment and humanitarian assistance to the world.

The fate of liberalism will not be determined by China, Russia or some *deus ex machina*, but within and by the West itself. The liberal international order may be gone, but liberalism itself has the potential to long outlive it and to shape global governance. However, that will require rethinking its nature and purpose. It would be foolish to imagine that liberal norms and institutions can be revived simply by countering Russian aggression, being tougher on China, or raising defence spending. More drastic action is needed, above all bringing integrity and generosity to Western policy-making. The collective West must demonstrate that it has drawn the right lessons from the suicidal statecraft that undermined its once dominant position in the world.

It must also show some self-belief. It is cruelly ironic that while Western governments have been preaching about "the rules-based international order", their own faith in liberal values has plummeted. This is evident not only in illiberal outliers like Hungary, but also in well-established democracies such as the United States, the United Kingdom, France and Germany. If liberalism falls out of favour in its own heartland, the likelihood of converts elsewhere is minuscule, as is the prospect of a global order influenced by liberal values. It is no coincidence that the heyday of liberalism's international appeal came in the 1990s when it was the dominant philosophy *within* Western democracies. Self-belief, but not self-entitlement, is indispensable to its future.

### A last word

One of the unhappy paradoxes of modern politics is that, at a time of extraordinary transformation, debates about global order and governance have become increasingly retrograde. Befuddled by the extent and speed of change, policy-makers have defaulted to replaying a series of "classic hits" on a constant loop – the "rules-based international order", multipolarity, "peace through strength", strategic containment, the Concert of great powers, the balance of power, and so on.

Such unreconstructed approaches promise nothing good. The world has moved on, and so must its governance. It is time we recast international order for the realities of this century, not the last. While not everything has to be reinvented, it is self-deceiving to think we can revert to standard prescriptions in response to challenges that are unprecedented in their character and scope. The generals of the past were sometimes accused of fighting the previous war, and to a large extent that is what we are doing today. Only worse. Because not only are we resorting to failed strategies and poor tactics, we are also missing or underestimating the main threats. No amount of military spending or strategic balancing will mitigate the escalating effects of climate change or help protect us against future pandemics. In an age of permanent technological revolution, old-fashioned geopolitical "truths" will hardly seem relevant if AI and disinformation are allowed to run amok.

We have a real opportunity to revitalize global governance and international society. But time's a wasting. As grim as today's world disorder looks, it could yet deteriorate further on multiple fronts. Indeed, we might even come to view the present era with some nostalgia, as a period of relative peace, and when the challenges before us still felt manageable. So we have a duty to seize the moment while we still can. If we fail to do so, it may be a very long time before we get another chance.

# NOTES

## Prologue: a parable of global disorder

1. Robert Ford, "Kamala Harris is just the latest victim of global trend to oust incumbents", *The Observer*, 10 November 2024, https://www.theguardian.com/global/2024/nov/10/kamala-harris-is-just-the-latest-victim-of-global-trend-to-oust-incumbents.
2. "We are inching ever closer to a Great Fracture in economic and financial systems and trade relations; one that threatens a single, open internet; with diverging strategies on technology and artificial intelligence; and potentially clashing security frameworks" – address by Antonio Guterres, UN General Assembly, 19 September 2023, https://www.un.org/sg/en/content/sg/speeches/2023-09-19/secretary-generals-address-the-general-assembly#:~:text=We%20are%20inching%20ever%20closer,and%20potentially%20clashing%20security%20frameworks.

## Introduction

1. Hedley Bull, *The Anarchical Society: A Study of Order in World Politics* (Palgrave, 3rd edition, 2002; originally published in 1977), 40.
2. *Ibid.*, 13.
3. Other terms to describe the current global crisis include "polycrisis" and a "confluence of calamities". See Adam Tooze, "Welcome to the world of the polycrisis", *Financial Times*, 28 October 2022, https://www.ft.com/content/498398e7-11b1-494b-9cd3-6d669dc3de33; and Nouriel Roubini, "Davos elites need to wake up to 'megathreats' the world is facing", *The Guardian*, 19 January 2023, https://www.theguardian.com/business/2023/jan/19/davos-megathreats-imf-economic-financial-challenges.
4. Steven Pinker, *Enlightenment Now: The Case for Reason, Science, Humanism and Progress* (Penguin, 2019).
5. Christopher Clark, *The Sleepwalkers: How Europe Went to War in 1914* (Penguin, 2014).
6. *Emissions Gap Report: No more hot air ... please!* UN Environment Programme, 24 October 2024, https://www.unep.org/resources/emissions-gap-report-2024, 33.
7. Larry Brilliant, Mark Smolinski, Lisa Danzig and Ian Lipkin, "Inevitable outbreaks: how to stop an age of spillovers from becoming an age of pandemics", *Foreign Affairs*, January/February 2023, https://www.foreignaffairs.com/world/inevitable-outbreaks-spillovers-pandemics.
8. According to the World Bank, 2020–30 is "set to be a lost decade" in global poverty reduction. As of October 2024, nearly 700 million people were living in extreme poverty, or on less than $2.15 a day, *Pathways out of the Polycrisis: Poverty, Prosperity, and Planet Report*, World Bank, October 2024, https://www.worldbank.org/en/publication/poverty-prosperity-and-planet.

9. See Richard Haass and Charles Kupchan, "The new Concert of Powers: how to prevent catastrophe and promote stability in a multipolar world", *Foreign Affairs*, 23 March 2021, https://www.foreignaffairs.com/articles/world/2021-03-23/new-concert-powers.
10. The term "Global South" is amorphous, describing some 134 countries, from major powers like China and India to the weakest and most backward of states. Yet it has become enshrined within the United Nations (for example, through the UN Office for South-South Cooperation – UNOSSC) and many governments find it useful to self-identify as part of the Global South.
11. Margaret Macmillan, *Nixon and Mao: The Week that Changed the World* (Random House, 2008).
12. John Ikenberry, *A World Safe for Democracy: Liberal Internationalism and the Crises of Global Order* (Yale, 2020), 258.
13. Thomas Hobbes, *The Leviathan* (Penguin, 1976 [original published in 1651]), 188.
14. As the founder of utilitarianism Jeremy Bentham put it: "The greatest happiness of the greatest number is the foundation of morals and legislation" (in *The Commonplace Book*).
15. William Burns, "A world transformed and the role of intelligence", 59th Ditchley Annual Lecture, 1 July 2023, https://www.ditchley.com/sites/default/files/Ditchley%20Annual%20Lecture%202023%20transcript.pdf.
16. Remarks by President Biden at the 2021 Virtual Munich Security Conference, 19 February 2021.

## 1. The rise and fall of the liberal order

1. John Ikenberry, *A World Safe for Democracy: Liberal Internationalism and The Crises of Global Order* (Yale, 2020), 180.
2. Charles Krauthammer, "The unipolar moment: America and the world 1990", *Foreign Affairs*, 1 January 1990, https://www.foreignaffairs.com/articles/1990-01-01/unipolar-moment.
3. Ikenberry, *A World Safe for Democracy*, 257.
4. In a mid-air collision, a Chinese J-8 interceptor fighter crashed, with the loss of the pilot, while the EP-3 had to make an emergency landing on Hainan, following which its crew was detained for 10 days. The incident had no lasting effect on US-China relations, which flourished in the years following.
5. "Russian-Chinese Joint Declaration on a Multipolar World and the Establishment of a New International Order", 23 April 1997, https://digitallibrary.un.org/record/234074?ln=en.
6. In October 1983, the United States launched a brief military invasion of Grenada, taking advantage of internal strife within the pro-Soviet People's Revolutionary Government.
7. See Fareed Zakaria, *The Post-American World* (Norton, 2009); Kishore Mahbubani, *The New Asian Hemisphere: The Irresistible Shift of Global Power to The East* (Public Affairs, 2008).
8. Andrei Kozyrev, "The lagging partnership", *Foreign Affairs*, May/June 1994, https://www.foreignaffairs.com/articles/russian-federation/1994-05-01/lagging-partnership.
9. George H. W. Bush, "Address to a joint session of the Congress on the Persian Gulf crisis and the budget deficit", 11 September 1990, https://bush41library.tamu.edu/archives/public-papers/2217.
10. Xi Jinping's address at the 19th Party Congress, 18 October 2017, https://www.chinadaily.com.cn/china/19thcpcnationalcongress/2017-11/04/content_34115212.htm.
11. As far back as 2013, Putin was already claiming that Russia and Ukraine were "one people" and that Ukraine was "part of our greater Russian world" – remarks to the Valdai International Discussion Club, 19 September 2013, http://en.kremlin.ru/events/president/news/19243.
12. Putin speech at the Munich Security Conference, 10 February 2007, http://en.kremlin.ru/events/president/transcripts/24034.

13. The term "suicidal statecraft" originated with the British historian Arnold Toynbee in his epic work *The Study of History*. It was later used by Zbigniew Brzezinski to describe the US-led invasion of Iraq. See Zbigniew Brzezinski, "George W. Bush's suicidal statecraft", *New York Times*, 13 October 2005, https://www.nytimes.com/2005/10/13/opinion/geo rge-w-bushs-suicidal-statecraft.html.
14. The "coalition of the willing" eventually expanded to 48 members, but only 4 countries participated in the invasion: the United States, the United Kingdom, Australia and Poland.
15. Martin Wolf, *The Crisis of Democratic Capitalism* (Penguin, 2023), 115–17.
16. Article 1 of the Budapest Memorandum committed Russia, the United States and the United Kingdom to "respect the independence and sovereignty and the existing borders of Ukraine". Under Article 2, they agreed to "refrain from the threat or use of force against the territorial integrity or political independence of Ukraine", https://treaties.un.org/Pages/showDetails.aspx?objid=0800000280401fbb.
17. Article 2 of the Treaty on Friendship, Cooperation and Partnership stated that the two countries "shall respect each other's territorial integrity and confirm the inviolability of their common borders", https://treaties.un.org/Pages/showDetails.aspx?objid=08000002803e6fae.
18. "We showed ourselves to be weak. And the weak get beaten" – Putin television address after the Beslan school massacre, 4 September 2004, http://www.en.kremlin.ru/events/president/transcripts/22589.
19. Hobbes, *The Leviathan*, 188.
20. The most serious sanctions related to the denial of advanced energy industry technology and investment. This ended a number of major projects, in particular the ExxonMobil-Rosneft venture in the Kara Sea.
21. "Obama, in dig at Putin, calls Russia 'regional power'", Reuters, 25 March 2014, https://www.reuters.com/article/us-ukraine-crisis-russia-weakness-idUSBREA2O19J20140325.
22. Russia's share of German gas imports grew from 38 per cent in 2014 to 55 per cent in 2022. See Noah Gordon, "Germany finally starts to turn from Russian gas", *Internationale Politik Quarterly*, 31 March 2022, https://ip-quarterly.com/en/germany-finally-starts-turn-russian-gas. In June 2021, Angela Merkel was able to secure US acquiescence for the Nordstream-2 gas pipeline to go ahead.
23. The Minsk agreements of September 2014 ("Minsk I") and February 2015 ("Minsk II") were intended to "freeze" the conflict between the Ukrainian government and Russian proxy forces in the Donbass. Their practical consequence, however, was to legitimize Moscow's de facto annexation of parts of southeast Ukraine. In time, this control prepared the way for the full Russian invasion of Ukraine in February 2022.
24. For a compelling account of Obama's hesitancy and its wider consequences, see Jeremy Bowen, *The Making of the Modern Middle East: A Personal History* (Picador, 2022), 206–210.
25. "Trump confirms he threatened to withdraw from NATO", Atlantic Council, 23 August 2018, https://www.atlanticcouncil.org/blogs/natosource/trump-confirms-he-threatened-to-withdraw-from-nato/; "Trump: EU is one of United States' biggest foes", *Politico*, 15 July 2018, https://www.politico.eu/article/donald-trump-putin-russia-europe-one-of-uni ted-states-biggest-foes/.
26. "We will lead not merely by the example of our power but by the power of our example", Biden inaugural address, 20 January 2021, https://www.whitehouse.gov/briefing-room/speeches-remarks/2021/01/20/inaugural-address-by-president-joseph-r-biden-jr/.
27. The recollections of former senior Trump administration officials are damning. See Jeffrey Goldberg, "James Mattis denounces President Trump, describes him as a threat to the Constitution", *The Atlantic*, 3 June 2020, https://www.theatlantic.com/politics/archive/2020/06/james-mattis-denounces-trump-protests-militarization/612640/; "John Bolton: ten biggest claims in his Donald Trump book", BBC News, 20 June 2020, https://www.bbc.co.uk/news/world-us-canada-53089609; and Fiona Hill's testimony to the Trump impeachment inquiry, *PBS*, 8 November 2019, https://www.pbs.org/newshour/politics/read-the-transcript-of-fiona-hills-full-testimony-in-the-impeachment-probe.

28. WHO Covid-19 dashboard, 26 May 2024, https://data.who.int/dashboards/covid19/deaths?n=o. An article in the medical journal, *The Lancet*, estimates the number of Covid-19-related deaths at 18.2 million between 1 January 2020 and 31 December 2021. See "Estimating excess mortality due to the COVID-19 pandemic: a systematic analysis of COVID-19-related mortality, 2020-21", *The Lancet*, 16 April 2022, https://www.thelancet.com/article/S0140-6736(21)02796-3/fulltext.

29. Gordon Brown, *Seven Ways to Change the World* (Simon & Schuster, 2021), 48.

30. According to UN Secretary-General Guterres, more than 130 countries had yet to receive a single vaccine dose by February 2021, with 10 countries accounting for 75 per cent of Covid-19 vaccinations. See "COVID-19 vaccination: 'wildly unfair': UN Secretary-General", UN News, 17 February 2021, https://news.un.org/en/story/2021/02/1084962. The situation improved slightly over the course of the year, but even by August the 30 poorest countries in the world had only managed to vaccinate an average of 2 per cent of their populations. See Kenan Malik, "The rich nations" take on the world post-pandemic? 'I'm all right, Jack'", *The Guardian*, 29 August 2021, https://www.theguardian.com/commentisfree/2021/aug/29/the-rich-nations-take-on-the-world-post-pandemic-im-all-right-jack.

31. The 2022 CHIPS and Science Act aimed to develop an indigenous semi-conductor industry through large-scale investment (USD 280 billion over ten years) in research and development, and manufacturing. Its main areas of focus were quantum computing, AI, clean energy and nanotechnology. See "The CHIPS and Science Act: here's what's in it", McKinsey, 4 October 2022, https://www.mckinsey.com/industries/public-sector/our-insights/the-chips-and-science-act-heres-whats-in-it.

32. Remarks by President Biden in Vilnius, 12 July 2023, https://www.whitehouse.gov/briefing-room/speeches-remarks/2023/07/12/remarks-by-president-biden-on-supporting-ukraine-defending-democratic-values-and-taking-action-to-address-global-challenges-vilnius-lithuania/. As of October 2024, total US military assistance to Ukraine amounted to $64.1 billion. See "US security cooperation with Ukraine", State Department press release, 21 October 2024, https://www.state.gov/u-s-security-cooperation-with-ukraine/.

33. "US opposes offering Ukraine a roadmap to NATO membership", *Financial Times*, 6 April 2023, https://www.ft.com/content/c37ed22d-e0e4-4b03-972e-c56af8a36d2e.

34. "Watch: Biden's disastrous few weeks … in 90 seconds", BBC News, 22 July 2024, https://www.bbc.co.uk/news/videos/cx028eq4qg1o.

35. Susan Shirk, *China: Fragile Superpower* (Oxford University Press, 2007), 239.

## 2. A world disorder

1. Ken Jowitt, *New World Disorder: The Leninist Extinction* (University of California, 1992), 264.

2. *Ibid.*, 283.

3. *Ibid.*, 263. See also Francis Fukuyama, "The end of history?", *The National Interest*, no. 16, Summer 1989, 3–18.

4. "… it is manifest that during the time men live without a common power to keep them all in awe, they are in that condition, which is called warre" – Hobbes, *The Leviathan*, 185.

5. Bruce Jones, "Instrument of order: does the UN Security Council matter in an era of Global South diplomacy and major power tensions?", Brookings, 3 June 2024, https://www.brookings.edu/articles/instrument-of-order/.

6. Bafundi Maronoti, "Revisiting the international role of the US dollar", *BIS Quarterly Review*, December 2022, https://www.bis.org/publ/qtrpdf/r_qt2212x.htm.

7. As Michael Kimmage has observed, "none of the usual descriptors of world order apply anymore: the international system is not unipolar or bipolar or multipolar" – in "The world Trump wants: American power in the new age of nationalism", *Foreign Affairs*, March/April 2025, https://www.foreignaffairs.com/united-states/world-trump-wants-michael-kimmage.

8. Deng Xiaoping's 24-character strategy translates as follows: "Observe calmly; secure our position; cope with affairs calmly; hide our capacities and bide our time; be good at maintaining a low profile; and never claim leadership".

9. Rush Doshi, *The Long Game: China's Grand Strategy to Displace American Order* (Oxford University, 2021).

10. "A global community of shared future: China's proposals and actions", State Council Information Office, September 2023, https://www.mfa.gov.cn/eng/xw/zyxw/202405/t20 240530_11332291.html. See also "Following the Vision of a Community with a Shared Future for Mankind and Bringing More Certainty to World Peace and Development", Prime Minister Li Qiang's speech at the Boao Forum, 30 March 2023, https://www.fmprc. gov.cn/eng/wjdt_665385/zyjh_665391/202303/t20230331_11052581.html.

11. Alexander Lukin, "Have we passed the peak of Sino-Russian rapprochement?", *The Washington Quarterly* 44:3 (2021), 162–7.

12. At the Anchorage 2+2 meeting in March 2021, the first high-level US-China encounter following Biden's election as president, State Councillor for Foreign Affairs Yang Jiechi questioned America's right to impose an interpretation of the rules-based international order "advocated by a small number of countries" – in *Nikkei Asia*, 19 March 2021, https:// asia.nikkei.com/Politics/International-relations/US-China-tensions/How-it-happened-Transcript-of-the-US-China-opening-remarks-in-Alaska.

13. Bobo Lo, "Turning point? Putin, Xi, and the Russian invasion of Ukraine", Lowy Institute Analysis, 25 May 2022, https://www.lowyinstitute.org/publications/turning-point-putin-xi-russian-invasion-ukraine.

14. Following the Spanish-American war of 1898, the United States acquired the Spanish overseas territories of Puerto Rico, Guam, the Philippines and, briefly, Cuba. The same year, it annexed Hawaii.

15. Eric Storm, "How Putin, Xi and now Trump are ushering in a new imperial age", *The Conversation*, 7 February 2025, https://theconversation.com/how-putin-xi-and-now-trump-are-ushering-in-a-new-imperial-age-248160.

16. *Mandate for Leadership: The Conservative Promise*, Heritage Foundation, April 2023.

17. As Stephen Walt puts it, "no other president has made his time in office so nakedly about himself" – in "How Trump will be remembered", *Foreign Policy*, 30 June 2025, https:// foreignpolicy.com/2025/06/30/trump-president-us-history.

18. Paul Kirby, "Trump says Nato's new 5% defence spending pledge a 'big win'", BBC News, 25 June 2025, https://www.bbc.co.uk/news/articles/cj4en8djwyko.

19. Sarah Smith, "EU and US agree trade deal, with 15% tariffs for European exports to America", BBC News, 27 July 2025, https://www.bbc.co.uk/news/articles/cx2xylk3d07o.

20. David Miliband, "Welcome to the age of impunity", address to the World Economic Forum, 24 January 2020, https://www.rescue.org/press-release/welcome-age-impunity-david-milibands-world-economic-forum-speech.

21. UN Charter, https://www.un.org/en/about-us/un-charter/full-text.

22. Bull, *The Anarchical Society*, 13.

23. "Universal Declaration of Human Rights (1948): drafting history", https://research.un.org/ en/undhr/draftingcommittee#s-lg-box-wrapper-3385355.

24. *Freedom in the World 2025: The Uphill Battle to Safeguard Rights*, Freedom House, February 2025, https://freedomhouse.org/sites/default/files/2025-02/FITW_World_2025_ Feb.2025.pdf.

25. "JD Vance attacks Europe over free speech and migration", BBC News, 14 February 2025, https://www.bbc.co.uk/news/articles/ceve3wl21x1o.

26. Thucydides, The Melian Dialogue, in *History of the Peloponnesian War.*

27. Yang Jiechi comments to Singapore Foreign Minister George Yeo at the ASEAN Ministerial meeting in Hanoi, July 2010 – in Joshua Kurlantzick, "The belligerents", *The New Republic*, 27 July 2011, https://newrepublic.com/article/82211/china-foreign-policy.

28. Bilahari Kausikan, "Navigating the new age of great-power competition: statecraft in the shadow of US-Chinese rivalry", *Foreign Affairs*, 11 April 2023, https://www.foreignaffairs.com/united-states/china-great-power-competition-russia-guide.
29. Matias Spektor, "In defense of the fence sitters: what the West gets wrong about hedging", *Foreign Affairs*, May/June 2023, https://www.foreignaffairs.com/world/global-south-defense-fence-sitters.
30. Shivshankar Menon, "Out of alignment: what the war in Ukraine has revealed about non-Western powers", *Foreign Affairs*, 9 February 2023, https://www.foreignaffairs.com/world/out-alignment-war-in-ukraine-non-western-powers-shivshankar-menon.
31. Linda Kinstler, "Are we witnessing the death of international law?", *The Guardian*, 26 June 2025, https://www.theguardian.com/law/2025/jun/26/are-we-witnessing-the-death-of-international-law.
32. Euan Graham, "The Hague tribunal's South China Sea ruling: empty provocation or slow-burning influence?", Council on Foreign Relations, 18 August 2016, https://www.cfr.org/councilofcouncils/global-memos/hague-tribunals-south-china-sea-ruling-empty-provocation-or-slow-burning-influence.
33. Michael Robbins, Amaney Jamal and Mark Tessler, "America is losing the Arab world: and China is reaping the benefits", *Foreign Affairs*, July/August 2024, https://www.foreignaffairs.com/united-states/america-losing-arab-world.
34. "Biden says ICC war crimes arrest warrant 'outrageous'", BBC News, 22 November 2024, https://www.bbc.co.uk/news/articles/c704y7gwr95o; also "US signals support for possible ICC sanctions over Israel warrants", BBC News, 21 May 2024, https://www.bbc.co.uk/news/articles/cp66e6ppzd0o.
35. "Imposing sanctions on the International Criminal Court", Executive Order 14203, The White House, 6 February 2025, https://www.whitehouse.gov/presidential-actions/2025/02/imposing-sanctions-on-the-international-criminal-court/.
36. "Oil vs human rights: Biden's controversial mission to Saudi Arabia", *Financial Times*, 15 June 2022, https://www.ft.com/content/b3c93eeb-9a79-49df-bd1a-3a82052319ff.
37. Niccolo Machiavelli, *The Prince* (Penguin, 2009 [original published in 1515]), 66.
38. Joint Statement of the Russian Federation and the People's Republic of China, 4 February 2022, http://www.en.kremlin.ru/supplement/5770.
39. Bull, *The Anarchical Society*, 40.
40. Francine Uenuma, "The 1983 military drill that nearly sparked nuclear war with the Soviets", *Smithsonian Magazine*, 27 April 2023, https://www.smithsonianmag.com/history/the-1983-military-drill-that-nearly-sparked-nuclear-war-with-the-soviets-180979980/.

## 3. Principles of a new internationalism

1. "Citizenship in a republic", Theodore Roosevelt speech to the Sorbonne, Paris, 23 April 1910, https://www.theodorerooseveltcenter.org/Learn-About-TR/TR-Encyclopedia/Culture-and-Society/Man-in-the-Arena.aspx.
2. Robert Kagan, "A superpower like it or not: why Americans must accept their global role", *Foreign Affairs*, March/April 2021, https://www.foreignaffairs.com/articles/united-states/2021-02-16/superpower-it-or-not.
3. "US Vice-President Vance shuns Scholz and meets AfD party leader instead", *Euronews*, 14 February 2025, https://www.euronews.com/2025/02/14/us-vice-president-vance-shuns-scholz-and-meets-afd-party-leader-instead.
4. Graham Allison, *Destined for War: Can America and China Escape Thucydides' Trap?* (Scribe, 2018), 29.
5. Richard Haass and Charles Kupchan propose a group of six: the United States, China, the European Union, India, Japan and Russia. Among multiple other issues, the lack of any representation from Africa or Latin America reinforces a stark North–South dichotomy.

See "The new Concert of Powers: how to prevent catastrophe and promote stability in a multipolar world", *Foreign Affairs*, 23 March 2021, https://www.foreignaffairs.com/articles/world/2021-03-23/new-concert-powers.

6. Antonio Guterres, "Secretary-General's address to the General Assembly", 19 September 2023, https://www.un.org/sg/en/content/sg/speeches/2023-09-19/secretary-generals-address-the-general-assembly.

7. See Amitav Acharya, "Understanding the emerging multiplex world order", University College of London, 1 July 2019, https://www.ucl.ac.uk/global-governance/news/2019/jul/understanding-emerging-multiplex-world-order.

8. Robert O'Brien, "The return of peace through strength: making the case for Trump's foreign policy", *Foreign Affairs*, July/August 2024, https://www.foreignaffairs.com/united-states/return-peace-strength-trump-obrien.

9. "China has become a scientific superpower", *The Economist*, 12 June 2024, https://www.economist.com/science-and-technology/2024/06/12/china-has-become-a-scientific-superpower.

10. See "America's assassination attempt on Huawei is backfiring", *The Economist*, 13 June 2024, https://www.economist.com/briefing/2024/06/13/americas-assassination-attempt-on-huawei-is-backfiring.

11. "DeepSeek: the Chinese AI app that has the world talking", BBC News, 27 January 2005, https://www.bbc.co.uk/news/articles/c5yv5976z9po.

12. Greg Torode, Eduardo Baptista and Tim Kelly, "China's aircraft carriers play 'theatrical' role but pose little threat yet", Reuters, 5 May 2023, https://www.reuters.com/world/chinas-aircraft-carriers-play-theatrical-role-pose-little-threat-yet-2023-05-05/.

13. Joseph Nye, "Get smart: combining hard and soft power", *Foreign Affairs*, July/August 2009, https://www.foreignaffairs.com/united-states/get-smart.

14. Jacob Poushter, Moira Fagan and Sneha Gubbala, "Climate change remains top global threat across 19-country survey", Pew Research Center, 31 August 2022, https://www.pewresearch.org/global/2022/08/31/climate-change-remains-top-global-threat-across-19-country-survey/.

15. Maximilian Kotz, Anders Levermann and Leonie Wenz, "The Economic Commitment of Climate Change", *Nature*, 17 April 2024, https://www.nature.com/articles/s41586-024-07219-0.

16. In his concept of a "multiplex world", Amitav Acharya focuses on the "interaction capacity" of diverse international actors. He describes "a broader pattern of interdependence, covering not just trade, but also investment flows, production networks, supply chains, and common ecological and other transnational challenges". See Amitav Acharya, Antoni Estevadeordal and Louis Goodman, "Multipolar or multiplex? Interaction capacity, global cooperation and world order", *International Affairs* 99:6 (November 2023), 2341.

17. Ian Bremmer, "Globalization isn't dead: the world is more fragmented, but interdependence still rules", *Foreign Affairs*, 25 October 2022, https://www.foreignaffairs.com/world/globalization-isnt-dead.

18. The WHO's definition, cited in "Globalization: definition, benefits, effects, examples – what is globalization?", *YouMatter*, 6 October 2020, https://youmatter.world/en/definition/definitions-globalization-definition-benefits-effects-examples/.

19. Trade and investment core statistics book, UK government, updated 22 February 2024, https://www.gov.uk/government/statistics/trade-and-investment-core-statistics-book/trade-and-investment-core-statistics-book.

20. For a superb analysis of the qualities of leadership, see Doris Kearns Goodwin, *Leadership: Lessons from the Presidents for Turbulent Times* (Viking, 2018).

21. "World's largest study of global climate related mortality links 5 million deaths a year to abnormal temperatures", Monash University press release, 8 July 2021, https://www.monash.edu/news/articles/worlds-largest-study-of-global-climate-related-mortality-links-5-million-deaths-a-year-to-abnormal-temperatures.

22. "Climate change and health", World Health Organization fact sheet, 30 October 2021, https://www.who.int/news-room/fact-sheets/detail/climate-change-and-health.

23. Ajit Niranjan, "Heatwave last summer killed 61,000 people in Europe, research finds", *The Guardian*, 10 July 2023, https://www.theguardian.com/environment/2023/jul/10/heatw ave-last-summer-killed-61000-people-in-europe-research-finds.

24. The COP 29 (2024) summit in Baku, Azerbaijan, showed how far developing nations still need to go before their interests are taken properly into account. They had sought $1.3 trillion in climate financing from developed nations, but received only a loose and heavily qualified promise of $300 billion. The summit communique also omitted any mention of transitioning away from fossil fuels. See David Vetter, "Developing nations and Nonprofits reject 'disaster' COP29 deal", *Forbes*, 25 November 2024, https://www.forbes.com/sites/ davidrvetter/2024/11/24/developing-nations-and-nonprofits-reject-disaster-cop29-clim ate-deal/.

25. See Martin Wolf, *The Crisis of Democratic Capitalism* (Penguin, 2023), 176–214.

26. Ryan Haas, "Ukraine presents opportunity to test China's strategic outlook", Brookings commentary, 1 March 2022, https://www.brookings.edu/articles/ukraine-presents-oppo rtunity-to-test-chinas-strategic-outlook/.

## 4. The United States, China and the making of a twenty-first-century relationship

1. Martin Jacques, *When China Rules the World: The Rise of the Middle Kingdom and the End of the Western World* (Allen Lane, 2009).

2. Susan Shirk, *China: Fragile Superpower* (Oxford University Press, 2007).

3. "America's leadership is what holds the world together" – remarks by President Joe Biden, White House, 20 October 2023, https://www.whitehouse.gov/briefing-room/speeches-remarks/2023/10/20/remarks-by-president-biden-on-the-unites-states-response-to-ham ass-terrorist-attacks-against-israel-and-russias-ongoing-brutal-war-against-ukraine/.

4. Trump presidential inaugural address, Washington DC, 20 January 2025, https://www.whi tehouse.gov/remarks/2025/01/the-inaugural-address/.

5. Biden presidential inaugural address, Washington DC, 20 January 2021, https://www.whi tehouse.gov/briefing-room/speeches-remarks/2021/01/20/inaugural-address-by-presid ent-joseph-r-biden-jr/.

6. At the 2025 NATO summit in The Hague, European member states pledged to spend 5 per cent of GDP on defence and defence-related priorities by 2035. If implemented – an unlikely prospect on past performance – it would mark a dramatic change. As late as 2021, only 6 alliance members had reached or exceeded the 2 per cent of GDP threshold agreed back in 2006 by NATO defence ministers.

7. Henry Foy and Demetri Sevastopulo, "US steps up pressure on European allies to harden China stance", *Financial Times*, 29 November 2022, https://www.ft.com/content/1ac33 4c2-4ef5-480e-9863-5d9f00daa16b.

8. Jamil Anderlini and Clea Caulcutt, "Europe must resist pressure to become 'America's followers', says Macron", Politico, 9 April 2023, https://www.politico.eu/article/emmanuel-macron-china-america-pressure-interview/.

9. Joe Leahy, James Kynge and Benjamin Parkin, "Ten years of China's Belt and Road: what has $1tn achieved?", *Financial Times*, 22 October 2023, https://www.ft.com/content/ 83501dd5-fe6d-4169-9d83-28a8cf46e681.

10. Shahar Hameiri and Lee Jones, "Why the West's alternative to China's international infrastructure is failing", *European Journal of International Relations*, 22 December 2023, https://journals.sagepub.com/doi/10.1177/13540661231218573.

11. "East Asia can't rely on the Indo-Pacific economic framework", *East Asia Forum*, 25 March 2024, https://eastasiaforum.org/2024/03/25/east-asia-cant-rely-on-the-indo-paci fic-economic-framework/.

12. "Xi Jinping tries to press China's advantage in Latin America", *The Economist*, 8 May 2025, https://www.economist.com/the-americas/2025/05/08/xi-jinping-tries-to-press-chinas-advantage-in-south-america.

13. The absence of a functioning Appellate Body has encouraged the practice of "appealing into the void", whereby countries are able to nullify adverse WTO rulings by challenging them in the knowledge that they cannot be reviewed and are therefore unenforceable. See Kristen Hopewell, "The world is abandoning the WTO: and America and China are leading the way", *Foreign Affairs*, 7 October 2024, https://www.foreignaffairs.com/united-sta tes/world-abandoning-wto-china-leading-way-kristen-hopewell.

14. Robert Greene, "China's dollar dilemma", Carnegie Endowment for International Peace, 3 October 2024, https://carnegieendowment.org/research/2024/10/chinas-dollar-dile mma?lang=en.

15. Lex Harvey, "How a Trump-fueled brain drain could be the rest of the world's brain gain", *CNN*, 1 June 2025, https://edition.cnn.com/2025/06/01/world/trump-brain-drain-harvard-intl-hnk.

16. Zongyuan Zoe Lu, "How China armed itself for the trade war: Beijing's high-risk approach to its economic confrontation with Washington", *Foreign Affairs*, 29 April 2025, https://www.foreignaffairs.com/united-states/how-china-armed-itself-trade-war.

17. Adam Posen, "The true dangers of Trump's economic plans: his radical agenda would wreak havoc on American businesses, workers and consumers", *Foreign Affairs*, 18 October 2024, https://www.foreignaffairs.com/united-states/true-dangers-trump-presidency-economic-plans.

18. "Trump's tariff turbulence is worse than anyone imagined", *The Economist*, 5 March 2025, https://www.economist.com/finance-and-economics/2025/03/05/trumps-tariffs-are-worse-than-anyone-imagined; Gregory Svirnovskiy, "Trump won't rule out a recession in 2025", Politico, 9 March 2025, https://www.politico.com/news/2025/03/09/trump-recess ion-tariffs-2025-economy-00220016.

19. Yan Xuetong, "Why China isn't scared of Trump: US-Chinese tensions may rise, but his isolationism will help Beijing", *Foreign Affairs*, 20 December 2024, https://www.foreignaffa irs.com/united-states/why-china-isnt-scared-trump.

20. Robert Keohane and Joseph Nye, "The end of the long American century: Trump and the sources of US power", *Foreign Affairs*, July/August 2025, https://www.foreignaffairs.com/united-states/end-long-american-century-trump-keohane-nye.

21. See opening of Chapter 3.

22. US *National Security Strategy*, October 2022, 23.

23. China's nuclear inventory in 2023 was estimated at 410 warheads, compared to Russia's 5,889 and the United States' 5,244. See "Nuclear weapons: who has what at a glance", Arms Control Association, June 2023, https://www.armscontrol.org/factsheets/Nuclearweapon swhohaswhat.

24. "China's lowest growth target in decades signals era of caution", *Financial Times*, 7 March 2023, https://www.ft.com/content/c51c202e-aff8-4019-a34e-a6f94baca024.

25. Roland Rajah and Alyssa Leng, "Revising down the rise of China", Lowy Institute Analysis, 14 March 2022, https://www.lowyinstitute.org/publications/revising-down-rise-china.

26. *Ibid*.

27. See Jude Blanchette and Ryan Haass, "Know your rival, know yourself: rightsizing the China challenge", *Foreign Affairs*, January/February 2025, https://www.foreignaffairs.com/united-states/know-your-rival-know-yourself-china.

28. See Xi Jinping, Report to the 20th Congress of the Chinese Communist Party, 16 October 2022, https://www.fmprc.gov.cn/eng/wjdt_665385/zyjh_665391/202210/t20221025_10791 908.html; also his report to the 19th Congress of the Chinese Communist Party, 18 October 2017, http://www.xinhuanet.com/english/special/2017-11/03/c_136725942.htm.

29. "How China measures national power", *The Economist*, 11 May 2023, https://www.econom ist.com/briefing/2023/05/11/how-china-measures-national-power.

30. Chinese Foreign Ministry spokesperson Mao Ning's press conference, 26 July 2023, http:// us.china-embassy.gov.cn/eng/fyrth/202307/t20230726_11118191.htm.

31. Mathias Spektor, "Rise of the nonaligned: who wins in a multipolar world?", *Foreign Affairs*, January/February 2025, https://www.foreignaffairs.com/united-states/rise-nonaligned-multipolar-world-matias-spektor.

32. Bernard Condon, "China's loans pushing world's poorest countries to brink of collapse", *Associated Press*, 18 May 2023, https://apnews.com/article/china-debt-banking-loans-financial-developing-countries-collapse-8df6f9fac3e1e758d0e6d8d5dfbd3ed6.

33. Adam Behsudi, "The 'rift is there': China vs the world on global debt", *Politico*, 11 April 2023, https://www.politico.com/news/2023/04/11/china-lending-imf-world-bank-00090588.

34. Patrick Greenfield and Fiona Harvey, "China and India should not be called developing countries, several Cop29 delegates say", *The Guardian*, 19 November 2024, https://www.theguardian.com/environment/2024/nov/19/china-india-developing-countries-cop29-climate-talks.

35. "Who's the big boss of the global south? In a dog-eat-dog world, competition is fierce", *The Economist*, 8 April 2024, https://www.economist.com/international/2024/04/08/whos-the-big-boss-of-the-global-south.

36. "China state media releases propaganda video mocking US coronavirus response", *ABC News*, 1 May 2020, https://www.abc.net.au/news/2020-05-01/china-state-media-propaga nda-video-mock-us-coronavirus/12204836.

37. "China blasts president of the Philippines for congratulating Taiwan election winner", Associated Press, 16 January 2024, https://apnews.com/article/china-philippines-taiwan-marcos-8f3b426f056d713a36b223300c083ae5.

38. Odd Arne Westad, "Sleepwalking toward war: will America and China heed the warnings of twentieth-century catastrophe?", *Foreign Affairs*, July/August 2024, https://www.foreign affairs.com/china/sleepwalking-toward-war-united-states.

39. In January 2023, the head of the US Air Mobility Command, Mike Minihan, foreshadowed a likely conflict as early as 2025; see "Air force general predicts war with China in 2025, tells officers to prepare by firing a 'clip' at a target, and 'aim for the head'", NBC News, 27 January 2023, https://www.nbcnews.com/politics/national-security/us-air-force-general-predicts-war-china-2025-memo-rcna67967. This followed earlier predictions of a mainland invasion of Taiwan by 2027 – in "China could invade Taiwan in next six years, top US admiral warns", *The Guardian*, 10 March 2021, https://www.theguardian.com/world/2021/mar/10/china-could-invade-taiwan-in-next-six-years-top-us-admiral-warns.

40. Wang Jisi, Hu Ran and Zhao Jianwei, "Does China prefer Trump or Harris? Why Chinese strategists see little difference between the two", *Foreign Affairs*, 1 August 2024, https://www.foreignaffairs.com/united-states/does-china-prefer-harris-or-trump.

41. "FBI director says China state hacker groups targeted US infrastructure", BBC News, 1 February 2024, https://www.bbc.co.uk/news/world-asia-68163172.

42. Seth Frantzman, "Why is China criticizing the US, Israel's war in Gaza?", *Jerusalem Post*, 21 February 2024, https://www.jpost.com/israel-hamas-war/article-788129.

43. See, for example, Matt Pottinger and Mike Gallagher, "No substitute for victory: America's competition with China must be won, not managed", *Foreign Affairs*, May/June 2024, https://www.foreignaffairs.com/united-states/no-substitute-victory-pottinger-gallagher.

44. Zhao Tong, "The perception gap and the China-US relationship", Asia-Pacific Leadership Network, 6 February 2023, https://www.apln.network/analysis/policy-briefs/the-percept ion-gap-and-the-china-us-relationship.

45. Helen Davidson, "Trump says Taiwan should pay the US for its defence as 'it doesn't give us anything'", *The Guardian*, 17 July 2024, https://www.theguardian.com/world/article/2024/jul/17/donald-trump-taiwan-pay-us-defence-china-national-convention.

46. Bobo Lo, "The Ukraine effect: demise or rebirth of the global order?", Lowy Institute Analysis, 11 May 2023, https://www.lowyinstitute.org/publications/ukraine-effect-dem ise-or-rebirth-global-order.
47. See Chapter 1, note 4.
48. Chloe Farand, "'Wind in the sails': US–China climate agreement can boost global action", *China Dialogue*, 22 November 2023, https://chinadialogue.net/en/climate/wind-in-the-sails-us-china-climate-agreement-can-boost-global-action/.
49. US-China trade reached an all-time high of USD 690 billion in 2022, before falling back to USD 575 billion in 2023 and USD 582 billion in 2024. See "Trade in goods with China", United States Census Bureau, https://www.census.gov/foreign-trade/balance/c5700.html
50. "The contentious US-China trade relationship", Council on Foreign Relations back-grounder, updated 14 April 2025, https://www.cfr.org/backgrounder/contentious-us-china-trade-relationship#chapter-title-0-1.
51. Chinese firms account for 69 per cent of extracted ore, over 90 per cent of refined miner-als, and nearly the entire global production of rare earth magnets. See Sarah Wu, "China's kingdom of rare earths", Drum Tower, *The Economist*, 15 August 2025.
52. "China hits back with limited response to Donald Trump's tariffs", *Financial Times*, 4 February 2025, https://www.ft.com/content/5653e2d6-2316-4316-9a7c-72cf4f7d86e5.
53. Yun Sun, "China is enjoying Trump 2.0: how the trade war is helping Beijing prepare for long-term competition", *Foreign Affairs*, 15 August 2025, https://www.foreignaffairs.com/china/china-enjoying-trump-20.
54. Greg Torode, Gerry Doyle and Laurie Chen, "US and China hold first informal nuclear talks in five years", Reuters, 21 June 2024, https://www.reuters.com/world/us-china-hold-first-informal-nuclear-talks-5-years-eyeing-taiwan-2024-06-21/.
55. Article VI of the NPT commits its signatories to "pursue negotiations in good faith on effec-tive measures relating to cessation of the nuclear arms race at an early date and to nuclear disarmament, and on a treaty on general and complete disarmament under strict and effec-tive international control", https://disarmament.unoda.org/wmd/nuclear/npt/text/.
56. Kevin Rudd, "China and the US: the case for managed strategic competition", Asia Policy Institute, 30 March 2022, https://asiasociety.org/policy-institute/china-and-us-case-managed-strategic-competition.

## 5. Powers in flux: adapting to change

1. Ivan Krastev, "Middle powers are shaping geopolitics", *Financial Times*, 18 November 2022, https://www.ft.com/content/0129492d-ac7f-4807-8050-2760a09e9ccc.
2. See Anders Fogh Rasmussen, "The transatlantic relationship is crumbling, says an ex-head of NATO", *The Economist*, 24 February 2025, https://www.economist.com/by-invitation/2025/02/24/the-transatlantic-relationship-is-crumbling-says-an-ex-head-of-nato.
3. Estimates vary as to the impact of Brexit on Britain's GDP, but the cost may be as high as 5 per cent. See John Springford, "The cost of Brexit to June 2022", Centre of European Reform, 21 December 2022, https://www.cer.eu/insights/cost-brexit-june-2022.
4. "Emmanuel Macron warns Europe: NATO is becoming brain-dead", *The Economist*, 7 November 2019, https://www.economist.com/europe/2019/11/07/emmanuel-macron-warns-europe-nato-is-becoming-brain-dead.
5. Anne-Elisabeth Moutet, "How Macron and Scholz broke the Franco-German alliance at the heart of the EU", *The Telegraph*, 24 March 2024, https://www.telegraph.co.uk/busin ess/2024/03/24/macron-scholz-broke-french-german-alliance-at-heart-eu/.
6. Treaty on European Union, https://eur-lex.europa.eu/legal-content/EN/TXT/?uri=CELEX:11992M/TXT.

7. An unfortunate example of this was EU High Representative Josep Borell's remarks to the European Diplomatic Academy on 13 October 2022: "Europe is a garden … Everything works. It is the best combination of political freedom, economic prosperity and social cohesion that … humankind has been able to build … Most of the rest of the world is a jungle, and the jungle could invade the garden". In fact, Borell's underlying point was sound: the Europeans could not wall themselves from the rest of the world, but "would have to be much more engaged with it". See https://www.eeas.europa.eu/eeas/european-diplomatic-academy-opening-remarks-high-representative-josep-borrell-inauguration-pilot_en.

8. See Emmanuel Martin, "The paradoxes of the EU's Africa policy", GIS, 28 June 2024, https://www.gisreportsonline.com/r/eu-africa-strategy/; also "Global Gateway risks diverting EU aid budget in key development sectors such as health and education", Oxfam press release, 9 October 2024, https://www.oxfam.org/en/press-releases/global-gateway-risks-diverting-eu-aid-budget-big-business.

9. Paul Taylor, "The EU has capitulated to Trump. But even this doesn't buy an end to the Transatlantic trade war", *The Guardian*, 28 July 2025, https://www.theguardian.com/commentisfree/2025/jul/28/eu-capitulated-donald-trump-transatlantic-trade-war.

10. As Ian Bond has observed, Europe "cannot afford to leave the defence of its interests to a president who is not interested in Europe, except as the target of attacks on its trade surpluses and inadequate military budgets. It needs to identify its own objectives and invest in achieving them, regardless of what Trump does" – in "Trump is back, worse than last time. Is Europe ready?", Centre for European Reform, 11 February 2025, https://www.cer.eu/insights/trump-back-worse-last-time-europe-ready.

11. Robert Zoellick, "Whither China? From membership to responsibility", remarks to the National Committee on US-China relations, 21 September 2005, https://www.ncuscr.org/fact/robert-zoellicks-responsible-stakeholder-speech/.

12. Joanne Lin, "India and multi-alignment: having one's cake and eating it too", Asialink, 21 February 2023, https://asialink.unimelb.edu.au/insights/india-and-multi-alignment-having-ones-cake-and-eating-it-too.

13. Hannah Ellis-Petersen, " 'Indian democracy fought back': Modi humbled as opposition gains ground", *The Guardian*, 9 June 2024, https://www.theguardian.com/world/article/2024/jun/09/indian-elections-democracy-modi-opposition-gains-analysis.

14. Ramachandra Guha, "India's feet of clay: how Modi's supremacy will hinder his country's rise", *Foreign Affairs*, March/April 2024, https://www.foreignaffairs.com/india/indias-feet-clay-modi.

15. "Why India isn't winning the contest with China", *The Economist*, 4 February 2025, https://www.economist.com/asia/2025/02/04/why-india-isnt-winning-the-contest-with-china.

16. "Narendra Modi is struggling to boost Indian growth", *The Economist*, 6 February 2025, https://www.economist.com/finance-and-economics/2025/02/06/narendra-modi-is-struggling-to-boost-indian-growth.

17. Inu Manak, "How India disrupts and navigates the WTO", Council on Foreign Relations, 10 February 2025, https://www.cfr.org/article/how-india-disrupts-and-navigates-wto.

18. In 2023, coal accounted for 56.3 per cent of India's primary energy consumption, oil 27.1 per cent, and natural gas 5.7 per cent. Renewables (solar, wind, hydropower) comprised less than 10 per cent. See Lydia Powell, Akhilesh Sati and Vinod Tomar, "India's energy profile: view from the South", Observer Research Foundation, 5 July 2024, https://www.orfonline.org/expert-speak/india-s-energy-profile-view-from-the-south. Worryingly, the growth of India's renewable energy industry has slowed. See Arunabha Ghosh, "Can India become a green superpower? The stakes of the world's most important energy transition", *Foreign Affairs*, July/August 2023, https://www.foreignaffairs.com/india/can-india-become-green-superpower.

19. Ashley Tellis, "America's bad bet on India: New Delhi won't side with Washington against Beijing", *Foreign Affairs*, 1 May 2023, https://www.foreignaffairs.com/india/americas-bad-bet-india-modi.

20. Happymon Jacob, "The shocking rift between India and the United States: can progress in the partnership survive Trump?", *Foreign Affairs*, 14 August 2025, https://www.foreignaffairs.com/india/shocking-rift-between-india-and-united-states.

21. Guha, "India's feet of clay".

22. Ashley Tellis, "India's great-power delusions: how New Delhi's grand strategy thwarts its grand ambitions", *Foreign Affairs*, July/August 2025, https://www.foreignaffairs.com/india/indias-great-power-delusions.

23. Chietigj Bajpaee, "India's never-ending quest for global status", The Interpreter, 10 October 2024, https://www.lowyinstitute.org/the-interpreter/india-s-never-ending-quest-global-status.

24. Supriya Gandhi, "Building a civilization-state", Global Currents, 15 May 2024, https://contendingmodernities.nd.edu/global-currents/building-a-civilization-state/.

25. Tellis, "India's great-power delusions".

26. David Elliott, "Middle powers: what are they and why do they matter?", World Economic Forum, 26 January 2024, https://www.weforum.org/agenda/2024/01/middle-powers-multilateralism-international-relations/. See also "Shaping cooperation in a fragmenting world", World Economic Forum White Paper, 15 January 2024, https://www.weforum.org/publications/shaping-cooperation-in-a-fragmenting-world/, 23.

27. "Shaping cooperation in a fragmenting world", World Economic Forum.

28. "Erdoğan says Türkiye is poised to ascend as global power", *Hurriyet*, 17 March 2024, https://www.hurriyetdailynews.com/erdogan-says-turkiye-poised-to-ascend-as-global-power-191695.

29. David Albright and Spencer Faragasso, "Post-attack assessment of the first 12 days of Israeli and US strikes on Iranian nuclear facilities", Institute for Science and International Security, 24 June 2025, https://isis-online.org/isis-reports/post-attack-assessment-of-the-first-12-days-of-israeli-strikes-on-iranian-nuclear-facilities.

30. See "Common understandings between China and Brazil on political settlement of the Ukraine Crisis", *Xinhua*, 23 May 2024, https://english.news.cn/20240523/8b0cc04f2c1d4e55a219c880567a2a9e/c.html.

31. Faith Mabera, "Ethiopia's Tigray conflict peace deal showcased the African Union's peace diplomacy, but several sticking points remain", Africa Up Close, Wilson Center, 15 February 2023, https://www.wilsoncenter.org/blog-post/ethiopias-tigray-conflict-peace-deal-african-union.

32. William Burns, "A world transformed and the role of intelligence", 59th Ditchley Annual Lecture, 1 July 2023, https://www.ditchley.com/sites/default/files/Ditchley%20Annual%20Lecture%202023%20transcript.pdf.

33. John Ainger and Jennifer Dlouhy, "Saudis resist restating fossil fuel transition pledge at COP29", Bloomberg UK, 16 November 2024, https://www.bloomberg.com/news/articles/2024-11-16/cop29-clash-brews-as-saudis-resist-restating-fossil-fuel-pledge.

34. Karen Young, "The Gulf goes green: can the fossil fuel giants lead the energy transition?", *Foreign Affairs*, 10 July 2023, https://www.foreignaffairs.com/persian-gulf/gulf-goes-green-fossil-fuel-energy-transition.

35. Jonathan Watts, "Optimism dries up in Amazon as Lula drifts from climate priorities", *The Guardian*, 25 January 2024, https://www.theguardian.com/environment/2024/jan/25/optimism-dries-up-amazon-lula-drifts-climate-priorities-brazil.

36. Francieli Barcellos, "'COP30 will be our last chance to avoid an irreversible rupture in the climate system', calls Lula at the final thematic session of the G20 Brasil leaders' summit", G20 Brasil 2024, 19 November 2024, https://www.g20.org/en/news/cop30-will-be-our-last-chance-to-avoid-an-irreversible-rupture-in-the-climate-system-calls-lula-at-the-final-thematic-session-of-the-g20-brasil-leaders-summit".

37. Marcio Astrini, "Is Brazil's Lula a climate leader? ", Climate Home News, 16 September 2024, https://www.climatechangenews.com/2024/09/16/is-brazils-lula-a-climate-leader/. Jonathan Watts, "Brazil's environmental governance is under threat – and Lula is siding

with oil industry", *The Guardian*, 31 May 2025, https://www.theguardian.com/environm ent/2025/may/31/brazil-environmental-movemen-lula-oil-industry; "Brazil is bashing its patron saint of the environment", *The Economist*, 9 July 2025, https://www.economist. com/the-americas/2025/07/09/brazil-is-bashing-its-patron-saint-of-the-environment.

38. It is richly ironic that preparations for COP 30 in Belem led to further major deforestation. See "Amazon forest felled to build road for climate summit", BBC News, 12 March 2025, https://www.bbc.co.uk/news/articles/c9vy191rgn1o.

39. Fareed Zakaria, *The Post-American World* (Norton, 2009), 2–5.

# 6. Flexible multilateralism

1. Bruce Jones, "Instrument of order: does the UN Security Council matter in an era of Global South diplomacy and major power tensions?", Brookings, 3 June 2024, https://www.brooki ngs.edu/articles/instrument-of-order/.

2. Stuart Patrick (ed.), *UN Security Council Reform: What the World Thinks*, report by Carnegie Endowment for International Peace, 28 June 2023, https://carnegieendowment.org/resea rch/2023/06/un-security-council-reform-what-the-world-thinks?lang=en#germany.

3. The one exception to the pattern of non-reform was the 1965 expansion in the number of non-permanent members from 6 to 10, increasing the overall size of the Security Council from 11 to 15.

4. Martin Mühleisen, "The Bretton Woods institutions in an era of geopolitical fragmentation", Atlantic Council, 9 October 2023, https://www.atlanticcouncil.org/in-depth-research-repo rts/issue-brief/the-bretton-woods-institutions-under-geopolitical-fragmentation/.

5. Kristalina Georgieva, "The price of fragmentation: why the global economy isn't ready for the shocks ahead", *Foreign Affairs*, September/October 2023, https://www.foreignaffairs. com/world/price-fragmentation-global-economy-shock.

6. As of October 2024, the EU-27's voting share in the IMF was 26.2 per cent of the total compared to a nominal combined GDP of $18.8 trillion. The respective figures for the United States and China were 17.4 per cent and $28.8 trillion, and 6.4 per cent and $18.5 trillion. In other words, the EU's voting share is four times larger than China's, despite their economies being roughly the same size. See Ousmene Mandeng, "Reversing international disintegration: the need for the EU to move", Bretton Woods Committee blog post, 11 October 2024, https://www.brettonwoods.org/article/reversing-international-financial-disintegration-the-need-for-the-eu-to-move.

7. Mia Mottley and Rajiv Shah, "How to revitalize the World Bank, the IMF, and the development finance system: the urgent need to update institutions built for a different era", *Foreign Affairs*, 7 April 2023, https://www.foreignaffairs.com/barbados/revitalize-world-bank-imf-development-finance-system-mia-mottley-raj-shah. Mottley, the Prime Minister of Barbados, is the driving force behind the "Bridgetown Initiative on the reform of the international development and climate finance architecture", https://www.bridget own-initiative.org/.

8. Fiona Harvey, "Billions more in overseas aid needed to avert climate disaster, say econo-mists", *The Guardian*, 17 April 2024, https://www.theguardian.com/business/2024/apr/ 17/billions-more-overseas-aid-climate-world-bank-imf-spring-summit.

9. Stephen Buranyi, "The WHO v coronavirus: why it can't handle the pandemic", *The Guardian*, 10 April 2020, https://www.theguardian.com/news/2020/apr/10/world-hea lth-organization-who-v-coronavirus-why-it-cant-handle-pandemic.

10. Larry Brilliant, Mark Smolinski, Lisa Danzig and Ian Lipkin, "Inevitable outbreaks: how to stop an age of spillovers from becoming an age of pandemics", *Foreign Affairs*, January/ February 2023, https://www.foreignaffairs.com/world/inevitable-outbreaks-spillovers-pandemics.

11. Claire Chaumont, "Five ways to reform the World Health Organization", Devex, 5 August 2020, https://www.devex.com/news/opinion-5-ways-to-reform-the-world-health-organ ization-97843.

12. John Ikenberry, "The G-7 becomes a power player", *Foreign Policy*, 31 August 2023, https:// foreignpolicy.com/2023/08/31/g7-geopolitics-alliance-west-democracies-us-europe- japan-free-world-liberal-order/.

13. Patrick Wintour, "Donald Trump repeats call for Russia to be readmitted at G7 sum- mit in Canada", *The Guardian*, 16 June 2025, https://www.theguardian.com/world/2025/ jun/16/donald-trump-repeats-call-for-russia-to-be-readmitted-at-g7-summit-in-canada. Russian membership was suspended in 2014 following its invasion and annexation of Crimea.

14. Ian Mitchell and Nancy Birdsall, "The unkept promises of Western aid: how donor coun- tries cook their books and let down the developing world", *Foreign Affairs*, 14 September 2022, https://www.foreignaffairs.com/world/unkept-promises-western-aid.

15. Of course, some countries have no desire to join the G-7. It suits India, for example, to preserve a distinct identity separate from the G-7.

16. Victor Cha, John Hamre and John Ikenberry, "How global governance can survive: with the right reforms, the G-7 can sustain the rules-based order", *Foreign Affairs*, 11 June 2025, https://www.foreignaffairs.com/united-states/how-global-governance-can-survive.

17. "Africa dominates list of the world's 20 fastest-growing economies in 2024 – African Development Bank says in macroeconomic report", African Development Bank Group, 16 February 2024, https://www.afdb.org/en/news-and-events/press-releases/africa-domina tes-list-worlds-20-fastest-growing-economies-2024-african-development-bank-says- macroeconomic-report-68751.

18. "The 17 goals", United Nations Department of Economic and Social Affairs, https://sdgs. un.org/goals.

19. "Brazil's President Lula launches the Global Alliance against Hunger and Poverty along- side 148 members, including 82 countries", presidential press release, 18 November 2024, https://www.gov.br/planalto/en/latest-news/2024/11/brazil2019s-president-lula-launc hes-the-global-alliance-against-hunger-and-poverty-alongside-148-members-including- 82-countries.

20. Paul Millar, "How the BRICS nations failed to rebuild the global financial order", *France24*, 24 August 2023, https://www.france24.com/en/economy/20230824-how-the-brics-nati ons-failed-to-rebuild-the-global-financial-order.

21. Charles Clover and Daria Mosolova, "Vladimir Putin's alternative to 'weaponised' dollar fails to excite Brics partners", *Financial Times*, 24 October 2024, https://www.ft.com/cont ent/77ddacad-2de7-4bdc-bac7-d5ec3af32781.

22. Alexander Gabuev and Oliver Stuenkel, "The battle for the BRICS: why the future of the bloc will shape global order", *Foreign Affairs*, 24 September 2024, https://www.foreignaffa irs.com/russia/battle-brics.

23. As of March 2025, there were nine EU candidate countries: Albania, Bosnia and Herzegovina, Georgia, Montenegro, North Macedonia, Serbia, Moldova, Ukraine and Türkiye, with Kosovo being a potential candidate. In November 2024, the government in Tbilisi suspended Georgia's EU accession process.

24. David Hutt, "ASEAN summit: is the bloc as we know it finished?", *Deutsche Welle*, 11 October 2022, https://www.dw.com/en/asean-summit-is-the-bloc-as-we-know-it-finis hed/a-63710529.

25. The last multilateral alliance in Asia was SEATO (Southeast Asia Treaty Organization), which grew out of the wars in Indochina. It contained only two Southeast Asian members (Thailand and the Philippines), and was disbanded in 1977.

26. Kishore Mahbubani, "Asia's third way: how ASEAN survives – and thrives – amid great- power competition", *Foreign Affairs*, March/April 2023, https://www.foreignaffairs.com/ southeast-asia/asias-third-way-asean-amid-great-power-competition.

27. Cameron Hill, "Assessing the Asian Infrastructure Investment Bank", DevpolicyBlog, 17 August 2022, https://devpolicy.org/assessing-the-asian-infrastructure-investment-bank-20220817/.

28. Russia's pseudo-multilateral approach is reminiscent of Soviet times, when the Warsaw Pact and COMECON were nominally multilateral bodies, but directed by Moscow.

29. Derek Grossman, "With ASEAN paralyzed, Southeast Asia seeks new security ties", RAND Blog, 18 September 2023, https://www.rand.org/pubs/commentary/2023/09/with-asean-paralyzed-southeast-asia-seeks-new-security.html; Thitinan Pongsudhirak, "The end of ASEAN as we know it", Project Syndicate, 12 October 2022, https://www.project-syndicate.org/commentary/asean-needs-realignment-for-new-geopolitical-realities-by-thiti nan-pongsudhirak-2022-10?gad_source=1.

30. Vietnam, in particular, has a big decision to make: whether to enhance security and defence ties with America or continue its "bamboo diplomacy", balancing relations with different external powers (China and Russia as well as the United States). See Prashanth Parameswaran, "Vietnam's 'bamboo diplomacy' faces shifting global currents", GIS, 28 May 2024, https://www.gisreportsonline.com/r/vietnam-bamboo-diplomacy/.

31. "We are bound together by common values: individual liberty, human rights, democracy and the rule of law" – *NATO 2022 Strategic Concept*, para 2, page 3, https://www.nato.int/strategic-concept/.

32. "Trump casts doubt on Article V commitment en route to NATO summit", *Politico*, 24 June 2025, https://www.politico.eu/article/donald-trump-nato-summit-sidesteps-article-5-mark-rutte-eu-defense-budget-russia-vladimir-putin-iran-israel-strikes-qatar.

33. See US Defence Secretary Pete Hegseth's remarks to the Ukraine Defence Contact Group, Brussels, 12 February 2025, https://www.defense.gov/News/Speeches/Speech/Article/4064113/opening-remarks-by-secretary-of-defense-pete-hegseth-at-ukraine-defense-contact/.

34. In February 2025, the British and French governments initiated a "coalition of the willing" to support Ukrainian sovereignty in anticipation that the United States would reduce its assistance to Ukraine. So far, however, the coalition has been more notional than real, with its commitments being largely declarative. See Claudia Major and Niklas Ebert, "Coalition of the willing", German Marshall Fund, 15 May 2025, https://www.gmfus.org/news/coalition-willing.

35. See Camille Grand, "The end of the 'imperial republic' and the future of the trans-atlantic alliance", *Brookings*, 23 June 2025, https://www.brookings.edu/articles/the-end-of-the-imperial-republic-and-the-future-of-the-transatlantic-alliance.

36. Daeun Kim and Kayla Orta, "Minilateralism: a newfound approach to bolstering the US-Indo-Pacific partnerships in emerging technology", *Asia Dispatches*, 26 March 2024, https://www.wilsoncenter.org/blog-post/minilateralism-newfound-approach-bolstering-us-indo-pacific-partnerships-emerging.

37. Hiroyuki Akita, "Why India wants a free hand, strategically speaking", Nikkei Asia, 13 August 2023, https://asia.nikkei.com/Spotlight/Comment/Why-India-wants-a-free-hand-strategically-speaking; also Tellis, "America's bad bet on India".

38. See Andrew Roth, "Stunning Signal leak reveals depths of Trump administration's loath-ing of Europe", *The Guardian*, 25 March 2025, https://www.theguardian.com/world/2025/mar/25/stunning-signal-leak-reveals-depths-of-trump-administrations-loathing-of-europe.

## 7. Thinking beyond the state

1. Bull, *The Anarchical Society*, 8.
2. *Ibid.*, 13.
3. See Andrew Hurrell, "The *Anarchical Society* 25 years on" (2002) in *Ibid.*, xv, xxii.

4. Meta, for example, has 3 billion users monthly, or two-thirds of the internet-connected world (and more than a third of the total global population). See Martyn Landi, "Facebook at 20: scandal, looming regulation and a future built around AI", *The Independent*, 4 February 2024, https://www.independent.co.uk/tech/facebook-mark-zuckerberg-meta-messenger-analytica-b2490099.html.

5. Ian Bremmer, "The technopolar paradox: the frightening fusion of tech power and state power", *Foreign Affairs*, 13 May 2025, https://www.foreignaffairs.com/united-states/tech nopolar-paradox-ian-bremmer-fusion-tech-state-power.

6. "Elon Musk's assault on the US federal bureaucracy", *Financial Times*, 10 February 2025, https://www.ft.com/content/f7665ee1-dcda-4c35-9209-735094054482.

7. This is true even in authoritarian regimes such as China. Beijing started developing renewable sources of energy not just because it identified a strategic necessity to reduce China's dependence on fossil fuels, but also because environmental pollution had become a contentious *political* question. Although its authority was not directly challenged, the Chinese Communist Party felt accountable for improving the dangerously poor air quality in major Chinese cities, such as Beijing.

8. Ian Bremmer, "The technopolar moment: how digital powers will reshape the global order", *Foreign Affairs*, November/December 2021, https://www.foreignaffairs.com/artic les/world/ian-bremmer-big-tech-global-order.

9. International arrivals in 2023 reached 1.3 billion, 88 per cent of pre-pandemic levels, and are expected to exceed these shortly. See "International tourism to reach pre-pandemic levels in 2024", UN Tourism, 19 January 2024, https://www.unwto.org/news/internatio nal-tourism-to-reach-pre-pandemic-levels-in-2024.

10. See Katie Lebling and Danielle Riedl, "Lessons from California's carbon dioxide removal policies", World Resources Institute, 11 September 2023, https://www.wri.org/insights/california-carbon-dioxide-removal-policies; also Andy Burnham, "Driving Greater Manchester towards net zero", Chamber UK, 7 November 2024, https://chamberuk.com/driving-greater-manchester-towards-net-zero/.

11. Bryony Gooch and Karl Matchett, "BP signs $25bn deal to redevelop Iraq's oil and gas fields as it slashes investments in renewable energy", *The Independent*, 26 February 2025, https://www.independent.co.uk/news/business/bp-cut-green-energy-oil-gas-trump-b2704853.html; Oliver Milman and Nina Lakhani, "Revealed: wealthy western countries lead in global oil and gas expansion", *The Guardian*, 24 July 2024, https://www.theguard ian.com/environment/article/2024/jul/24/new-oil-gas-emission-data-us-uk.

12. Damian Carrington, "World's top climate scientists expect global heating to blast past 1.5C target", *The Guardian*, 8 May 2024, https://www.theguardian.com/environment/article/2024/may/08/world-scientists-climate-failure-survey-global-temperature.

13. *Emissions Gap Report*, 33.

14. Fiona Harvey, "Backroom deals and betrayal: how late $300bn deal left nobody happy", *The Guardian*, 26 November 2024, https://www.theguardian.com/environment/2024/nov/26/how-late-deal-left-a-sense-of-dissatisfaction-and-betrayal-at-cop29-baku.

15. In her capacity as Executive Secretary of the UN Framework Convention on Climate Change.

16. Christiana Figueres, "I understand climate scientists' despair – but stubborn optimism may be our only hope", *The Guardian*, 9 May 2024, https://www.theguardian.com/com mentisfree/article/2024/may/09/climate-scientists-despair-stubborn-optimism-paris-2015-climate. Emphasis in original.

17. *Emissions Gap Report*, 11. For a breakdown of the differing consequences of various temperature rises, see "Comparing climate impacts at 1.5C, 2C, 3C and 4C", UN Climate Summit, 25 April 2023, https://unclimatesummit.org/comparing-climate-impacts-at-1-5c-2c-3c-and-4c/.

18. *Renewables 2024: Analysis and Forecast to 2030*, International Energy Agency, October 2024, https://www.iea.org/reports/renewables-2024, 7–8.

19. "Renewable power remains cost-effective amid fossil fuel crisis", International Renewable Energy Agency (IRENA) press release, 13 July 2022, https://www.irena.org/news/pressr eleases/2022/Jul/Renewable-Power-Remains-Cost-Competitive-amid-Fossil-Fuel-Crisis.

20. "The future of work in the green economy", World Economic Forum, 12 June 2023, https:// www.weforum.org/agenda/2023/06/the-future-of-work-in-the-green-economy/.

21. *Global EV Outlook: Moving towards Increased Affordability*, International Energy Agency, April 2024, https://www.iea.org/reports/global-ev-outlook-2024.

22. Bill McGuire, "The big takeaway from Cop27? These climate conferences just aren't work-ing", *The Guardian*, 20 November 2022, https://www.theguardian.com/commentisfree/2022/nov/20/big-takeaway-cop27-climate-conferences-arent-working. The debacle of COP29, hosted by Azerbaijan (90 per cent dependent on fossil fuels), has only increased the pressure to reform the COP process. See "Open letter on COP reform to all states that are parties to the convention", Club of Rome, 15 November 2024, https://www.clubofrome.org/cop-reform-2024/.

23. Cynthia Stahl and Alan Cimorelli, *Environmental Public Policy Making Exposed: A Guide for Decision Makers and Interested Citizens* (Springer, 2020), 50.

24. "The Inflation Reduction Act: here's what's in it", McKinsey, 24 October 2022, https://www.mckinsey.com/industries/public-sector/our-insights/the-inflation-reduct ion-act-heres-whats-in-it.

25. "Republican districts dominate US clean technology investment boom", *Financial Times*, 13 August 2023, https://www.ft.com/content/06fcd3dd-9c39-48d3-bb08-6d75d34b5ed1.

26. This is by no means inconceivable. As British Prime Minister (1979–90), Margaret Thatcher was one of the first world leaders to highlight the dangers of climate change, although she later recanted her views.

27. *Strategies for Affordable and Fair Clean Energy Transitions*, World Energy Outlook Special Report, International Energy Agency, May 2024, https://www.iea.org/reports/strategies-for-affordable-and-fair-clean-energy-transitions, 14–18.

28. Helena Horton, "British climate action plan unlawful, high court rules", *The Guardian*, 3 May 2024, https://www.theguardian.com/environment/article/2024/may/03/britain-clim ate-action-plan-unlawful-high-court.

29. "Shell: Netherlands court orders oil giant to cut emissions", BBC News, 26 May 2021, https://www.bbc.co.uk/news/world-europe-57257982.

30. Isabella Kaminski, "Shell's successful appeal will not end climate lawsuits against firms, say experts", *The Guardian*, 14 November 2024, https://www.theguardian.com/environment/2024/nov/14/shell-successful-appeal-will-not-end-climate-lawsuits-against-firms-say-experts.

31. Claire Brown, "Young people are worried about climate change – and that is affecting their future plans", *Wall Street Journal*, 17 October 2024, https://www.wsj.com/articles/young-people-are-worried-about-climate-changeand-thats-affecting-their-future-plans-de0f7cd3. See also Alec Kennedy, Brian Kennedy and Cary Funk, "Gen Z, millennials stand out for climate activism, social media engagement with issue", Pew Research Center report, 26 May 2021, https://www.pewresearch.org/science/2021/05/26/gen-z-millenni als-stand-out-for-climate-change-activism-social-media-engagement-with-issue/.

32. The case against Shell was brought by 6 climate action groups *and* 17,000 private citizens.

33. The term "Big Tech" normally refers to the big five tech companies – Amazon, Apple, Meta (formerly Facebook), Alphabet (incorporating Google) and Microsoft. But it can also apply to big Chinese tech companies, such as Alibaba, Baidu, ByteDance and Tencent.

34. Joseph Nye, "The end of cyber-anarchy? How to build a new digital order", *Foreign Affairs*, January/February 2022, https://www.foreignaffairs.com/articles/russian-federation/2021-12-14/end-cyber-anarchy.

35. Ian Bremmer and Mustafa Suleyman, "The AI power paradox: can states learn to govern Artificial Intelligence – before it's too late?", *Foreign Affairs*, September/October 2023, https://www.foreignaffairs.com/world/artificial-intelligence-power-paradox.

36. The Bletchley Declaration by Countries Attending the AI Safety Summit, 1–2 November 2023, https://www.gov.uk/government/publications/ai-safety-summit-2023-the-bletchley-declaration/the-bletchley-declaration-by-countries-attending-the-ai-safety-summit-1-2-november-2023.

37. "Executive Order on the Safe, Secure and Trustworthy Development and Use of Artificial Intelligence", 30 October 2023.

38. "AI Act enters into force", European Commission, 1 August 2024, https://commission.europa.eu/news/ai-act-enters-force-2024-08-01_en. "The Digital Services Act", European Commission, https://commission.europa.eu/strategy-and-policy/priorities-2019-2024/europe-fit-digital-age/digital-services-act_en.

39. "Remarks by the Vice President at the Artificial Intelligence Summit in Paris, France", 11 February 2025, https://www.presidency.ucsb.edu/documents/remarks-the-vice-president-the-artificial-intelligence-action-summit-paris-france.

40. In June 2025, the market capitalization of each of Nvidia, Microsoft and Apple exceeded USD 3 trillion. If they were sovereign nations, they would all rank in the top ten by GDP. See Lyle Daly, "The largest companies by market cap in June 2025", *The Motley Fool*, updated 2 July 2025, https://www.fool.com/research/largest-companies-by-market-cap/.

41. Mustafa Suleyman, "Containment for AI: how to adapt a Cold War strategy for a new threat", *Foreign Affairs*, 23 January 2024, https://www.foreignaffairs.com/world/containment-artificial-intelligence-mustafa-suleyman.

42. See Sam Freedman, "Technology vs Democracy: the origins and ideology of Muskworld", *Comment is Freed*, 12 February 2025, https://samf.substack.com/p/technology-vs-democracy.

43. See, for example, "Americans' views of technology companies", Pew Research Center, 29 April 2024, https://www.pewresearch.org/internet/2024/04/29/americans-views-of-technology-companies-2/.

44. *Winning the Race: America's AI Action Plan*, The White House, July 2025, https://www.whitehouse.gov/wp-content/uploads/2025/07/Americas-AI-Action-Plan.pdf.

45. See US National Security Strategy, October 2022, 32; also Chris Miller, *Chip War: The Fight for The World's Most Critical Technology* (Scribner, 2022), xix.

46. Mackinder's original 1919 aphorism was: "Who rules East Europe commands the Heartland; who rules the Heartland commands the World Island; who rules the World Island commands the world".

47. "Tech giants are putting $500 bn into 'Stargate' to build up AI in US", BBC News, 22 January 2025, https://www.bbc.co.uk/news/articles/cy4m84d2xz2o.

48. "DeepSeek sends a shockwave through markets", *The Economist*, 27 January 2025, https://www.economist.com/business/2025/01/27/deepseek-sends-a-shockwave-through-markets.

49. Other models include the European Organization for Nuclear Research and the International Atomic Energy Agency. See "AI needs regulation, but what kind, and how much?", *The Economist*, 20 August 2024, https://www.economist.com/schools-brief/2024/08/20/ai-needs-regulation-but-what-kind-and-how-much.

50. John Villasenor, "DeepSeek shows the limits of US export controls on AI chips", Brookings, 29 January 2025, https://www.brookings.edu/articles/deepseek-shows-the-limits-of-us-export-controls-on-ai-chips/.

51. Aziz Huq, "A world divided over artificial intelligence: geopolitics gets in the way of global regulation of powerful technology", *Foreign Affairs*, 11 March 2024, https://www.foreignaffairs.com/united-states/world-divided-over-artificial-intelligence.

52. In the run-up to the 2024 US presidential election, Donald Trump's interview with the podcaster Joe Rogan gained more than 40 million views on YouTube, nearly three times the audience for Kamala Harris's appearance on Fox News. See "Donald Trump vs the media … round 2!", BBC Americast, 6 December 2024, https://www.bbc.co.uk/sounds/play/m0025ldh.

53. See Peter Pomerantsev, "Elon Musk and the new world order: the hijacking of the global conversation", *The Guardian*, 12 January 2025, https://www.theguardian.com/technology/2025/jan/12/elon-musk-and-the-new-world-order-the-hijacking-of-the-global-conversation.

54. Glenn Kessler, Salvador Rizzo and Meg Kelly, "Trump's false and misleading claims total 30,573 over 4 years", *Washington Post*, 24 January 2021, https://www.washingtonpost.com/politics/2021/01/24/trumps-false-or-misleading-claims-total-30573-over-four-years/.

55. Ruth Marcus, "Big Tech's power surge", *Washington Post*, 20 January 2025, https://www.washingtonpost.com/opinions/2025/01/20/trump-elon-musk-zuckerberg-bezos/?utm_medium=email&utm_source=newsletter&utm_campaign=wp_opinions_pm.

56. Mark Zuckerberg, Meta post, 7 January 2025, https://www.facebook.com/zuck/videos/its-time-to-get-back-to-our-roots-around-free-expression-were-replacing-fact-che/1525382954801931/.

57. Chris Stokel-Walker, "A new era of lies: Mark Zuckerberg has just ushered in an extinction-level event for truth on social media", *The Guardian*, 7 January 2025, https://www.theguardian.com/commentisfree/2025/jan/07/new-era-of-lies-mark-zuckerberg-meta-social-media.

58. Emily Bell, "Trump, Musk and Zuckerberg have declared war on facts and truth. The pushback must start now", *The Guardian*, 11 January 2025, https://www.theguardian.com/commentisfree/2025/jan/11/trump-musk-zuckerberg-war-on-facts-truth-pushback-now.

59. Dominick Mastrangelo, "Bannon on Musk, Zuckerberg: 'We'll break these guys eventually'", *The Hill*, 20 January 2025, https://thehill.com/homenews/media/5095165-bannon-attacks-musk-zuckerberg/.

60. In April 2024, Congress passed a bill aimed at forcing ByteDance to sell its controlling stake in the social media platform TikTok. This move reflected a bipartisan consensus on the need to counter Chinese influence in America. The ban has been temporarily suspended pending Trump's efforts to set up a deal.

61. "In Britain, and across Europe, free speech … is in retreat" – JD Vance speech at the 2025 Munich Security Conference, 13 February 2025, https://foreignpolicy.com/2025/02/18/vance-speech-munich-full-text-read-transcript-europe/.

62. China accounts for a quarter of the global revenue of Elon Musk's Tesla company – see Amy Hawkins, "Tesla's path in China clears as Musk courts both Trump and Xi", *The Guardian*, 22 November 2024, https://www.theguardian.com/technology/2024/nov/22/elon-musk-tesla-china-us-relationship-trump-xi-jinping; Another key figure in US-China tech relations is Jensen Huang, CEO of Nvidia. See "Move over, Tim Cook, Jensen Huang is America Inc's new China envoy", *The Economist*, 17 July 2025, https://www.economist.com/business/2025/07/17/move-over-tim-cook-jensen-huang-is-america-incs-new-china-envoy.

63. Not long before his death in November 2023, Henry Kissinger co-wrote an article with Graham Allison proposing "an advisory group consisting of US and Chinese scientists". This would be a Track II process (i.e. involving non-government participants), whereby "individuals [are] chosen for their judgment and fairness although not formally endorsed by their government". See "The path to AI arms control: America and China must work together to avoid catastrophe", *Foreign Affairs*, 13 October 2023, https://www.foreignaffairs.com/united-states/henry-kissinger-path-artificial-intelligence-arms-control. According to reports, a number of these "Kissinger dialogues" have since taken place – see "Is Xi Jinping an AI doomer?", *The Economist*, 25 August 2024, https://www.economist.com/china/2024/08/25/is-xi-jinping-an-ai-doomer.

64. There are various definitions of civil society. Here the term refers to political engagement by individuals as well as by civil society organizations. See EUR-Lex, https://eur-lex.europa.eu/EN/legal-content/glossary/civil-society-organisation.html.

65. Henry Mance, "Britain has had enough of experts, says Gove", *Financial Times*, 3 June 2016, https://www.ft.com/content/3be49734-29cb-11e6-83e4-abc22d5d108c.

66. Sarah Gilbert and Catherine Green, *Vaxxers: The Inside Story of the Oxford AstraZeneca Vaccine and The Race against the Virus* (Hodder & Stoughton, 2021).

67. Richard Wilson, "Citizens' assemblies could work wonders for Labour and Britain – but only if they're more than a talking shop", *The Guardian*, 16 July 2024, https://www.theguardian.com/commentisfree/article/2024/jul/16/citizens-assemblies-labour-britain. See also Wolf, *The Crisis of Democratic Capitalism*, 338–41.

## Epilogue: tomorrow's world

1. Policy statement by Olaf Scholz to the German Bundestag, 27 February 2022, https://www.bundesregierung.de/breg-en/service/archive/policy-statement-by-olaf-scholz-chancellor-of-the-federal-republic-of-germany-and-member-of-the-german-bundestag-27-february-2022-in-berlin-2008378.

2. Colin Meisel, "Accelerating change but not necessarily an inflection point", Stimson Center, 20 February 2024, https://www.stimson.org/2024/accelerating-change-but-not-necessarily-an-inflection-point/.

3. See, for example, Matt Pottinger and Mike Gallagher, "No substitute for victory: America's competition with China must be won, not managed", *Foreign Affairs*, May/June 2024, https://www.foreignaffairs.com/united-states/no-substitute-victory-pottinger-gallagher.

4. Andrea Kendall-Taylor and Richard Fontaine, "The axis of upheaval: how America's adversaries are uniting to overturn the global order", *Foreign Affairs*, May/June 2024, https://www.foreignaffairs.com/china/axis-upheaval-russia-iran-north-korea-taylor-fontaine.

5. Lionel Barber and Henry Foy, "Putin says liberalism has 'become obsolete'", *Financial Times*, 28 June 2019, https://www.ft.com/content/670039ec-98f3-11e9-9573-ee5cbb98ed36.

# INDEX

9/11   20, 29, 30, 143

Able Archer, NATO exercise (1983)   49
accountability, in governance   10, 113, 128,
      129, 136, 139, 141–2, 147
adaptability, in multilateral
      organizations   120–1, 124
adapting to decline   92–9; *see also*
      major powers
Afghanistan
   International Security Assistance Force
      (ISAF)   28
   Taliban   21, 26, 28, 41
   US-led military intervention (2002–21),
      Operation "Enduring Freedom"   4,
      21, 24, 28, 29, 46, 55, 57, 74, 103
Africa   27, 42, 82, 83, 96, 101, 111
African Union (AU)   64–5, 104, 115, 124
"age of empires"   39
"age of impunity" (David Miliband)   40
Al-Qaeda   29, 127
Alibaba   136, 170
all-of-society approach to problem
      solving   10, 126
Alphabet   36, 126, 170; *see also* Google
Alternative für Deutschland (AfD)   121
Amazon (company)   126, 137, 170
Amazon basin   59, 106, 165
"America-first"   8, 24, 40, 145, 147,
      148; *see also* "Make America
      Great Again"
"anarchical society" (Hedley Bull)   1, 33,
      49, 125
Anglo-Iranian Oil Company   126; *see
      also* BP
arms control   34, 89, 95, 163
artificial intelligence (AI)   3, 133–9
   governance   133–36
Asia-Pacific Economic Cooperation
      (APEC)   86

Asian Infrastructure and Investment Bank
      (AIIB)   112, 119
al-Assad, Bashir
   use of chemical weapons
      (2013)   24, 45, 79
Association of Southeast Asian Nations
      (ASEAN)   105, 116, 117–20, 124
Attlee, Clement   61
Australia   37, 68, 76, 81, 103, 114, 117,
      119, 155
Australia–United Kingdom–United States
      (AUKUS)   76, 85, 122
"axis of upheaval" (China, Russia, Iran,
      North Korea)   148

Baidu   136, 170
balance of power   56, 105, 151
   Bismarckian balance of power   5, 36
   strategic balancing   104–5
Balkan conflicts (Bosnia,
      Kosovo)   16, 17, 42
ballistic missile defence *see* missile defence
"Beijing Consensus" *see* "China model"
Belt and Road Initiative (BRI)   57, 75,
      99, 112
Bezos, Jeff   137
Bharatiya Janata Party (BJP)   100
Biden, Joe   6, 11, 20, 25, 28–9, 55, 65, 74,
      75, 123, 157
   and Artificial Intelligence (AI)   134
   and China   28, 84, 86, 88
   concept of "democracy versus autocracy"
      *see* concept of "democracy versus
      autocracy"
   and Gaza   29, 103
   and Inflation Reduction Act (IRA) *see*
      Inflation Reduction Act (IRA)
   and the International Criminal Court
      (ICC)   46
   and Israel   29, 103

175